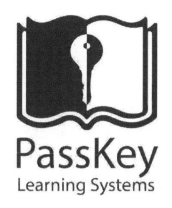

PassKey
Learning Systems

EA Review

Part 3: Representation

Enrolled Agent Study Guide

May 1, 2023-February 29, 2024
Testing Cycle

Joel Busch, CPA, JD
Christy Pinheiro, EA, ABA®
Thomas A. Gorczynski, EA, USTCP

Executive Editor: Joel Busch, CPA, JD

PassKey Learning Systems EA Review Part 3 Representation Enrolled Agent Study Guide (May 1, 2023-February 29, 2024 Testing Cycle)

ISBN 13: 978-1-935664-90-1

First Printing. April 15, 2023.

Official website: ***www.PassKeyOnline.com***

This study guide is designed for exam candidates who will take their exams in the May 1, 2023-February 29, 2024 testing cycle.

Note: Prometric will NOT TEST on any legislation or court decisions passed after December 31, 2022. For exams taken between May 1, 2023-February 29, 2024, all references on the examination are to the Internal Revenue Code, forms and publications, as amended through December 31, 2022. Also, unless otherwise stated, all questions relate to the calendar year 2022. Questions that contain the term 'current tax year' refer to the calendar year 2022.

This page intentionally left blank.

Table of Contents

This page intentionally left blank.

Praise for the PassKey EA Review Series

(Real customers, real names, public testimonials)

Perfect review book!
A. Mietzner
This EA review is great! It goes into detail. Explains why. When you do the practice test, it actually details the answer for learning and retaining! Definitely recommend!

Fantastic textbooks and video resources.
Vino Joseph Philip
Comprehensive and accurate video lessons are available online, and testing is also available for each course. I passed all three exams on the first attempt after using Passkey's resources.

Passed on the first attempt!
William Collins
I passed the first time with the Part 2 [textbook] for the EA SEE 2 exam. I also used the Part 1 textbook and passed that EA exam on the first try as well. Great resources!

I highly recommend these materials
Tosha H. Knelangeon
Using only the [PassKey] study guide and the workbook, I passed all three EA exams on my first try. I highly recommend these materials. As long as you put in the time to read and study all the information provided, you should be well-prepared.

I passed on the first try.
Jake Bavaro
I recently passed the first part of the EA exam using just the textbook and a separate practice test workbook. The textbook is very easy to read and understand. Although I have a background in accounting and tax, someone with little or no knowledge of either should be able to grasp all of the various topics covered in the book. I really do believe that it is a superior preparation resource.

I passed all three parts the first time taking them.
Sheryl Reinecke
I passed all three parts the first time. I read each chapter and the review quiz at the end of each chapter. Before taking the real exam, I did the practice exams in the additional workbook. I feel the material adequately prepared me for success in passing the exam.

Outstanding Material!
E. De La Garza
If you're looking to pass the EA exam with minimal expense, I recommend the PassKey system.

You can pass.
Vishnu Kali Osirion
I really rushed studying for this section. These authors make tax law relevant to your day-to-day experiences and understandable. You can pass the exam with just this as a resource. I do recommend purchasing the workbook as well, just for question exposure. The questions in the book and in the workbook are pretty indicative of what's on the exam. This is a must-buy. Cheers.

Absolute Best Purchase
Sharlene D.
This book was definitely worth the purchase. The layout was great, especially the examples! Reading the book from front to back allowed me to pass [Part 2]. I also recommend purchasing the workbook or subscribing to the material on their website for this section.

Excellent explanations!
Janet Briggs
The best thing about these books is that each answer has a comprehensive explanation about why the answer is correct. I passed all three EA exams on the first attempt.

PassKey was the only study aid that I used
Stephen J Woodard, CFP, CLU, ChFC
The [PassKey] guides were an invaluable resource. They were concise and covered the subject matter succinctly with spot-on end-of-chapter questions that were very similar to what I encountered on the exams.

Amazing!
Sopio Svanishvilion
PassKey helped me pass all three parts of the Enrolled Agent exam. They are a "must-have" if you want to pass your EA exams.

I passed all three with Passkey.
Swathi B.R.
I went through the online membership, read the whole book, solved all the questions, and passed the EA exam on my first attempt. For all three [parts], I referred to Passkey EA Review. Wonderful books.

Passed all 3 Parts!
Kowani Collins
Thank you so much for providing this resource! I have passed all 3 parts of the SEE exam. PassKey allowed me to study on my own time and take the exam with confidence. Thank you for providing such thorough and easy-to-follow resources!

Introduction

Congratulations on taking the first step toward becoming an enrolled agent, a widely respected professional tax designation. The Internal Revenue Service licenses enrolled agents, known as EAs, after candidates pass a competency exam testing their knowledge of federal tax law. As an enrolled agent, you will have the same representation rights as a CPA, with the ability to represent taxpayers in IRS audits and appeals—an EA's rights are unlimited before all levels and offices of the IRS.

The PassKey study guide series is designed to help you study for the EA exam, which is formally called the *IRS Special Enrollment Examination* or *"SEE."*

EA Exam Basics

The EA exam consists of three parts, which candidates may schedule separately and take in any order they wish. The computerized exam covers all aspects of federal tax law, with Part 1 testing the taxation of individuals; Part 2 testing the taxation of businesses; and Part 3 testing representation, practice, and procedures.

Each part of the EA exam features 100 multiple choice questions, with no written answers required. The exam will include some experimental questions that are not scored. You will not know which of the questions count toward your score and which do not.

> **Computerized EA Exam Format**
>
> **Part 1: Individual Taxation–100 questions**
>
> **Part 2: Business Taxation–100 questions**
>
> **Part 3: Representation, Practice, and Procedures–100 questions**

You will have 3.5 hours to complete each part of the exam. The actual seat time is four hours, which allows time for a pre-exam tutorial and a post-exam survey. An on-screen timer counts down the amount of time you have to finish. The testing company Prometric exclusively administers the EA exam at thousands of testing centers across the United States and in certain other countries. You can find valuable information and register online at *https://www.prometric.com/IRS*.

Prometric Testing Center Procedures

The testing center is designed to be a secure environment. The following are procedures you will need to follow on test day:

1. Check in about a half-hour before your appointment time and bring a current, government-issued ID with a photo and signature. If you do not have a valid ID, you will be turned away and will have to pay for a new exam appointment. Refunds will not be issued by Prometric if you forget to bring a proper ID with you.

2. The EA exam is a closed-book test, so you are not allowed to bring any notes or reference materials into the testing room. The center supplies sound-blocking headphones if you want to use them.

3. No food, water, or other beverages are allowed in the testing room.

4. You will be given scratch paper and a pencil to use, which will be collected after the exam.

5. You will be able to use an on-screen calculator during the exam, or Prometric will provide you with a handheld calculator. You cannot bring your own calculator into the examination room.

6. Before entering the testing room, you may be scanned with a metal detector wand.

7. You will need to sign in and out every time you leave the testing room.

8. You are not allowed to talk or communicate with other test-takers in the exam room. Prometric continuously monitors the testing room via video, physical walk-throughs, and an observation window.

> **Important Note:** Violation of any of these procedures may result in the disqualification of your exam. In cases of cheating, the IRS says candidates are subject to consequences that include civil and criminal penalties.

> **Break Policy:** The Special Enrollment Exam (SEE) now includes one scheduled 15-minute break. You may choose to decline the scheduled break and continue testing. If you choose to take the scheduled break, you will leave the testing room, adhering to all security protocols. You are allowed to take additional unscheduled breaks; however, the exam clock will continue to count down during any unscheduled break.

Exam-takers who require special accommodations under the Americans with Disabilities Act (ADA) must contact Prometric directly to obtain an accommodation request. The test is administered in English; a language barrier is not considered a disability.

Exam Content

Each year, using questions based on the prior calendar year's tax law, the IRS introduces multiple new versions of each part of the EA exam. If you fail a particular part of the exam and need to retake it, do not expect to see identical questions the next time.

Prometric's website includes broad content outlines for each exam part. When you study, make sure you are familiar with the items listed, which are covered in detail in your PassKey guides. Questions from older exams are available on the IRS website for review. Be aware that tax law changes every year, so be familiar with recent updates.

Your PassKey study guides present an overview of all the major areas of federal taxation that enrolled agents typically encounter in their practices and are likely to appear on the exam. Although our guides are designed to be comprehensive, we suggest you also review IRS publications and try to learn as much as you can about tax law in general, so you are well-equipped to take the exam.

In addition to this study guide, we highly recommend that all exam candidates read:

- **Publication 17**, *Your Federal Income Tax* (for Part 1 of the exam), and
- **Circular 230**, *Regulations Governing Practice before the Internal Revenue Service* (for Part 3 of the exam)

You may download these publications for free from the IRS website.

> **Note:** Some exam candidates take *Part 3: Representation, Practice, and Procedures* first rather than taking the tests in order, since the material in Part 3 is considered less complicated. However, test-takers should know that several questions pertaining to taxation of *Individuals* (Part 1) and *Businesses* (Part 2) are often included on the Part 3 exam.

Exam Strategy

Each multiple-choice question has four answer choices. There are several different question formats. During the exam, you should read each question thoroughly to understand precisely what is being asked. Be particularly careful when the problem uses language such as "not" or "except."

Format One–Direct Question
Which of the following entities are required to file Form 709, United States Gift Tax Return?
A. An individual B. An estate or trust C. A corporation D. All of the above
Format Two–Incomplete Sentence
Supplemental wages do not include payments for:
A. Accumulated sick leave B. Nondeductible moving expenses C. Vacation pay D. Travel reimbursements paid at the federal government's per diem rate
Format Three–All of the Following Except
Five tests must be met for you to claim an exemption for a dependent. Which of the following is *not* a requirement?
A. Citizen or Resident Test B. Member of Household or Relationship Test C. Disability Test D. Joint Return Test

If you are unsure of an answer, you may mark it for review and return to it later. Try to eliminate clearly wrong answers from the four possible choices to narrow your odds of selecting the right answer. But be sure to answer every question, even if you have to guess, because all answers left incomplete will be marked as incorrect. Each question is weighted equally.

There may also be a limited number of questions that have four choices, with three incorrect statements or facts and only one with a correct statement or fact, which you would select as the right answer.

With 3.5 hours allotted for each part of the exam, you have about two minutes per question. Try to answer the questions you are sure about quickly, so you can devote more time to those that include calculations or that you are unsure about. Allocate your time wisely. To familiarize yourself with the computerized testing format, you may take a tutorial on the Prometric website. The tutorial illustrates what the test screens look like.

Scoring Methods

The EA exam is not graded on a curve. The IRS determines scaled scores by calculating the number of questions answered correctly from the total number of questions in the exam and converting to a scale that ranges from 40 to 130. The IRS has set the scaled passing score at 105, which corresponds to the minimum level of knowledge deemed acceptable for EAs.

After you finish your exam and submit your answers, you will exit the testing room, and a Prometric staff member will print results showing whether you passed or failed. Test results are automatically shared with the IRS, so you do not need to submit them yourself. Test scores are confidential and will be revealed only to you and the IRS. If you pass, your printed results will show a passing designation but not your actual score. The printout also will not indicate which specific questions you answered correctly or incorrectly.

If you fail, you will receive a scaled score, so you will be able to see how close you are to the minimum score of 105. You will also receive the following diagnostic information to help you know which subject areas to concentrate on when studying to retake the exam:

- Level 1: Area of weakness where additional study is necessary.
- Level 2: Might need additional study.
- Level 3: Clearly demonstrated an understanding of the subject area.

These diagnostic indicators correspond to various sections of each part of the exam. If necessary, you may take each part of the exam up to four times during the current testing window. You will need to re-register with Prometric and pay fees each new time you take an exam part. Due to the global pandemic, the IRS extended the two-year carryover period to three years for passing all three parts of the exam.

Example: Janice passed Part 1 of the EA exam on November 15, 2020. Subsequently Janice passed Part 2 on February 15, 2021. Janice has until November 15, 2023 to pass the remaining part (part 3). Otherwise, she loses credit for Part 1. Janice has until February 15, 2024 to pass all other parts of the examination before she loses credit for Part 2.

Applying for Enrollment

Once you have passed all three parts of the EA exam, you can apply to become an enrolled agent. The process includes an IRS review of your tax compliance history. Failure to timely file or pay personal income taxes can be grounds for denial of enrollment.

The IRS Return Preparer Office will review the circumstances of each case and make determinations on an individual basis. You may not practice as an EA until the IRS approves your application and issues you an enrollment card, a process that takes up to 60 days or more.

Successfully passing the EA exam can launch you into a fulfilling and lucrative new career. The exam requires intense preparation and diligence, but with the help of PassKey's comprehensive *EA Review*, you will have the tools you need to learn how to become an enrolled agent.

We wish you much success.

Ten Steps for the EA Exam

STEP 1: Learn

Learn more about the enrolled agent designation, and explore the career opportunities that await you after passing your EA exam. In addition to preparing income tax returns for clients, EAs can represent individuals and businesses before the IRS, just as attorneys and CPAs do. A college degree or professional tax background is not required to take the EA exam. Many people who use the PassKey study guides have had no prior experience preparing tax returns, but go on to rewarding new professional careers.

STEP 2: Gather Information

Gather more information before you launch into your studies. You will find valuable information about the exam itself on the Prometric testing website at www.prometric.com/IRS. Be sure to download the official Candidate Information Bulletin, which takes you step-by-step through the registration and testing process.

STEP 3: Obtain a PTIN

PTIN stands for "Preparer Tax Identification Number." Before you can register for your EA exam, you must obtain a PTIN from the IRS. The PTIN sign-up system can be found at www.irs.gov/ptin. You will need to create an account and provide personal information. Foreign-based candidates without a Social Security number are also required to have a PTIN in order to register to take the exam; they will need to submit additional paperwork with their Form W-12 (PTIN Application and Renewal).

STEP 4: Register with Prometric

Once you have your PTIN, you may register for your exam on the Prometric website by creating an account to set up your user ID and password. You must also complete Form 2587, Application for Special Enrollment Examination.

STEP 5: Schedule Your Test

After creating an account, you can complete the registration process by clicking on "Scheduling." Your exam appointment must be scheduled within one year from the date of registration. You can choose a test site, time, and date that are convenient for you. Prometric has test centers in most major metropolitan areas of the United States, as well as in many other countries.

You may schedule your exam through the website or by calling Prometric directly Monday through Friday (some centers have Saturday testing). The testing fee is nonrefundable. Once you've scheduled, you'll receive a confirmation number. Keep it for your records because you will need it to reschedule (which may incur a charge), cancel, or change your appointment.

STEP 6: Adopt a Study Plan

Focus on one exam part at a time, and adopt a study plan that covers each unit of your PassKey guides. You'll need to develop your own individualized study program. The period of time you'll need to prepare for each exam is truly unique to you, based on how much prior tax preparation experience you have and your current level of tax knowledge, how well you understand and retain the information you read, and how much time you have to study for each test.

For those without prior tax experience, a good rule of thumb is to study *at least* 60 hours for each of the three exam sections. Part 2: Businesses may require additional study preparation, as evidenced by the lower pass rates. One thing is true for all candidates: for each of the tests, start studying well in advance of your scheduled exam date.

STEP 7: Get Plenty of Rest and Good Nutrition

Get plenty of rest, exercise, and good nutrition prior to the EA exam. You'll want to be at your best on exam day.

STEP 8: Test Day

Be sure to arrive early at the test site. Prometric advises arriving at least 30 minutes before your scheduled exam time. If you miss your appointment and are not allowed to take the test, you'll forfeit your fee and have to pay for a new appointment. Remember to bring a government-issued ID with your name, photo, and signature. Your first and last name must exactly match the first and last name you used to register for the exam.

STEP 9: During the Exam

This is when your hard work finally pays off. Focus and don't worry if you don't know the answer to every question, but make sure you use your time well. Give your best answer to every question. All questions left blank will be marked as wrong.

STEP 10: Congratulations. You Passed!

After celebrating your success, you need to apply for your EA designation by filling out Form 23, *Application for Enrollment to Practice Before the Internal Revenue Service*. Once your application is approved, you'll be issued an enrollment card, and you'll officially be a brand-new enrolled agent!

This page intentionally left blank.

Essential Tax Law Updates for Representation

Here is a quick summary of some of the essential tax figures for the enrolled agent exam cycle that runs from May 1, 2023-February 29, 2024.

> **Study Note:** Congress may enact additional legislation that will affect taxpayers after this book goes to print. Prometric will NOT TEST on any legislation or court decisions passed after December 31, 2022. For exams taken between May 1, 2023-February 29, 2024, all references on the examination are to the Internal Revenue Code, forms and publications, as amended through December 31, 2022.

Important Legislation for the 2022 Tax Year:

- The *Inflation Reduction Act of 2022* was signed into law on August 16, 2022. The bill includes dozens of expanded or extended tax credits and additional funding for the IRS.

- The *SECURE Act 2.0* was signed into law on December 29, 2022, as part of the *Consolidated Appropriations Act of 2023*. This bill added more than ninety new retirement plan provisions that affect individuals and businesses. Most of these provisions do not go into effect until 2023, but there are some provisions that are retroactive.

Due Date: Taxpayers will have until Tuesday, April 18, 2023 to file their 2022 return because the Emancipation Day holiday in Washington, D.C. falls on Sunday, April 16, 2023 and will be celebrated on Monday, April 17, 2023. The extended deadline is October 16, 2023, because October 15 falls on a Sunday in 2023.

FBAR penalties: For the purposes of the "non-willful" civil penalty, on February 28, 2023, in a 5-4 decision, the United States Supreme Court ruled that this penalty applies per FBAR report - not for each reportable foreign account. Therefore, even if an individual has multiple reportable foreign bank accounts with a "non-willful" FBAR violation, only one civil penalty can be imposed on the taxpayer for the year. Prior to this decision, there was a split in the lower courts about whether the non-willful civil penalty could be imposed per FBAR report or for each reportable foreign account.

Passport Revocation threshold: The IRS can certify a taxpayer has "seriously delinquent tax debt," which can lead to the denial and/or revocation of a taxpayer's passport. The threshold in 2022 is $55,000, which includes penalties and interest.

Penalty relief for prior late filings: An automatic waiver and abatement of penalties for tax year 2019 and 2020 returns that were filed by September 30, 2022 applies under IRS Notice 2022-36. This relief applies to Forms 1040, 1120, 1120-S, and 1065. It does not apply to Forms 990, 1041 or 706.

Late filing penalties: If an individual taxpayer files their return more than 60 days after the due date, or extended due date, the minimum penalty is the smaller of $450 (for 2022) or 100% of the unpaid tax.

Lookback periods for refund claims extended: On February 27, 2023, the IRS issued Notice 2023-21, providing relief with respect to lookback periods for claims for credit or refund for returns with due dates postponed due to COVID-19. Due to the COVID-19 pandemic, the IRS postponed federal tax return filing and payment obligations that were due to be performed on or after April 1, 2020, and before July 15, 2020, to July 15, 2020. The IRS also postponed due dates and payment dates for Form 1040 with an original due date of April 15, 2021 to May 17, 2021. As a result of this notice, the applicable refund period statute of limitations period for these tax years will start with the revised (later) COVID-19 dates and *not* from the original (pre-COVID extended) due dates.

Form 1099-MISC, Form 1099-NEC: These forms and instructions have been converted from an annual revision to continuous use. Both the forms and instructions will be updated as needed.

Form 1099-K: The reporting requirement for Form 1099-K, Payment Card and Third-Party Network Transactions, was reduced to $600 for tax year 2022 by the *American Rescue Plan of 2021*. However, on December 23, 2022, the IRS announced a delay in the new 1099-K reporting threshold for third-party settlement organizations (TPSOs). This means that for tax year 2022, the previous Form 1099-K reporting threshold of $20,000 in payments and/or over 200 transactions will remain in effect.

E-file Application Changes: On September 25, 2022, the IRS implemented a new electronic fingerprinting process for EFIN applications. Each new Principal and Responsible Official listed on a new e-file application, or added to an existing application, is required to schedule an appointment with Fieldprint®, the IRS authorized vendor (if the applicant is not an EA, CPA, or attorney). Prior to this date, the IRS had been relying on fingerprint cards for conducting background checks on tax practitioners. The IRS will not process fingerprint cards postmarked after August 15, 2022.

Tax Pro Accounts: The IRS recently launched Tax Pro Accounts, which lets tax professionals submit an authorization request to a taxpayer's IRS Online Account. This includes both power of attorney (Form 2848) and tax information authorization requests (Form 8821). Most requests record immediately to the CAF database. Taxpayers can then review, approve and sign the request electronically. IRS Publication 5533-A explains how to submit authorizations using a Tax Pro Account.

E-file Mandates for Businesses: The Taxpayer First Act of 2019, authorized the IRS to issue regulations that would reduce the aggregate number of information returns that would trigger a mandatory efile requirement for most businesses. The Taxpayer First Act (TFA) included a phased threshold to require employers filing a certain number of information returns to do so electronically. On February 23, 2023, The Department of the Treasury and the Internal Revenue Service published final regulations amending the rules for filing returns and other documents electronically. These regulations will require certain filers to e-file beginning in 2024. The final regulations:

- Reduce the 250-return threshold to require electronic filing by filers of 10 or more returns in a calendar year. The final regulations also create several new regulations to require e-filing of certain returns and other documents not previously required to be e-filed;
- Require filers to aggregate almost all information return types covered by the regulation to determine whether a filer meets the 10-return threshold and is required to e-file their information returns. Earlier regulations applied the 250-return threshold separately to each type of information return covered by the regulations;
- Eliminate the e-filing exception for income tax returns of corporations that report total assets under $10 million at the end of their taxable year, and
- Require partnerships with more than 100 partners to e-file information returns, and they require partnerships required to file at least 10 returns of any type during the calendar year to also e-file their partnership return.

ID Verification: On February 21, 2022, the IRS announced that it put new features in place for IRS Online Account registration. The IRS has two options for customers to sign up for IRS online accounts without the use of any biometric data, including facial recognition.

- **Without using biometric data** – Taxpayers will have the option of verifying their identity during a live, virtual interview with agents, using no biometric data.

- **Using biometric data** – Taxpayers will still have the option to verify their identity automatically through the use of biometric verification. For taxpayers who select this option, new requirements are in place to ensure images provided are deleted for the account being created.

Prior biometric data stored, including files that were already collected from customers who previously created an IRS Online Account, will be permanently deleted by March 11, 2022.

Due Diligence Preparer Penalty (6695(g)): The penalty for failure to meet the due diligence requirements on tax returns containing EITC, CTC/ACTC/ODC, the AOTC, and/or HOH status filed for 2022 is $560 per failure.

Internet platform for Form 1099 filings: The Taxpayer First Act required the IRS to develop an Internet portal by January 1, 2023. The new Information Returns Intake System (IRIS) went live on January 25, 2023, and will be available to replace the current system: Filing Information Returns Electronically (FIRE). Currently, IRIS will accept Forms 1099 only for tax year 2022 and later. The FIRE system also remains open for the filing of Forms 1099 and other information returns through at least the end of current filing season.[1]

Form 1040-X and Direct Deposit: The Internal Revenue Service announced on February 9, 2023 that taxpayers electronically filing their Form 1040-X, Amended U.S Individual Income Tax Return, will for the first time be able to select direct deposit for their refund.

New S Corporation Simplified Relief Procedure: On October 11, 2022, the IRS released Rev. Proc. 2022-19, which allows S corporations (or QSub parent) and their shareholders to obtain relief for certain matters without requesting a private letter ruling (PLR).

Extension of the Two-Year Carryover Period for EA Exam Candidates: The IRS has extended the two-year period to three years. For example, if a candidate passed Part 1 on November 15, 2020, then subsequently passed Part 2 on February 15, 2021, that candidate has until November 15, 2023, to pass the remaining part. Otherwise, the candidate loses credit for Part 1. The candidate has until February 15, 2024 to pass all other parts of the examination or will lose credit for Part 2.

Form 1024 for Nonprofit Exemptions: Electronic filing of Form 1024, *Application for Recognition of Exemption Under Section 501(a) or Section 521 of the Internal Revenue Code*, was made mandatory upon the release of Revenue Procedure 2022-08 on January 3, 2022.[2] The form and user fee must be submitted online on www.pay.gov. The required user fee for Form 1024 is $600 for 2022.

"Perfection Periods" for Rejected Submissions: The IRS provides a "transmission perfection period" for rejected returns. Individual returns are given a 5-day perfection period, while most business returns are given a 10-day perfection period; however, the Transmission Perfection Period for an extension to file Form 4868, 7004, or 8868 is five days.

---

[1] Taxpayer Advocate Service's 2022 Annual Report to Congress (ARC), Publication 2104. Also see Publication 5717, IRIS Taxpayer Portal User Guide.
[2] Organizations applying for §501(c)(3) exempt status on Form 1023 have been required to file Form 1023 electronically since 2020 per Revenue Procedure 2020-8.

Unit 1: Legal Authority of the IRS

> **More Reading:**
> Circular 230, Regulations Governing Practice Before the Internal Revenue Service
> Publication 947, Practice Before the IRS and Power of Attorney
> Publication 1, Your Rights as a Taxpayer

Part 3 of the EA exam concerns the ethics, laws, and regulations that govern the tax profession: rules that tax practitioners must follow; standards that the tax profession is held to; who may represent taxpayers before the IRS; IRS procedures for assessment, collection, audit, and appeals; and penalties that tax preparers face if they violate the law.

Specifically, Part 3 of the exam is broken down into the following sections and the corresponding percentage of questions:[3]

1. **Practices and Procedures – 26 questions**

2. **Representation before the IRS – 25 questions**

3. **Specific Areas of Representation – 20 questions**

4. **Filing Process – 14 questions**

Issues of ethics, practice, and representation are dealt with in detail in Treasury Department Circular No. 230, Regulations Governing Practice before the Internal Revenue Service.[4] All practitioners who represent taxpayers before the IRS are subject to the rules and regulations outlined in Circular 230. Paid preparers are a cornerstone of the U.S. tax system. They prepare approximately 60% of all tax returns filed, and their actions have an enormous impact on the Internal Revenue Service's ability to administer tax laws effectively.

Federal Tax Law

The Internal Revenue Code (IRC) is the main body of tax law of the United States. The IRC is enacted by Congress and published as Title 26, the Internal Revenue Code of the United States Code. The Federal courts interpret the IRC in judicial opinions, by the Treasury Department in Treasury Regulations, and in other administrative guidance published by the IRS.

Other tax laws are promulgated by individual states, cities, and municipalities. However, not all Federal tax law is located in Title 26 of the United States Code. FBARs and most international financial reporting laws are promulgated in the *Bank Secrecy Act,* a provision of Title 31. Although the *Bank Secrecy Act* was focused initially on financial institutions, the law has been expanded by Congress beyond the regulation of banks.

---

[3] These specifications are listed in the current Enrolled Agent Special Enrollment Examination Candidate Information Bulletin, which is available for download on the official Prometric website.

[4] Regulations governing practice before the IRS are also set forth in Title 31, Code of Federal Regulations, Subtitle A, Part 10, as published in pamphlet form as Treasury Department Circular No. 230 on June 12, 2014.

In 2003, The Financial Crimes and Enforcement Network (FinCEN) delegated enforcement authority regarding the FBAR to the Internal Revenue Service (IRS).

> **Note:** The IRS Enrolled Agent exam deals only with federal laws and not with the laws of any individual state or municipality. However, some state laws directly affect federal tax reporting. An example of this would be community property laws, which determine how much income each spouse is required to report on a separate return.

Tax law is determined by all three branches of our federal government, although the legislative branch (Congress) has the primary function of originating tax laws. The executive branch (the president) is responsible for income tax regulations, revenue rulings, and revenue procedures. The judicial branch is responsible for court decisions. The U.S. courts also have the responsibility for determining whether or not a particular tax law is constitutional.

THREE BRANCHES OF GOVERNMENT

Legislative
Makes laws

Executive
Carries out laws

Judicial
Evaluates laws

The IRS and U.S. Treasury Department
are part of the **Executive branch.**

The U.S. Treasury Department (which includes the Internal Revenue Service) is part of the **executive branch** of the U.S. government. The U.S. Treasury collects taxes through the Internal Revenue Service. The president has veto powers, which means he can stop legislation from becoming law (subject to a veto override by a two-thirds vote in both the House of Representatives and the Senate).

The Internal Revenue Service is the federal agency that enforces tax law. In other words, the IRS is the "collection arm" of the U.S. Treasury Department, which is responsible for paying various government expenses. The Internal Revenue Service administers the Internal Revenue Code enacted by Congress.

The IRS itself does not *enact* any tax statute—that is the job of the U.S. Congress. The IRS takes the specifics of the laws ratified by Congress and translates them into detailed regulations, rules, and procedures.

The IRS produces several kinds of documents that provide guidance to taxpayers, including the following:

1. Treasury Regulations
2. Revenue Rulings
3. Revenue Procedures
4. Private letter rulings
5. Technical advice memoranda (also called "TAMs")
6. IRS notices

Each of these can factor into "substantial authority," which means the authority to serve as the basis for interpretation of current tax law and to establish precedents for the future. Treasury Regulations define substantial authority as existing when "the weight of authorities for the tax treatment of an item is substantial in relation to the weight of authorities supporting contrary positions."

The weight given an authority depends on its "relevance and persuasiveness" and the type of document providing the authority. For example, a revenue ruling is accorded greater weight than a private letter ruling (other than to whom the private letter ruling was issued to) addressing the same issue. Newer pronouncements also carry greater weight than older ones.

> **Example:** Jesse is an enrolled agent. He used a decades-old court case as authority to claim a large business deduction on his client's corporate tax return. Jesse did not realize that a higher court had later overturned the case. Therefore, the source that he used to base his deduction was outdated and invalid. Under audit, his client's business deduction was disallowed, and the client was also assessed an accuracy-related penalty. Jesse could also be assessed a preparer penalty for his negligence.

The **primary** authority for any tax position is the **Internal Revenue Code**.[5] Other sources of tax law that factor into "substantial authority" include the following:

- Temporary and final Treasury Regulations (but not proposed regulations),[6]
- Court cases,
- Administrative pronouncements,
- Tax treaties, and
- Congressional intent, as reflected in committee reports.

This list was later expanded to include private letter rulings, technical advice memoranda, IRS information or press releases, notices, and any other similar documents published by the IRS in the Internal Revenue Bulletin.

---

[5] Primary authority also consists of decisions by the U.S. Supreme Court, which is the highest court in the land.
[6] Taxpayers generally may not rely on proposed regulations for planning purposes, except if there are no applicable final or temporary regulations in force and there is an express statement in the preamble to the proposed regulations that taxpayers may rely on them currently.

Note that *"substantial authority"* does *not* include official IRS publications or IRS form instructions. Many IRS publications are not updated every year, and reliance on IRS publications does not constitute substantial authority for purposes of avoiding understatement penalties.[7]

> **Note:** the IRS announced that all future frequently asked questions (FAQs) posted on irs.gov would be issued as a Fact Sheet as part of an IRS press release. By doing this, these FAQs can constitute authority for a tax return position. Please note that general content on the IRS webpage does NOT constitute substantial authority.

The possibility that a return will not be audited or, if audited, that an item will not be raised on audit, is not relevant in determining whether the substantial authority standard (or the reasonable basis standard) is satisfied.

Treatises and articles in legal periodicals are not considered substantial authority under this statute. An authority no longer remains an authority if it is overruled or modified by a body with the power to overrule or modify it.

Treasury Regulations

Treasury regulations are the U.S. Treasury Department's official interpretations of the Internal Revenue Code. The IRC authorizes the Secretary of the Treasury to "prescribe all needful rules and regulations for enforcement" of the code.[8] All regulations are written by the IRS's Office of the Chief Counsel and approved by the U.S. Treasury Secretary.

The courts give weight to Treasury regulations and will generally uphold the regulations so long as the IRS's interpretation is *reasonable* and does not contradict any provisions in the IRC. Treasury regulations are first published in the Federal Register. After publication in the Federal Register, regulations are organized by subject matter and codified in a separate publication called the Code of Federal Regulations (CFR). The three types of Treasury regulations are:

1. **Legislative Regulations,**
2. **Interpretive Regulations, and**
3. **Procedural Regulations.**

Legislative regulations are created when Congress expressly delegates the authority to the Treasury secretary or the commissioner of the IRS to provide the requirements for a specific provision of the IRC. A legislative regulation has a higher degree of authority than an *interpretive regulation*. In general, legislative regulations carry the same authority as the law itself.

---

[7] IRS Publications generally explain the law in more easy-to-understand language than the actual primary law for taxpayers and their advisors. They typically highlight changes in the law and provide examples illustrating IRS positions on matters. IRS publications are non-binding on the IRS and do not necessarily cover all positions for a given issue. While a good source of general information, IRS publications should not be cited to sustain a position (IRM 4.10.7.2.8).

[8] The Internal Revenue Service (IRS) is responsible for administering and enforcing the internal revenue laws and related statutes, except those relating to alcohol, tobacco, firearms, and explosives.

However, a legislative regulation may be overturned if any of the following conflicts apply:

- It is outside the power delegated to the U.S. Treasury.
- It conflicts with a specific statute.
- It is deemed unreasonable or unconstitutional by the courts.

Interpretive regulations are issued under the IRS's general authority to interpret the IRC. An interpretive regulation only explains the meaning of a portion of the code. Unlike a legislative regulation, there is no grant of authority for the promulgation of an interpretive regulation, so these regulations may be challenged on the grounds that they do not reflect Congressional intent.

Procedural regulations concern the administrative provisions of the code and are issued by the commissioner of the IRS and not the Secretary of the Treasury. They often concern minor issues, such as when notices should be sent to employees or how to file certain IRS forms.

> **Note:** The IRS is **legally bound** by its regulations, but the courts are **not.** Official regulations have the force of law, unless they are overly broad in relation to the statute or are deemed unconstitutional by the courts. U.S. Treasury regulations are authorized by law, but U.S. courts are not obligated to follow any of the IRS' administrative interpretations.

Classification of Treasury Regulations

Regulations are further classified as proposed, temporary, or final:

- **Proposed regulations** are open to commentary from the public. Various versions of proposed regulations may be issued and withdrawn before a final regulation is issued. Proposed regulations have minimal practical effect. A taxpayer may not rely on proposed treasury regulations unless they contain an express statement permitting reliance. Unlike temporary regulations, proposed regulations do not expire.
- **Temporary regulations** remain in effect for three years. They provide immediate guidance to the public and IRS employees prior to publishing final regulations. Temporary regulations are effective immediately upon publication in the Federal Register.[9]
- **Final regulations** are issued when a regulation becomes an official Treasury decision. Final regulations are effective immediately upon publication in the Federal Register. They are the highest authority issued by the Treasury Department. Final regulations have the effect of law.

Revenue Rulings and Revenue Procedures

The IRS issues **revenue rulings** and **revenue procedures** to inform and guide taxpayers. Neither has the force of Treasury Department regulations, but they may be used as authority. A revenue ruling typically states the IRS position, while a revenue procedure provides instructions concerning that position.

---

[9] Unlike proposed regulations, temporary regulations go into effect immediately upon publication in the Federal Register, but they expire within three years of enactment (with the exception of temporary regulations issued prior to 1989).

Revenue rulings are intended to promote the uniform application of the IRC. The national office of the IRS issues revenue rulings, which are published in the Internal Revenue Bulletin and the Federal Register. A revenue ruling is not binding in Tax Court or any other U.S. court. However, taxpayers can use revenue rulings as guidance to avoid certain accuracy-related IRS penalties.

The numbering system for revenue rulings corresponds to the year the ruling was issued. Thus, for example, revenue ruling 2022-1 was the first revenue ruling issued in 2022. Revenue procedures are official IRS statements of procedure that affect the rights or duties of taxpayers under the IRC. A revenue procedure may be cited as authority, but it does not have the force of law.

> **Study Note:** A **revenue ruling** may announce that taxpayers may deduct certain automobile expenses. A **revenue procedure** will then explain how taxpayers must deduct, allocate, or calculate these automobile expenses.

IRS Written Determinations

IRS Written Determinations are determinations the IRS is required to make open to public inspection. There are many types of official IRS correspondence and determinations. We will discuss the most common types in the subsequent section.

Technical Advice Memorandum (TAM)

A Technical Advice Memorandum is written guidance furnished by the IRS Office of Chief Counsel upon the request of an IRS director. A request for a TAM generally stems from an examination of a taxpayer's return, a consideration of a taxpayer's claim for a refund or credit, or any other matter involving a specific taxpayer under the jurisdiction of the territory manager or the area director. Technical advice memoranda are issued only on closed transactions and provide the interpretation of the proper application of tax laws, tax treaties, regulations, revenue rulings, or other precedents. TAMs are not published in the Internal Revenue Bulletin.

The advice rendered represents the position of the IRS, but it only relates to the specific case in question. Technical advice memoranda are made public after all the private information has been removed that could identify a particular taxpayer.

> **Example:** Valley Dairy Farm, Inc. is a farming corporation with 55 employees. The company usually gives its employees a holiday ham at the end of the year. Because of dietary restrictions, some of the employees requested gift certificates instead of a holiday ham. In 2022, the business provided a holiday gift certificate with a face value of thirty-five dollars that was redeemable at several local grocery stores. Valley Dairy Farm excluded the value of the gift certificate from the employee's wages, and deducted the full amount as a business expense, arguing that it was a de minimis fringe benefit under Code §132. The IRS disagreed, and determined that the gift certificates were essentially "cash equivalents," and not excludable from the employee's gross income. The full amounts of the gift certificates were taxable as wages to the employees, and subject to payroll taxes for both the employer and the employee (example based on TAM-108577-04).

> **Example:** Manhattan Literacy, Inc. is a 501(c)(3) tax-exempt organization that also has an affiliated 501(c)(4) organization, Manhattan Lobbyists, Inc. The 501(c)(4) organization did substantial lobbying activities for political candidates in New York. Although the organizations were separate legal entities, both organizations shared a website. Manhattan Lobbyists used pages on the website to distribute political campaign endorsements. While the Manhattan Lobbyists' website contains its own logo and address, they also contain the 501(c)(3)'s banner and related links. A website is a form of communication, and as a charitable entity, Manhattan Literacy is prohibited from disseminating any information that favors or opposes a particular candidate for public office. The IRS determines that Manhattan Literacy (the 501(c)(3) organization) had engaged in prohibited political activity by sharing its website with Manhattan Lobbyists, its affiliated 501(c)(4) organization. Manhattan Literacy was found to have impermissibly intervened in a political campaign by distributing campaign endorsements on its website (example based on TAM 200908050).

Private Letter Ruling (PLR)

A taxpayer who has a specific question regarding tax law may request a private letter ruling (PLR) from the IRS. A PLR is a written statement issued to a taxpayer that interprets and applies tax laws to the taxpayer's specific case. It is issued to communicate the tax consequences of a particular transaction before the transaction is completed or before the taxpayer's return is filed.

A PLR is legally binding on the IRS, but only if the taxpayer fully and accurately described the proposed transaction in the request and carried out the transaction as described. In addition, it is only binding on the IRS for the particular taxpayer who requested the ruling.

PLRs are made public after the taxpayer's private, identifiable information has been redacted (removed or blacked out). A private letter ruling is not free. The minimum fee for most PLRs start at $10,000 and up (per request), with some requests requiring an even higher fee.

> **Example:** Robert is age 31 and permanently disabled. On March 1, Robert inherits a traditional IRA valued at over $1.5 million when his elderly father dies. Because Robert is disabled, he is eligible for public benefit programs, such as Medicaid. Robert does not want to risk losing Medicaid or his other state disability benefits, so his financial advisor suggests that he transfer the inherited IRA funds into a special needs trust of which he will be the beneficiary. The financial advisor recommends that Robert request a Private Letter Ruling from the IRS *before* initiating the transfer to make sure there would be no unintended Federal tax consequences to Robert. The IRS rules favorably, holding in the PLR that if the inherited IRA is transferred to a special needs trust, the transfer would neither trigger a taxable event nor be considered a gift to the trust (example based on PLR 201116005).

IRS Notices

An official IRS notice is a public pronouncement that may contain guidance involving substantive interpretations of the IRC or other provisions of the law.

Information commonly published in IRS notices includes:

1. Weighted average interest rate updates
2. Inflation adjustment factors
3. Changes to IRS regulations
4. Tax provisions related to presidentially declared disaster areas
5. IRS requests for public comments on changes to regulations, rulings, or procedures
6. Internal Revenue Bulletin items

The Internal Revenue Bulletin (IRB) is the authoritative source of official IRS tax guidance. It is a weekly collection of items of substantial interest to the professional tax community. The IRB announces official IRS rulings and publishes Treasury decisions, executive orders, tax conventions, significant legislation, and certain court decisions.

Anyone may search the IRS website, *www.irs.gov,* for past issues of the IRB. Issues are available in both HTML and PDF file formats. The IRS often releases individual items in advance of their publication in the IRB. Tax professionals may subscribe to the IRS GuideWire service to receive automated email notifications about these items.

Internal Revenue Manual

The Internal Revenue Manual (IRM) is the single official compilation of policies, delegated authorities, procedures, instructions, and guidelines relating to the organization, functions, administration, and operations of the IRS. IRS employees primarily use it to guide them in all facets of operations.

The manual currently includes sections on the processing of tax submissions, examinations, collection, and appeals. Criminal investigations, legal advice, and litigation in the courts are also included in the manual. The IRM is public information and can be searched and read directly on the IRS website. The IRM is not considered "substantial authority" for positions taken on tax matters; however, IRS employees are required to follow it when working on taxpayer matters.

IRS Publications and Forms

The IRS disseminates information to both taxpayers and preparers through its official publications. For example, Publication 17 covers the general rules for filing a federal income tax return for individuals. Publication 17 supplements information contained in the tax form instruction booklet and explains the law in more detail, so it is an important document for taxpayers who prepare their own income tax returns.

Although the information in publications is drawn from the Internal Revenue Code, Treasury Regulations, and other primary sources of authority, publications themselves are not "authority." Taxpayers and preparers may not rely on IRS publications to avoid accuracy-related penalties.

Example: Alvan Bobrow took $65,000 out of his traditional IRA account, intending to replace that money within 60 days, in order to have the transaction treated as an indirect IRA rollover, rather than a taxable distribution. Just before the sixty-day rollover deadline elapsed, Alvan took another distribution from a second IRA, (IRA-2), and placed those funds into IRA-1. Alvan's tax return was later chosen for audit and his second purported rollover was invalidated under the once-per-year indirect rollover rule. The taxpayer had relied on information in IRS Publication 590, but the information in the publication was incorrect at the time. The court determined that the publication did not provide substantial authority for Mr. Bobrow's position. Mr. Bobrow lost his case. See Bobrow v. Commissioner (T.C. Memo 2014-21)

Note: In *Bobrow v. Commissioner,* a U.S. Tax Court judge famously declared, *"Taxpayers rely on IRS guidance at their own peril."* Judge Joseph W. Nega wrote that IRS guidance was not "binding precedent" or "sufficient authority" to excuse the taxpayer from penalties. The IRS later revised the publication at issue.

Study Note: The Enrolled Agent exam is based mainly on IRS publications, and exam candidates will not be tested on court cases unless the law has already made its way into an IRS publication. Similarly, exam candidates will not be tested on any *pending* tax law or legislation. The exam is based on tax law from the prior year. However, EA candidates must understand the basics of tax law, the U.S. court system, and how it relates to taxpayers and tax professionals.

Tax Forms and Schedules

IRS tax forms and schedules are used by taxpayers to report financial information to the IRS and calculate taxes to be paid or disclose other information as required by the Internal Revenue Code. There are hundreds of forms and schedules in use. Many have accompanying instructions for taxpayers. Forms, schedules, and instructions are updated whenever necessary due to changes in the tax code.

All publications, forms, and instructions are listed and available for download on the IRS website at *www.irs.gov,* usually in both HTML and PDF file formats. Updated versions of publications are listed with the date revisions were made, so taxpayers can know they are using the most current information. Due to the growth in electronic filing and the availability of free access to tax forms online, the IRS no longer mails paper tax publications or paper forms to taxpayers.

Court Decisions

Often, taxpayers and tax preparers will disagree with the IRS's interpretation of the IRC. In these cases, it is up to the courts to determine Congressional intent or the constitutionality of tax law, or the IRS position that is being challenged. There are many instances where tax laws are disputed or even overturned.

Court decisions then serve as guidance for future tax decisions. In most instances, the IRS chooses whether or not to acquiesce to a court decision. This means that the IRS may decide to ignore the court's ruling and continue with its regular policies regarding the litigated issue.

The IRS is not bound to change its interpretation of the tax law due to a loss in court. The only exception to this rule is the U.S. Supreme Court, whose decisions the IRS is obligated to follow.

The IRS does not announce acquiescence or nonacquiescence in every case. When it does announce its position, the IRS publishes its acquiescence or nonacquiescence in the Internal Revenue Bulletin in an "action on decision." The issuance of a nonacquiescence usually reflects that the IRS does not agree with the result reached by the U.S. Tax Court, and will continue to challenge the decision. The IRS may also retroactively revoke acquiescence to any case.

> **Example:** In the tax case *Jacobs v. Commissioner*, the U.S. Tax Court concluded that the pregame meals provided to the Boston Bruins professional hockey team were not subject to the then 50% meal limit. The Bruin's attorneys successfully argued that the meals were *de minimis* fringe benefits under §132(e)(2). The Tax Court held in favor of the Bruins' owners, holding that they were entitled to the deduction because the team's pre-game meals were provided at "employer-operated eating facilities," which qualified as an employee fringe benefit. The IRS later issued a partial acquiescence to the case, stating that the IRS would follow *Jacobs* only with respect to cases involving sports teams in which the material facts are substantially identical to those present in *Jacobs*.

Freedom of Information Act Requests (FOIA)

The Freedom of Information Act (FOIA) is a law designed to ensure public access to U.S. government records.[10] Upon written request, federal agencies, including the IRS, are required to disclose requested records, unless they can be withheld under certain exceptions allowed in the FOIA. Under the terms of the act, agencies may charge reasonable fees for searching, reviewing, and copying records that have been requested.

All IRS records are subject to FOIA requests. However, FOIA does not require the IRS to release all documents that are subject to FOIA requests. The IRS may withhold information pursuant to exemptions contained in the FOIA statute. The exemptions protect against the disclosure of information that would harm: national security, the privacy of individuals, the proprietary interests of business, the functioning of the government, and other vital recognized interests. Exclusions involve sensitive law enforcement records related to criminal activities, FBI counterintelligence, and international terrorism investigations.

When a record contains some information that qualifies as exempt, the entire record is not necessarily exempt. Instead, the FOIA specifically provides that any portions of a record that can be set apart must be provided to a requester after deletion of the exempt portions.

The IRS generally has 20 business days to say whether it will comply with an FOIA request. When a request is denied, the IRS must give the reason for denial and explain the right to appeal to the head of the agency.

---

[10] For more information, see The Freedom of Information Act Guide to Treasury Records at *www.treasury.gov* and Freedom of Information Act (FOIA) Guidelines at *www.IRS.gov.*

A taxpayer may contest the fees charged in processing a records request. The IRS will copy the requested records and send the taxpayer a bill for the fees. A taxpayer may appeal other types of adverse determinations under the FOIA, such as the failure of the IRS to conduct an adequate search for requested documents.

A person whose request was granted in part and denied in part may appeal the part that was denied. If the IRS has agreed to disclose some but not all of the requested documents, the filing of an appeal does not affect the release of the documents that can be disclosed.

Taxpayer Bill of Rights

The IRS must adhere to the Taxpayer Bill of Rights as described in the *IRS Restructuring and Reform Act of 1998.* This law was designed to better communicate to taxpayers their existing statutory and administrative protections. The Taxpayer Bill of Rights groups the dozens of rights in the Internal Revenue Code, and the Internal Revenue Manual into ten fundamental rights to make them clear, understandable, and accessible both to taxpayers and IRS employees. These rights are detailed in *Publication 1, Your Rights as a Taxpayer.* These rights are as follows:[11]

1. The Right to Be Informed: Taxpayers have the right to know what they need to do to comply with the tax laws. They are entitled to clear explanations of the laws and IRS procedures in all tax forms, instructions, publications, notices, and correspondence. They have the right to be informed of IRS decisions about their tax accounts and to receive clear explanations of the outcomes.

Note: Certain notices must include the amount (if any) of the tax, interest and certain penalties the taxpayer owes and must explain why he or she owes these amounts (IRC §7522).

2. The Right to Quality Service: Taxpayers have the right to receive prompt, courteous, and professional assistance in their dealings with the IRS, to be spoken to in a way they can easily understand, to receive clear and easily understandable communications from the IRS, and to speak to a supervisor about inadequate service.

Note: When collecting tax, the IRS should treat a taxpayer with courtesy. Generally, the IRS should only contact a taxpayer between 8 a.m. and 9 p.m. The IRS should not contact a taxpayer at their place of employment if the IRS knows, or has reason to know, that their employer does not allow this kind of contact (IRC §6304).

3. The Right to Pay No More than the Correct Amount of Tax: Taxpayers have the right to pay only the amount of tax legally due, including interest and penalties, and to have the IRS apply all tax payments properly.

---

[11] Examples drawn from the Taxpayer Advocate Service's *What the Taxpayer Bill of Rights Means for You.*

Note: If a taxpayer believes he or she has overpaid his taxes can file a refund claim asking for the money back (IRC §6402).

4. The Right to Challenge the IRS's Position and Be Heard: Taxpayers have the right to raise objections and provide additional documentation in response to formal IRS actions or proposed actions; to expect that the IRS will consider their timely objections and documentation promptly and fairly, and to receive a response if the IRS does not agree with their position.

Note: If a taxpayer is notified his return has a mathematical or clerical error, he has 60 days to tell the IRS that he disagrees. If the IRS is not persuaded, it will issue a notice proposing a tax adjustment. The notice provides a taxpayer the right to challenge the proposed adjustment in Tax Court by filing a petition within 90 days of the date of the notice (IRC §6213(b)).

5. The Right to Appeal an IRS Decision in an Independent Forum: Taxpayers are entitled to a fair and impartial administrative appeal of most IRS decisions, including many penalties, and have the right to receive a written response regarding the Independent Office of Appeals' decision. Taxpayers generally have the right to take their cases to court.

The *Taxpayer First Act of 2019* (TFA) expanded a taxpayer's appeals rights even further. In cases where a request for Appeals consideration is denied, the IRS must notify taxpayers of the denial with a written statement explaining the reasons for the denial. Taxpayers also have the right to protest the IRS's decision not to send a case to Appeals.

Note: If the IRS has sent a taxpayer a notice proposing additional tax, the taxpayer may dispute the proposed adjustment in the U.S. Tax Court before he has to pay the tax (IRC §6213).

6. The Right to Finality: Taxpayers have the right to know the maximum amount of time they have to challenge the IRS's position, as well as the maximum amount of time the IRS has to audit a particular tax year or collect a tax debt. Taxpayers have the right to know when the IRS has finished an audit.

Note: The IRS generally has ten years from the assessment date to collect unpaid taxes from a taxpayer (IRC §6502).

7. The Right to Privacy: Taxpayers have the right to expect that any IRS inquiry, examination, or enforcement action will comply with the law and be no more intrusive than necessary, and will respect all due process rights, including search and seizure protections, and will provide, where applicable, a collection due process hearing.

Note: The IRS should not seek intrusive and extraneous information about a taxpayer's lifestyle during an audit if there is no reasonable indication that he has unreported income (IRC §7602(e)).

8. The Right to Confidentiality: Taxpayers have the right to expect that any information they provide to the IRS will not be disclosed unless authorized by the taxpayer or by law. Taxpayers have the right to expect appropriate action will be taken against employees, return preparers, and others who wrongfully use or disclose taxpayer return information.

> **Note:** In general, the IRS may not disclose a taxpayer's tax information to third parties unless he gives explicit permission (IRC §6103). There are exceptions for law enforcement and other limited scenarios.

9. The Right to Retain Representation: Taxpayers have the right to retain an authorized representative of their choice to represent them in their dealings with the IRS. Taxpayers have the right to seek assistance from a Low-Income Taxpayer Clinic if they cannot afford representation.

> **Note:** A taxpayer may select a qualified representative person to represent him in an interview with the IRS. The IRS cannot force the taxpayer to attend with his representative (IRC §7521(c)) if the representative is qualified to practice before the IRS.

10. The Right to a Fair and Just Tax System: Taxpayers have the right to expect the tax system to consider facts and circumstances that might affect their underlying liabilities, ability to pay, or ability to provide information timely. Taxpayers have the right to request assistance from the Taxpayer Advocate Service if they are experiencing financial difficulty or if the IRS has not resolved their tax issues properly and timely through its normal channels.

> **Note:** The IRS cannot levy (seize) all of a taxpayer's wages to collect his unpaid tax. A portion will be exempt from levy to allow payment of basic living expenses (IRC §6334).

IRS Divisions

The IRS has four main operating divisions. These are:

1. **Large Business & International Division (LB&I):** This division serves corporations, including S corporations, and partnerships, with assets in excess of $10 million. This is the division of the IRS that audits large corporate taxpayers and partnerships, including publicly traded companies like Ford, Apple, Coca-Cola, etc.
2. **Small Business/Self-Employed Division (SB/SE):** This division serves small corporations and partnerships with assets less than $10 million; filers of gift, estate, excise, employment, and fiduciary returns; individuals filing an individual Federal income tax return with accompanying Schedule C, Schedule E, Schedule F, and Form 2106, *Employee Business Expenses.*[12]
3. **Wage and Investment Division:** This division serves individuals with wage and investment income only (not including international tax returns), filing an individual Federal income tax return without accompanying Schedule C, E, or F.
4. **Tax-Exempt and Government Entities Division:** This division serves three distinct taxpayer segments: employee plans (including IRAs), exempt organizations, and government entities.

---

[12] Miscellaneous itemized deductions were eliminated for most taxpayers under the Tax Cuts and Jobs Act, so Form 2106 is only applicable to very narrow circumstances (Armed Forces reservists, qualified performing artists, fee-basis state or local government officials, or employees with impairment-related work expenses).

Taxpayer Advocate Service

The Taxpayer Advocate Service (TAS) is an independent organization within the IRS, whose goal is to help taxpayers resolve problems with the IRS. A taxpayer may be eligible for TAS assistance when he or she is facing a number of different situations involving economic harm or significant delays in resolving a tax issue.

The Taxpayer Advocate Service is free and confidential, and available for businesses and individuals. TAS has at least one office in every U.S. state and the District of Columbia, and Puerto Rico.

There are local TAS offices where taxpayers can meet face-to-face with advocates, a video conferencing service for areas where there are no nearby offices, and toll-free telephone service. The quickest contact method is by fax, but a taxpayer may also submit *Form 911, Request for Taxpayer Advocate Service Assistance.* TAS may be able to help a taxpayer who is experiencing a problem with the IRS and:

1. The problem with the IRS is causing financial difficulties for the taxpayer, his family, or his business;
2. The taxpayer faces (or his business is facing) an immediate threat of adverse action; or
3. The taxpayer has repeatedly tried to contact the IRS, but no one has responded, or the IRS has not responded by the date promised.

When the Taxpayer Advocate Service evaluates a taxpayer's request for assistance, it will use the following criteria to determine whether to intervene:

- The taxpayer is experiencing economic harm or is about to suffer economic harm.
- The taxpayer is facing an immediate threat of adverse action.
- The taxpayer will incur significant costs if relief is not granted (including fees for professional representation).
- The taxpayer will suffer irreparable injury or long-term adverse impact if relief is not granted.
- The taxpayer has experienced a delay of more than 30 days to resolve a tax account problem.
- The taxpayer did not receive a response or resolution to his problem or inquiry by the date promised.
- A system or procedure has either failed to operate as intended or failed to resolve the taxpayer's problem or dispute within the IRS.
- The manner in which the tax laws are being administered raise considerations of equity, or have impaired or will impair the taxpayer's rights.
- The National Tax Advocate determines compelling public policy warrants assistance to an individual or group of taxpayers.

The Taxpayer Advocate Service will generally ask the IRS to stop certain collection activities while a taxpayer's request for assistance is pending (such as lien filings, levies, and seizures).

Example: Shirley filed an amended tax return for a prior year, because she found an error on the return that would result in a refund. She has an outstanding balance for the prior tax year and has been receiving IRS collection notices. Shirley's expected refund would fully pay her balance due and leave her with a small refund. The official processing time for *Form 1040X, Amended U.S. Individual Tax Return*, is eight to twelve weeks. However, she has been waiting for more than nine months for her refund to be processed. She has contacted the IRS numerous times but was never given a reason for the delay. Shirley may request intervention from the Taxpayer Advocate Service.

Unit 1: Study Questions

(Test yourself and then check the correct answers at the end of this chapter.)

1. Treasury regulations are published in _____.

A. The Congressional Notes
B. The Federal Register
C. The Office of Appeals
D. The IRS Newswire

2. The IRS generally has _____ to say whether it will comply with an FOIA request.

A. 7 business days
B. 14 business days
C. 20 business days
D. 30 business days

3. Which of the following statements regarding revenue rulings is *correct?*

A. Revenue rulings cannot be used to avoid certain IRS penalties.
B. Revenue rulings can be used to avoid certain IRS penalties.
C. Revenue rulings are not authority for tax return positions.
D. Revenue rulings cannot be overturned by a court.

4. A private letter ruling is legally binding on the IRS if:

A. The taxpayer that received the private letter ruling, fully and accurately described the proposed transaction in his request and carried out the transaction as described.
B. The IRS is notified of any discrepancies on a taxpayer's return.
C. The taxpayer goes to the Tax Court and requests a formal decision.
D. None of the above.

5. Which of the following types of Treasury regulations have the *highest level* of authority?

A. Revenue regulations.
B. Procedural regulation.
C. Interpretive regulation.
D. Legislative regulation.

6. Of the following sources of information, which cannot factor into "substantial authority" for Federal Tax Law purposes?

A. Final regulations.
B. Legal opinion printed in a law school journal.
C. Congressional intent, as reflected in committee reports.
D. Technical advice memorandum.

7. Which branch of government is the main source of tax law in the United States?

A. Legislative.
B. Executive.
C. Judicial.
D. All three branches contribute equally to the creation and adoption of tax law.

8. An IRS revenue officer has a question about a collection procedure involving a taxpayer. He should consult:

A. The Internal Revenue Manual.
B. The Internal Revenue Bulletin.
C. Publication 594, the IRS Collection Process.
D. The Congressional Record.

9. Connor is having serious financial difficulties. Of the following situations, which is most likely to warrant intervention by the Taxpayer Advocate Service?

A. Connor's home is in foreclosure, and he is worried he will be unable to pay his federal income tax liability by the due date.
B. Connor has experienced a few, short delays in trying to contact the IRS by telephone.
C. Connor has waited for months for the IRS to discharge the lien on his property, which must be removed immediately, or else the sale of the property will fall through.
D. Connor has received an IRS Notice of Federal Tax Lien that his bank account will be subject to levy if he does not pay his federal tax liability.

10. In matters of tax law, the IRS must acquiesce in all decisions rendered by the:

A. U.S. Tax Court
B. U.S. District Court
C. U.S. Court of Appeals
D. U.S. Supreme Court

11. Which of the following would have the <u>highest</u> authority in establishing a precedent for tax law for all taxpayers?

A. Private letter ruling.
B. Treasury regulation.
C. IRS publication.
D. Technical advice memorandum.

Unit 1: Quiz Answers

1. The answer is B. Treasury regulations are published in the Federal Register and codified in Title 26 of the Code of Federal Regulations. Treasury Regulations are the highest administrative authority issued by the Treasury Department.

2. The answer is C. The IRS has 20 business days to say whether it will comply with an FOIA request. When a request is denied, the IRS must give the reason for denial and explain the right to appeal to the head of the agency.

3. The answer is B. Revenue rulings can be used to avoid certain accuracy-related IRS penalties. Taxpayers may rely on revenue rulings as official IRS guidance on an issue to make a decision regarding taxable income, deductions, and how to avoid certain IRS penalties.

4. The answer is A. A private letter ruling (PLR) is binding on the IRS if the taxpayer fully and accurately described the proposed transaction in his request and carried out the transaction as described.

5. The answer is D. A legislative regulation is authorized by Congress to provide the material requirements of a specific IRC provision. If written correctly, a legislative regulation carries the same authority as the Internal Revenue Code itself. It can only be overturned if it is outside the power delegated to the U.S. Treasury; it conflicts with a specific statute, or it is deemed unreasonable by the courts.

6. The answer is B. A legal opinion printed in a law journal does not have substantial authority. Sources of substantial authority are as follows: the Internal Revenue Code, temporary and final regulations, court cases, administrative pronouncements, tax treaties, Congressional intent as reflected in committee reports, proposed regulations, private letter rulings, technical advice memoranda, IRS information or press releases, IRS notices, and any other similar documents published by the IRS in the Internal Revenue Bulletin.

7. The answer is A. Although both the judicial and executive branches play important roles in interpreting, implementing, and enforcing tax laws, the legislative branch (Congress) is the main source of tax law in the United States. *Congress* is responsible for passing tax laws, which are published as the Internal Revenue Code, issued separately as Title 26 of the United States Code.

8. The answer is A. The Internal Revenue Manual (IRM) is the single official compilation of policies, delegated authorities, procedures, instructions, and guidelines relating to the organization, functions, administration, and operations of the IRS. It is the resource primarily used by IRS employees to guide them in all facets of operations.

9. The answer is C. The Taxpayer Advocate will likely intervene if Connor has waited for months for the IRS to discharge the lien on his property, which must be removed immediately, or else the sale of the property will fall through. The Taxpayer Advocate Service is designed to attempt to resolve issues when a taxpayer has a serious problem with the IRS or has experienced a serious delay. There are specific criteria used to determine whether taxpayer assistance is warranted, and the example in the correct answer is drawn from an actual case. On Form 911, Request for Taxpayer Advocate Service Assistance, a taxpayer must indicate one or more of the following reasons he is asking for help:

- He is experiencing economic harm or is about to suffer economic harm.
- He is facing an immediate threat of adverse action.
- He will incur significant costs if relief is not granted (including fees for professional representation).
- He will suffer irreparable injury or long-term adverse impact if relief is not granted.
- He has experienced a delay of more than 30 days to resolve a tax account problem.
- He has not received a response or resolution to his problem or inquiry by the date promised.
- A system or procedure has either failed to operate as intended, or failed to resolve the taxpayer's problem or dispute with the IRS.
- The manner in which the tax laws are being administered raises concerns of equity, or has impaired or will impair the taxpayer's rights.

10. The answer is D. The Internal Revenue Service must obey all decisions rendered by the highest court of the land, the U.S. Supreme Court. Although case law helps set precedent and will influence the IRS in its regulations, policies, and procedures, the IRS is not obligated to change its regulations in matters of tax law that are decided by other U.S. courts, including the U.S. Tax Court.

11. The answer is B. A Treasury regulation is the Treasury Department's official interpretation of the Internal Revenue Code. It has substantial authority in establishing a precedent for tax law.

Unit 2: Practice Before the IRS

> **More Reading:**
> Circular 230, Regulations Governing Practice Before the Internal Revenue Service
> Publication 947, Practice Before the IRS and Power of Attorney
> Publication 470, Limited Practice Without Enrollment
> Publication 5227, A Guide to the Annual Filing Season Program

"Practice before the IRS" includes all matters connected with a presentation before the IRS, or relating to a taxpayer's rights, privileges, or liabilities under laws or regulations administered by the IRS. Representation, or "practice before the IRS," is defined in *Publication 947, Practice Before the IRS and Power of Attorney.* "Practice before the IRS" includes:

1. Corresponding and communicating with the IRS

2. Representing a taxpayer at conferences, hearings, or meetings with the IRS

3. Preparing and filing documents with the IRS

4. Rendering written advice with respect to any entity, transaction, plan or arrangement, or other plan or arrangement having a potential for tax avoidance or evasion.

U.S. citizenship is not required to practice before the IRS.

> **Example:** Anika is a CPA. Her client, Samuel, has a large tax debt from a prior year. Samuel does not wish to communicate directly with the IRS, but he wants to set up an installment agreement. Anika has Samuel sign Form 2848, giving her power of attorney, and calls the IRS on his behalf to set up the installment agreement for him. This action is considered practice before the IRS.

In a significant loss for the IRS, the U.S. Court of Appeals for the District of Columbia upheld a lower court's decision that the IRS did not possess the legal authority to regulate tax return preparers. The issue centered on whether the "practice of representatives" included the mere preparation of tax returns.

The appeals court ruled it did not, and the IRS chose not to appeal the decision. This means that tax return preparation, in and of itself, does not constitute "practice before the IRS" under current law.[13]

Current federal law imposes no competency or licensing requirements on paid tax return preparers (although there are some states that now impose mandatory education or licensing requirements). Credentialed individuals who may prepare tax returns, including attorneys,

---

[13] The relevant court case is *Loving v. IRS,* No. 13-5061, D.C. Circuit Court of Appeals. At the time of this book's printing, the current version of Circular 230 (issued in June 2014) has not yet been updated to reflect the changes necessitated by the *Loving v. IRS decision,* including removal of the RTRP education and competency requirements. However, Publication 947 was more recently revised, and now states that unenrolled return preparers may represent a taxpayer before the IRS, but only if they participate in the Annual Filing Season Record of Completion (AFSP) program. In addition, they may only represent a taxpayer with respect to returns prepared and signed by the unenrolled preparer.

certified public accountants (CPAs), and enrolled agents (EAs), are generally required to pass competency tests and take continuing education courses.

Volunteers who prepare tax returns as part of the Volunteer Income Tax Assistance and Tax Counseling for the Elderly programs also must pass competency tests.

However, the vast majority of paid preparers are non-credentialed and are not required to pass competency tests, take any courses in tax return preparation, or follow prescribed standards of conduct.[14]

Enrolled Practitioners

The IRS defines "enrolled practitioners" as attorneys, CPAs, enrolled agents, enrolled retirement plan agents, or enrolled actuaries authorized to practice before the IRS. Only attorneys, CPAs, and EAs have *unlimited rights* to represent taxpayers before the IRS.

Other individuals may qualify to practice temporarily or engage in limited practice before the IRS. However, they are not referred to as "enrolled practitioners." The following individuals may represent taxpayers and practice before the IRS <u>by virtue of their licensing</u> unless they are currently under suspension or disbarment:

1. **Attorneys:** An attorney who is a member in good standing of the bar of any state, possession, territory, commonwealth, or of the District of Columbia.

2. **Certified Public Accountants (CPAs):** A CPA who is duly qualified to practice as a CPA in any state, possession, territory, commonwealth, or the District of Columbia.

3. **Enrolled Agents (EAs):** An enrolled agent with active status may represent clients before any office of the IRS. Like attorneys and CPAs, EAs are unrestricted as to which taxpayers they can represent and what types of tax matters they can handle.

4. **Enrolled Actuaries:** The practice of an individual enrolled as an actuary by the Joint Board for the Enrollment of Actuaries is limited to certain Internal Revenue Code sections that relate to his or her area of expertise, principally those sections governing employee retirement plans.

5. **Enrolled Retirement Plan Agents (ERPAs):** The practice of an enrolled retirement plan agent is limited to certain Internal Revenue Code sections that relate to his or her area of expertise, principally those sections governing employee retirement plans.

Note: The IRS **Office of Professional Responsibility** (OPR) has responsibility for matters related to practitioner conduct, discipline, disciplinary proceedings, and sanctions. The **Return Preparer Office** (RPO) is responsible for the issuance of PTINs, acting on applications for enrollment, and administering AFSP testing and continuing education for designated groups.

---

[14] The National Taxpayer Advocate 2023 Purple Book states that most non-credentialed preparers do not participate in the IRS' voluntary AFSP program.

Annual Filing Season Program (AFSP)

The IRS replaced its now-defunct RTRP program with the voluntary Annual Filing Season Program (AFSP) program.[15] Non-credentialed return preparers can elect to voluntarily demonstrate completion of basic filing season tax preparation and other tax law training by participating in the program.

The AFSP program is designed to encourage competence and education among unenrolled tax preparers. To receive an annual "record of completion," a preparer must normally have:

- A minimum of 18 hours of continuing education from an IRS-approved continuing education provider, including a six-hour "Annual Federal Tax Refresher" (AFTR) course.
- Passed a knowledge-based comprehension test administered by the CE provider at the end of the AFTR course.
- A current preparer tax identification number (PTIN).
- Consented to the "duties and restrictions relating to practice before the IRS" in Circular 230. This consent gives the IRS the authority to regulate those individuals who receive the record of completion.

Circular 230 has not yet been updated to include all the IRS's AFSP program information, which was designed to replace the now-defunct RTRP program. Normally the record of completion has to be applied for no later than April 15 for the year in which the preparer wants it to apply.

Exempt Individuals

Certain individuals may obtain the AFSP Record of Completion without taking the annual refresher tax course and exam, assuming they took at least fifteen hours of qualifying continuing education courses during the year. The following unenrolled preparers are exempt from the AFSP "annual refresher" course:

1. **State-based return preparer program participants:** Return preparers who are active registrants of state-based programs, such as the Oregon Board of Tax Practitioners, California Tax Education Council, and the Maryland State Board of Individual Tax Preparers.
2. **SEE Part I Test-Passers:** Tax practitioners who have passed the Special Enrollment Exam Part I within the past two years.
3. **VITA/TCE volunteers:** VITA and TCE volunteers who are quality reviewers, instructors, and return preparers with active PTINs.
4. **Other accredited tax-focused credential-holders:** The Accreditation Council for Accountancy and Taxation's Accredited Business Accountant/Advisor (ABA) and Accredited Tax Preparer (ATP) programs.

AFSP participants are included in a public, searchable database of tax return preparers on the IRS website. The *Directory of Federal Tax Return Preparers with Credentials and Select*

---

[15] Individuals who passed the now-defunct Registered Tax Return Preparer exam are exempt from the six-hour federal tax law refresher course. They only need 15 hours of continuing education each year to obtain an *Annual Filing Season Program – Record of Completion.* Other Individuals will need a total of 18 hours of continuing education hours. An AFTR course does not count toward enrolled agent continuing education requirements.

Qualifications includes the name, city, state, zip code, and credentials of attorneys, CPAs, EAs, ERPAs, and enrolled actuaries with a valid PTIN, as well as AFSP Record of Completion holders. An individual may choose to opt-out of being listed in the directory.

Currently, Annual Filing Season Program participants have *limited* practice rights before the IRS. AFSP participants may only represent clients whose returns they prepared and signed; and only before revenue agents, customer service representatives, and similar IRS employees, including the Taxpayer Advocate Service.

Only unenrolled preparers that participate in the IRS's Annual Filing Season Program (AFSP) will have these limited representation rights. Unenrolled preparers who do not participate in this annual program will no longer have the authority to represent clients before the IRS.

Unenrolled Tax Return Preparers

Individuals who prepare tax returns for other taxpayers but who are not EAs, CPAs, attorneys, ERPAs, or enrolled actuaries are called "unenrolled preparers." In general, unenrolled preparers have no practice rights before the IRS, unless they are AFSP participants.

Unenrolled tax return preparers that have current AFSP certificates may represent taxpayers in a limited capacity, but only during an IRS examination of the taxable year or period covered by the tax return or claim of refund they themselves prepared and signed.

This representation may occur only before revenue agents, customer service representatives, or similar officers and employees of the IRS, including the Taxpayer Advocate Service.[16] Unenrolled tax return preparers cannot do any of the following:

- Represent taxpayers before appeals officers, revenue officers, counsel, or similar officers or employees of the IRS or Department of Treasury
- Execute closing agreements
- Extend the statutory period for tax assessments or collection of tax
- Execute waivers
- Execute claims for refund
- Sign any document on behalf of a taxpayer

Unenrolled preparers who do not have an AFSP certificate are allowed to prepare tax returns for compensation, but they may not represent taxpayers before any level of the IRS, regardless of whether they prepared the return or not.[17]

---

[16] The IRS believes in a mandatory competency standard for federal tax return preparers. To this end, legislation continues to be their priority. In the interim, however, the AFSP program recognizes the efforts of unenrolled return preparers to improve their professional competency through continuing education. Subject to certain states (such as California, Oregon and Maryland) that require unenrolled return preparers to be specially licensed by their states, anyone with a PTIN can prepare a federal tax return, but for those preparers with a PTIN who also work to ready themselves for the filing season through educational efforts, the AFSP program affords them a level of differentiation from the rest of the marketplace.

[17] According to current IRS regulations, only unenrolled return preparers who hold a record of completion for BOTH the tax return year under examination and the year the examination is conducted may represent under the following conditions: Unenrolled return preparers may represent taxpayers only before revenue agents, customer service representatives, or similar officers and employees of the Internal Revenue Service (including the Taxpayer Advocate Service) and only during an examination of the taxable year or period covered by the tax returns they prepared and signed (Publication 947).

> **Example:** Wilfred is an unenrolled tax preparer, and he does not hold any formal licensing or have an AFSP certificate. Wilfred's client, Hester, is now being audited by the IRS. The IRS is examining Hester's income tax returns for 2020, 2021, and 2022 returns. Wilfred prepared all the tax returns under examination. However, since Wilfred is not an enrolled practitioner and does not have an AFSP certificate, he may not represent Hester before the IRS. Wilfred must refer Hester to an enrolled practitioner if she wishes to be represented.

> **Example:** Zelma is an unenrolled tax preparer with an AFSP certificate. She has always prepared tax returns for her client, Leo. On February 1, 2022, Leo receives an audit notice from the IRS for his prior year return, which Zelma prepared. Zelma can represent Leo before the IRS and respond to the notice, because she has a current AFSP certificate, and she prepared the return.

Limited Practice Due to 'Special Relationship'

Other individuals who are not enrolled practitioners may represent taxpayers before the IRS because of a special relationship with the taxpayer, without having prepared the tax return in question.

1. **An individual (self-representation):** An individual may always represent himself before the IRS, provided he has appropriate identification, such as a driver's license. He does not have to file a written declaration of qualification and authority. Even a disbarred individual may represent himself before the IRS. Disbarred practitioners are also allowed to represent family members, or act as fiduciaries for an estate or trust if a court appoints them.

2. **A family member:** An individual may represent members of his or her immediate family. For this purpose, family members include a spouse, child, parent, brother, or sister of the individual.

3. **An officer:** A bona fide officer of a corporation (including a parent, subsidiary, or affiliated corporation), association, organized group, or governmental agency may represent its corporation, association, organized group, or governmental agency before the IRS.

4. **A partner:** A general partner may represent the partnership before the IRS, but a limited partner may not.

5. **An employee:** A regular full-time employee can represent his employer. An employer can be an individual, partnership, corporation, association, trust, receivership, guardianship, estate, or organized group, or a governmental unit, agency, or authority.

6. **A fiduciary:** A fiduciary (trustee, executor, personal representative, administrator, receiver, or guardian) is considered to be the taxpayer and not a representative of the taxpayer.

7. **Qualifying Student or Law Graduate working in a LITC or STCP:** A taxpayer may authorize a student who works in a qualified Low Income Taxpayer Clinic (LITC) or Student Tax Clinic Program (STCP) to represent them under a special appearance authorization issued by the Taxpayer Advocate Service.

8. **Authorization for Special Appearances:** In rare circumstances, the Commissioner of the IRS or a delegate will authorize a person who is not otherwise eligible to practice before the IRS to represent another person for a particular matter. The request is made to the Office of Professional Responsibility (OPR). If granted, the written consent will detail the specific circumstances related to the appearance.

Example: Rich was a tax attorney who was disbarred because of felony embezzlement. A disbarred individual is not eligible to represent other taxpayers before the IRS. Rich was audited by the IRS in 2022. Despite being disbarred, Rich may still represent himself before the IRS during the examination of his own return. Rich may also represent a close family member, like his own child or his spouse.

Example: Leia is a 21-year-old accounting student. She is not an enrolled practitioner. Leia lives with her brother, Brandon, who is 32 and self-employed. Leia prepares her brother's tax return. Brandon is later audited by the IRS. Leia may represent her brother before the IRS, if Brandon signs a Form 2848, granting his sister representation rights. Leia will have all the rights that an enrolled practitioner would have, but only with respect to her brother's tax issues.

Example: Nicolette is a full-time payroll bookkeeper for her employer, Green Lawn Landscaping. The IRS sent her employer a notice regarding some delinquent payroll tax returns. Nicolette may file Form 2848, *Power of Attorney and Declaration of Representative*, and speak with the IRS on her employer's behalf. Even though Nicolette is not an enrolled preparer, she may represent Green Lawn Landscaping before the IRS because of the employee-employer relationship.

Example: Milton was named the executor of his mother's estate after she passed away. He is not an accountant or a tax professional, but Milton is allowed to represent his mother's estate before every level of the IRS because he is the fiduciary for her estate.

Example: Bartholomew's mother is being audited by the IRS. Bartholomew is an accountant who works as a controller for a manufacturing firm, but he is not a CPA or an enrolled agent. He does not have a PTIN because he does not prepare tax returns for compensation. He does prepare his mother's return, but he does not charge her for doing so. Even though Bartholomew is not enrolled to practice before the IRS, he is allowed to represent his mother because of their family relationship.

Persons Ineligible to Practice Before the IRS

Individuals not previously described are generally not eligible to practice before the IRS. Corporations, associations, partnerships, and other entities are not eligible to practice before the IRS. Even if named in a power of attorney as a representative, an individual will not be recognized if he has lost his eligibility to practice before the IRS.

Reasons for losing eligibility include suspension or disbarment by the OPR, being placed in inactive retirement status, and not meeting the requirements for renewal of enrollment, such as continuing professional education.

Actions That Are Not "Practice" Before the IRS

"Practice before the IRS" *does not* include:

1. Representation of taxpayers before the U.S. Tax Court: The Tax Court has its own rules of practice and its own rules regarding admission to practice.

2. Merely appearing as a witness for the taxpayer: In general, individuals who are not practitioners may appear before the IRS as witnesses—but they may not advocate for the taxpayer.

3. The preparation of a tax return (preparers do not practice before the IRS when they simply assist in the preparation of tax returns).

Example: James and Lenora are neighbors and lifelong friends. James is a retired bookkeeper, and he prepares Lenora's tax return for free. Later, Lenora is audited by the IRS. James is not an enrolled practitioner, and he cannot represent Lenora before the IRS. However, he is allowed to appear as a witness and provide information on her behalf. James cannot "advocate" for his friend.

Example: Valentina is a bookkeeper that does not have any type of professional licensing. Valentina's cousin, Diego, is audited by the IRS. Diego does not speak English very well, so Valentina offers to assist with information exchange during the audit. Valentina is not considered to be practicing before the IRS because she is merely serving as a translator when the taxpayer does not speak English. Valentina will be allowed to translate for her cousin, but she cannot advocate for him.

Tax Return Preparers

The IRS defines tax return preparers as individuals who participate in the preparation of tax returns for taxpayers for compensation. This includes preparers who are in business, casual or part-time preparers who receive fees for preparing tax returns, and certain e-file providers.

All paid tax return preparers must register with the IRS and obtain a preparer tax identification number (PTIN). The PTIN is a nine-digit number that preparers must use when they prepare and sign a tax return or a claim for refund.

The use of a PTIN is mandatory on all federal tax returns and claims for refund prepared by paid tax preparers.[18] Specifically, Circular 230 states that "any individual who for compensation prepares or assists with the preparation of all, or substantially all of a tax return or claim for refund" must have a PTIN.

Tax preparers who register for a PTIN must undergo a limited tax compliance check to ensure they have filed their own personal and business tax returns.

---

[18] As a PTIN expires every December 31, a preparer who renews their PTIN after December 31 may not prepare a tax return in the following year until the PTIN is issued.

The PTIN requirement applies to all enrolled agents and many attorneys and CPAs. Attorneys and CPAs do not need to obtain PTINs if they do not prepare federal tax returns, even if they represent clients in a federal tax matter.

Example: Trudy is a licensed attorney who specializes in employment law. She does not prepare tax returns for compensation. In 2022, Trudy is hired by Johnathan, a business owner who wants to contest a negative worker classification audit by the IRS. The IRS determined that Johnathan was improperly classifying his employees as independent contractors in order to avoid paying payroll taxes, but Johnathan vehemently disagrees. Johnathan has already received a Notice of Deficiency from the IRS, so Trudy files a petition in U.S. Tax Court on his behalf, and she will also represent him before the Tax Court if the case goes to trial. Although Trudy is representing her client in court in an IRS-related matter, she is not required to obtain a PTIN, because she does not prepare tax returns.

Multiple individuals cannot share one PTIN. A PTIN is assigned to a single preparer to identify that he is the preparer of a particular return. A PTIN cannot be transferred to another preparer, even if the practice is later sold. An applicant must be at least 18 years old to obtain a PTIN. Felony convictions and failure to meet federal tax obligations may affect an individual's ability to obtain a PTIN.

In the past, all paid preparers were required to pay a fee to renew their PTINs online. A group of tax preparers filed a class-action suit against the IRS, arguing that the agency's decision to charge the PTIN fee was arbitrary and capricious. The U.S. Court of Appeals for the District of Columbia Circuit ruled on March 1, 2019 that the IRS had authority under the *Independent Offices Appropriations Act* to charge a fee for PTINs. The PTIN fee is currently $30.75 and is non-refundable.

Third Party Designee	Do you want to allow another person to discuss this return with the IRS? See instructions . . . . □ **Yes.** Complete below. □ **No**					
	Designee's name		Phone no.		Personal identification number (PIN)	

Sign Here

Under penalties of perjury, I declare that I have examined this return and accompanying schedules and statements, and to the best of my knowledge and belief, they are true, correct, and complete. Declaration of preparer (other than taxpayer) is based on all information of which preparer has any knowledge.

	Your signature	Date	Your occupation	If the IRS sent you an Identity Protection PIN, enter it here (see inst.)
Joint return? See instructions. Keep a copy for your records.	ALEXANDER JONES	3/1/2023	DOCTOR	
	Spouse's signature. If a joint return, **both** must sign.	Date	Spouse's occupation	If the IRS sent your spouse an Identity Protection PIN, enter it here (see inst.)
	Phone no.		Email address	

Paid Preparer Use Only

Preparer's name	Preparer's signature	Date	PTIN	Check if:
JENNIFER SMITH, EA	Jennifer Smith, EA	3/1/2023	P12345678	☒ Self-employed
Firm's name SMITH TAX SERVICE			Phone no. 555-222-3333	
Firm's address 123 MAIN ST, ANYTOWN NV 89100			Firm's EIN 56-1112222	

Go to *www.irs.gov/Form1040* for instructions and the latest information.

Form **1040** (2022)

Preparers who fail to list a valid PTIN on tax returns they sign are subject to penalties. Preparers may also be subject to disciplinary action by the Office of Professional Responsibility. In order to renew a PTIN in 2022, a preparer must attest that they have a written information security plan (WISP).

Supervised Preparers

Supervised preparers are also required to have PTINs. These are individuals who do not sign tax returns as paid return preparers but are:

1. Employed by a law firm, EA office, or CPA practice; and
2. Are directly supervised by an attorney, CPA, EA, ERPA, or enrolled actuary who signs the returns prepared by the supervised preparer as the paid tax return preparer.
3. Supervised preparers may not:
   a. Sign any tax return they prepare or assist in preparing.
   b. Represent taxpayers before the IRS in any capacity.
   c. Identify themselves as Circular 230 practitioners.
   d. When applying for or renewing a PTIN, supervised preparers must provide the PTIN of their supervisor.

Exceptions to PTIN Requirements

An individual who prepares a tax return with no agreement for compensation is not considered a tax return preparer for IRS purposes. This is true even if the individual voluntarily receives a gift or a favor in return. The *agreement* for compensation is the deciding factor as to whether the IRS considers an individual a tax return preparer.

> **Example:** Skye is a CPA who specializes in business valuation and audit services. She works for an accounting firm with a tax division, but Skye does not prepare tax returns, because she only does audit work. Skye is not required to obtain a PTIN as long as she does not prepare tax returns. Lorene is an enrolled agent who works for the same accounting firm. She also does not prepare tax returns. Lorene only does some bookkeeping, and occasional tax planning. Unlike her co-worker Skye, Lorene is required to have a PTIN, even though she does not prepare tax returns, because she is an enrolled agent. All enrolled agents are required to have a PTIN.

> **Example:** Melanie is a retired CPA who only prepares tax returns for her close family members. She does not charge her family to prepare their tax returns. Sometimes, a family member will give Melanie a gift in return. This year, her sister gave her home-baked cookies, and her niece gave her a sweater. However, Melanie did not ask for any presents or expect them. She is not a tax return preparer for IRS purposes, and she is not required to obtain a PTIN.

An individual is not considered an income tax return preparer and would not be required to obtain a PTIN in the following instances:

- A person who gives an opinion about events that have not happened (such as tax advice for a business that has not been created).
- A person who furnishes typing, copying, or mechanical assistance.
- A person who prepares the return of his employer (or of an officer or employee of the employer) by whom the person is regularly and continuously employed.
- A fiduciary who prepares a tax return for a trust or estate.

- An unpaid volunteer who provides tax assistance under Volunteer Income Tax Assistance (VITA), Low Income Taxpayer Clinic (LITC), or Tax Counseling for the Elderly (TCPE) programs.
- An employee of the IRS who performs official duties by preparing a tax return for a taxpayer who requests it.

Note: Do not confuse a PTIN with an EFIN, which is an electronic filing identification number. An EFIN is a number issued by the IRS to individuals who have been approved as authorized IRS e-file providers. Although most tax preparers must use IRS e-file, some preparers are ineligible for the e-file program. Currently, the IRS e-file program does not accept foreign preparers without Social Security numbers who live and work abroad. These preparers must still obtain a PTIN, but they are not required to e-file their clients' returns since they are not eligible for an EFIN.

Example: Ingrid is a bookkeeper for Superb Realty Services, Inc. She is a full-time employee, and she prepares the payroll checks and payroll tax returns for all of the employees of Superb Realty Services. As a full-time employee, Ingrid is not considered a tax return preparer since her employer is ultimately responsible for the accuracy of the company's payroll tax returns. Ingrid is not required to obtain a PTIN.

Example: Quincy is an EA. He has a valid PTIN. He employs an administrative assistant, Madeline, who performs data entry during the tax filing season. At times, clients call and provide Madeline with information, which she records in the system. Using the data Madeline has entered, Quincy meets with his clients and provides tax advice as needed. He then prepares and signs their returns. Madeline is not a tax return preparer and is not required to have a PTIN.

Example: Ernie is a retired tax accountant, and he does not have a PTIN, because he stopped preparing returns several years ago. This year, Ernie decides to volunteer at a Tax Counseling for the Elderly (TCE) site, where he prepares individual tax returns for lower-income seniors for free. In this capacity, Ernie is not a tax return preparer and is not required to have a PTIN.

Example: Kelsey is a licensed CPA. His neighbor, Helena, consults with Kelsey about a bakery business she is thinking about starting. Kelsey gives Helena an opinion regarding the potential business and taxes. In this case, the IRS does not consider Kelsey a tax return preparer. This is because Kelsey is merely giving an opinion about events that have not yet happened.

The "Substantial Portion" Rule

Only the person who prepares all or a "substantial portion" of a tax return is considered the preparer of the return. Preparers of income, estate, and gift tax returns are all subject to the rule. With regards to tax preparation firms, only one person in a firm will be deemed the "signing preparer," but both the firm and the person with primary responsibility can be penalized if the return contains an unreasonable position. A person who merely gives advice or prepares a portion of a tax return is considered to have prepared only that portion.

If more than one individual is involved in the preparation of a tax return, the person with the primary responsibility for the overall accuracy of the return is considered the preparer and must sign the return. In order to identify who is responsible for a substantial portion of the return, the following guidelines may be used.

A portion of a tax return is not typically considered to be "substantial" if it involves only amounts of gross income, amounts of deductions, or amounts on the basis of which credits are determined that are:

- Less than $10,000, or
- Less than $400,000 and less than 20% of the adjusted gross income on the return.

Usually, a single IRS schedule would not be considered a substantial portion of a tax return unless it represents a major portion of the income. One example of this may be a business taxpayer with a Schedule C that represents a majority of the income on the return.

Example: Emilio and Kristy are equal partners in Sunbelt Tax Services, LLC, where they both work as enrolled agents. In March, Kristy finishes a few tax returns that Emilio had started before he left on vacation. Six months later, one tax return comes up for audit, and it is determined that the return has a gross valuation misstatement for a large deduction. Emilio prepared Schedule C on the return, and Kristy prepared the rest of the return. Schedule C represents 95% of the income and expenses shown on the return. Therefore, for purposes of any potential preparer penalty, Emilio is considered the preparer of this return, since he completed the schedule that represents the majority of the income and expenses on the return.

Example: Kaufman Accountancy, Inc. is a mid-sized CPA firm that offers audit and tax services to large businesses and wealthy individuals. William Smith is a wealthy real estate investor that hires Kaufman Accountancy to prepare his individual tax return. William owns 25 rental properties, as well as several investments in limited partnerships. His return is extremely complex, and two accountants in the firm, David and Nicole, work together to complete it. The most complex part of the return was the Schedule E, which was completed by David, and included the partnership flow-through income, as well as the rental income. This Schedule accounted for 90% of the income reported on William's return. As the preparer of the Schedule E, David is considered the accountant with primary responsibility for the accuracy of the return.

Enrolled Agent Licensing

As outlined in Circular 230, there are two tracks to become an enrolled agent. An individual may receive the designation by passing a three-part exam, or by virtue of past employment with the IRS.

1. Exam Track: For the first track, an EA candidate must apply for a PTIN and register to take the Special Enrollment Examination (SEE), also known as the EA exam, by filling out *Form 2587, Application for Special Enrollment Examination.* A candidate then must:

- Achieve passing scores on all three parts of the SEE.
- File *Form 23, Application for Enrollment to Practice before the Internal Revenue Service,* to apply for enrollment within one year from the date of passing the exam. Form 23 can now be submitted online, and the fee can be paid at *www.pay.gov.*

- Pass a background check conducted by the IRS: the tax compliance check makes sure the applicant has filed all necessary tax returns and has no outstanding tax liabilities. The suitability check determines whether an applicant has engaged in any conduct that would justify suspension or disbarment.

2. Previous Experience Track: For the second track, an EA candidate must possess a minimum of five years of past service with the IRS that includes technical experience as outlined in Circular 230. The application must be made within three years from the date the employee left the IRS. Factors considered with this second track are the length and scope of employment and the recommendation of the superior officer. The applicant then must:
- Apply for enrollment on Form 23.
- Pass a background check, which includes a tax compliance check and a suitability check.

Former IRS employees who become enrolled agents without taking the EA exam may be granted limited or unlimited representation rights. The IRS's Return Preparer Office (RPO) makes the determination on applications for enrollment to practice.

The RPO provides oversight of competency testing, enrollment, renewal, and continuing education of enrolled agents. Once an individual's application is approved, the IRS will issue an enrollment card, and enrollment becomes effective on that date.

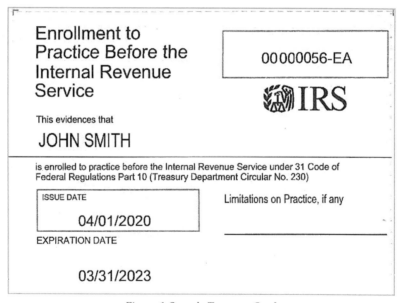

Figure 1-Sample Treasury Card

Denial of Enrollment

Any individual who is involved in disreputable or criminal conduct is subject to disciplinary action or denial of enrollment. Disreputable acts alone may be grounds for denial of enrollment, even after the candidate has passed the EA exam. Failure to timely file tax returns or to pay one's taxes may also be grounds for the Return Preparer Office to deny any application for enrollment.

The IRS must inform the applicant of the reason they are denied enrollment. The applicant may then file a written appeal to the Office of Professional Responsibility (OPR) within 30 days from the date of the notice. The appeal must be filed along with the candidate's reasoning why the enrollment application should be accepted.

> **Example:** Sheldon passed all three parts of the EA exam and filed Form 23, requesting enrollment. Because he had failed to file numerous tax returns in the past, his application was denied. Sheldon filed an appeal with the OPR, explaining he had failed to file on time because he had been seriously injured years ago. He attached supporting evidence, including copies of medical bills and a letter from his doctor. Sheldon also provided evidence that all his tax returns had been properly filed after his recovery. The OPR accepted Sheldon's appeal and granted him enrollment.

> **Example:** Martin passed all three parts of the EA exam, and wants to become an enrolled agent. However, six years ago, Martin was convicted of embezzlement and felony wire fraud. He served a year in prison and was ordered to pay restitution to his victims. The felony offense is grounds for denial of enrollment. Martin submits application, but it is denied, based on his past felony offense.

Renewal of Enrollment

Enrolled agents must renew their enrollment status every three years. To renew, an EA must file Form 8554, *Application for Renewal of Enrollment to Practice before the Internal Revenue Service*, and submit the required fee. Enrolled agents that do not renew their enrollment, may not practice before the IRS.

The three successive enrollment years preceding the effective date of renewal is referred to as the IRS "enrollment cycle." Applications for renewal of enrollment must be submitted between November 1 and January 31, prior to April 1 of the year that the next enrollment cycle begins. The last digit of a practitioner's Social Security number determines when he must renew enrollment. The IRS sends a reminder notice when an EA is due for renewal. However, an enrolled agent is not excused from the obligation to renew if he does not receive the notice. It is the practitioner's responsibility to apply for renewal by filing Form 8554. If the candidate's SSN ends in:

SSN ends in:	Renewal Cycle	Renewal Application Period[19]	Renewal Cycle Expiration
7, 8, 9, or no SSN	2021-2024	November 1, 2023 - January 31, 2024	March 31, 2024
0, 1, 2, 3	2022-2025	November 1, 2024 - January 31, 2025	March 31, 2025
4, 5 or 6	2023-2026	November 1, 2025 - January 31, 2026	March 31, 2026

---

[19] From IRS Publication 5186, available at: https://www.irs.gov/pub/irs-pdf/p5186.pdf.

EAs who do not have an SSN (such as foreign preparers who work overseas) must use the "7, 8, or 9" renewal schedule. As part of the renewal process, the IRS will check the practitioner's filing history to verify that he has filed and paid all federal taxes on time.

If the enrolled agent owns or has an interest in a business, the IRS will also check the tax compliance history of the business. In addition, the IRS will check that the EA has completed all necessary professional continuing education requirements. An EA must inform the Return Preparer Office of an address change within 60 days of a move.

Continuing Education for Enrolled Agents

During each three-year enrollment cycle, an EA must complete 72 hours of continuing education (CE) credit. A minimum of 16 hours, including two hours of ethics or professional conduct, must be completed during each enrollment year.

The IRS conducts random CE audits of EAs by requesting copies of their continuing education certificates of completion for the past three years. Recipients of these letters will be asked to mail or fax the documents within 30 days. The first month of enrollment begins the CE requirement for a new EA. The practitioner must complete two hours of CE for each month enrolled, and two hours of ethics for the enrollment year. Enrollment for any part of a month is considered enrollment for the entire month. The initial CE Requirements for EAs in their first enrollment cycle are:

- **2 hours of CE for every month enrolled**
- **2 hours of ethics annually (no exceptions)**

> **Note:** Generally, newly enrolled EAs will not need 72 hours of CE because they will not have been enrolled for all three years of the cycle. The 16-hour yearly minimum may not apply to them for at least one of the three years of the cycle.

When an EA's new three-year enrollment cycle begins, the practitioner will be required to satisfy the full 72-hour continuing education credit requirement. A 2-hour ethics course must be taken <u>every year</u>. An enrolled agent may not take additional ethics courses in the current year and neglect to take them in future years.

> **Example:** Charisse passed all three parts of the EA exam on July 1, 2022. She submitted her application for enrollment and received her Treasury card and license number on September 1, 2022 (2 months later). This was the third year of the enrollment cycle based on her SSN. She is required to take two hours of CE for <u>each month</u> before January 1, 2023, which equals eight hours for the period of September through December, 2022. Two of those hours must be on the topic of ethics. Charisse attends a national tax conference on December 19, 2022. She takes a 2-hour ethics course as well as an additional 10 hours of CE on various tax topics. She has fulfilled her CE requirements for the year. Since her initial enrollment came during the final year of the enrollment cycle, Charisse must renew her enrollment status in 2023 and will be subject to the full 72-hour CE requirement during her subsequent renewal periods.

Note: If an enrolled agent *retakes* and passes the SEE again since their last renewal, the EA is only required to take 16 hours of CE (continuing education), including two hours of ethics, during the last year of their current enrollment cycle.

CE Providers: Individuals and companies who wish to offer continuing education to EAs must pay a registration fee and apply as providers with the IRS. Providers are issued a provider number and may display a logo that says: "IRS Approved Continuing Education Provider." Course providers must renew their status every year.

Approved Programs: Qualifying programs include traditional seminars and conferences, as well as correspondence or individual self-study programs on the Internet, so long as they are approved courses of study by approved providers.

In order to qualify as CE, a course must be designed to enhance professional knowledge in federal taxation or federal tax-related matters. Courses related to state taxation do not meet the IRS requirement unless at least 80% of the program material consists of a comparison of federal and state tax laws.

Contact Hours: Continuing education programs are measured in terms of contact hours. The shortest recognized program is one hour. In order for a course to qualify for CE credit, it must feature at least 50 minutes of continuous participation. Individual segments at conferences and conventions are considered one total program. For example, two 90-minute segments (180 minutes) at a continuous conference will count as **three** "contact hours."

Example: Stephanie is an enrolled agent who signs up for a half-day federal tax update class. The instructor starts the class promptly at 8 a.m. and lectures until 9:40 a.m., when the class takes a 20-minute break. The instructor resumes the class at 10 a.m., and it runs until 11:40 a.m. when the class is recessed. Stephanie will receive four CE credits because she completed four 50-minute segments of instruction, worth one contact hour each.

Instructor Credit: An enrolled agent may receive continuing education credit for serving as an instructor, discussion leader, or speaker on federal tax matters for approved educational programs. One hour of CE credit is awarded for each contact hour completed. Two hours of CE credit is awarded for actual subject preparation time for each contact hour completed as an instructor, discussion leader, or speaker at such programs. The maximum credit for instruction and preparation may not exceed six hours annually.

Verifying CE Hours: After completing CE coursework, an EA will receive a certificate from the course provider. The course provider will also report completed continuing education to the IRS, using the PTINs of the individual participants.

Tax preparers may check their online PTIN accounts to see a display of the CE programs they have completed, as reported by providers. EAs are required to keep track of their own records related to continuing education hours for four years following the date of renewal.

CE Waiver

An EA may request a full or partial waiver of CE requirements from the RPO. Qualifying circumstances may include:

- Health issues
- Extended active military duty
- Absence from the United States for employment or other reasons
- Other reasons on a case-by-case basis

The request for a waiver must be accompanied by appropriate documentation, such as medical records or military paperwork. If the request is denied, the enrolled agent will be placed on the inactive roster. If the request is accepted, the EA will receive an updated enrollment card reflecting his renewal.

> **Example:** Benedict is an EA who is also an Army reservist. He was called to active duty in a combat zone for two years. During his deployment, Benedict was unable to complete his CE requirements for his enrolled agent license. Benedict contacted RPO and requested a waiver based on his current active-duty military service. RPO grants the waiver. Benedict later returns to the United States after an honorable discharge. Benedict is free to begin preparing tax returns as an enrolled agent again.

Inactive and Terminated EAs

RPO notifies any EA who fails to comply with the requirements for eligibility for renewal of enrollment. A notice will be sent via first-class mail explaining the reason for noncompliance.

The notice further provides the preparer an opportunity to furnish the requested information, such as missing CE credits, in writing. An EA has 60 days from the date of the notice to respond to this initial notice. If no response is received, the EA will be moved to inactive status.

To be eligible for renewal after missing one full enrollment cycle, an EA must pay fees for both the prior and current renewal cycles and verify that the required CE hours have been taken. To have his termination status reconsidered, an EA must file a written protest within 30 days and provide a valid reason for not renewing on time. Reasons may include serious illness or extended travel out of the country.

Losing the Eligibility to Practice

Practitioners may lose their eligibility to practice before the IRS for the following reasons, among others:

- Failure to meet the annual continuing education requirements for enrollment (for EAs).
- Failure to renew a PTIN.
- Requesting to be placed on inactive/retirement status.
- Being disciplined by state regulatory agents. For example, an attorney who has been disbarred from practice at the state level or a CPA whose license has been revoked or

suspended at the state level is disbarred from practice at the federal level, and cannot practice before the IRS as long as their disbarment, revocation, or suspension is active.

> **Example:** Aileen is an enrolled agent. On January 25, 2022, the Office of Professional Responsibility disbarred Aileen for stealing a client's tax payments and preparing tax returns with false deductions for multiple clients. Aileen's enrolled agent status is revoked for at least five years. After five years, Aileen may try to petition for reinstatement, but reinstatement would be solely at the IRS' discretion.

> **Example:** Jose is a tax attorney who practiced in New York. On March 3, 2022, Jose was convicted of a felony after a domestic assault case when he attacked his neighbor with a deadly weapon. Jose is later disbarred as an attorney, which means he can no longer practice either at the state level, or before the IRS.

Unit 2: Study Questions

(Test yourself and then check the correct answers at the end of this chapter.)

1. Rose's tax return is under audit. All of the following persons are permitted to represent Rose before the examination division of the IRS **except:**

A. Paula, Rose's best friend, who is a licensed attorney in the state where Rose lives.
B. Gary, who is Rose's brother, who is neither an attorney, CPA, nor an enrolled agent.
C. Harold, Rose's boyfriend. Harold has an AFSP certificate, and he is an unenrolled return preparer, but he did not prepare the return under audit.
D. Rosalie, who is Rose's mother. Rosalie is a retired accountant with an inactive CPA license.

2. Cameron is an enrolled agent who takes a continuing education class from an approved IRS provider. The class runs continuously from 9 a.m. until 11:45 a.m., when there is a break for lunch. How many CE credits will Cameron receive for the morning session of the class?

A. One
B. Two
C. Three
D. Four

3. Everett is an EA with a PTIN. His firm employs a bookkeeper named Fernanda. Fernanda gathers client receipts and invoices and organizes and records all information for Everett. She does not use Everett's professional tax return software, but she does use the firm's bookkeeping software. Everett then uses the information that his bookkeeper has compiled and prepares all the client tax returns. Which of the following statements is correct?

A. Fernanda needs to have a PTIN, and she is required to become an EA or AFSP.
B. Fernanda needs to have a PTIN, but she is not required to become an EA.
C. Fernanda is a supervised preparer and needs to have a PTIN.
D. Fernanda is not a tax return preparer and is not required to have a PTIN.

4. Denise and Gabriela are cousins. Gabriela must appear before the IRS for an examination. Denise wants to appear before the IRS on her cousin's behalf, though she is not an enrolled practitioner. Which of the following statements is correct?

A. Denise may appear before the IRS as a witness and communicate information.
B. Denise may advocate for Gabriela to the best of her ability.
C. Denise may represent Gabriela before the IRS without Gabriela being present.
D. Denise may not appear before the IRS in any capacity.

5. What is the "enrollment cycle" for enrolled agents?

A. The enrollment cycle is the year after the effective date of renewal.
B. The enrollment cycle means the three successive enrollment years preceding the effective date of renewal.
C. The enrollment cycle is the method by which the RPO approves EA exam candidates.
D. The enrollment cycle is the method Prometric uses to choose EA exam questions.

6. The IRS's public directory of tax return preparers includes listings for:

A. Practitioners with a current PTIN, as well as practitioners who are inactive status.
B. All current and past PTIN holders.
C. Enrolled agents and CPAs with a current PTIN.
D. All enrolled practitioners with a current PTIN, as well as AFSP Record of Completion holders.

7. Which of the following individuals is required to obtain a PTIN?

A. A CPA who does not prepare any tax returns.
B. An EA who works for a CPA firm, but does not sign any tax returns.
C. A tax attorney who only does representation of clients in the U.S. court system.
D. A retired accountant who prepares tax returns for free for his family.

8. Which of the following individuals does *not* qualify as an enrolled practitioner?

A. Certified public accountant.
B. Enrolled actuary.
C. Registered tax return preparer.
D. Attorney.

9. Gabriela is an EA. Her records show that she had the following hours of qualified CE during the year:
- January 2, 2022, seven hours: Federal tax CE.
- May 3, 2022, one hour: Ethics.
- December 20, 2022, nine hours: Federal tax CE.

Has Gabriela met her minimum yearly CE requirements?

A. Gabriela has met all her minimum yearly CE requirements.
B. Gabriela has met her ethics requirement, but not the minimum CE requirement for the year.
C. Gabriela has not met her ethics requirements.
D. None of the above.

10. Johnny passed all three parts of the EA exam, and applied immediately by filing Form 23. When does his official enrollment take effect?

A. The date he applies for enrollment with the IRS.
B. The date listed on his enrollment card.
C. The date he receives his enrollment card.
D. The day he passes all three parts of the EA exam.

11. Matthew is a full-time bookkeeper for Parkway Partnership. He is not an EA, attorney, or CPA. Parkway requests that Matthew represent the partnership in connection with an IRS audit. Which of the following statements is correct?

A. Matthew is allowed to represent the partnership before the IRS.
B. Matthew is not allowed to represent the partnership before the IRS.
C. Matthew is allowed to represent individual partners before the IRS.
D. Matthew must have an AFSP certificate to represent the partnership before the IRS.

12. Which of the following is considered a tax return preparer under Circular 230 regulations?

A. A full-time bookkeeper working for an employer who prepares payroll tax returns.
B. A retired attorney who prepares tax returns under the VITA program.
C. A full-time teacher who also prepares tax returns for pay, part-time from home.
D. A secretary who furnishes typing, reproducing, or mechanical assistance.

13. Barry helps his best friend, Jose, who does not speak English fluently. Barry appears before the IRS and translates for Jose at an IRS examination. Which of the following statements is correct?

A. Barry is not considered to be practicing before the IRS.
B. Jose must sign a power of attorney form authorizing Barry to represent him.
C. Barry is considered to be practicing before the IRS.
D. The IRS prohibits unrelated persons from being present at an IRS examination.

14. Khan is a CPA who employs Lynne, an accounting student, to assist in preparing tax returns. Lynne prepares several of the easier tax returns, but Khan reviews and signs all of the returns. Which of the following statements is correct?

A. Lynne and Khan can share one PTIN.
B. Lynne is required by law to sign the returns that she has prepared.
C. Lynne is required to obtain a PTIN.
D. Lynne cannot assist with the preparation of tax returns until she becomes a CPA.

15. Enrolled agents must complete continuing education credits for renewed enrollment. Which of the following best describes the *minimum* yearly credit requirements?

A. A minimum of 72 hours must be completed in each year of an enrollment cycle.
B. A minimum of 24 hours must be completed in each year of an enrollment cycle.
C. A minimum of 16 hours must be completed for the entire enrollment cycle, on any topic.
D. A minimum of 16 hours must be completed in each year of the enrollment cycle, including two hours of ethics.

16. All of the following are potential grounds for denial of enrollment except:

A. Failure to timely file tax returns.
B. Failure to pay taxes.
C. A candidate who is only 18 years old.
D. Felony convictions.

17. "Practice before the IRS" does not include:

A. Communicating directly with the IRS on behalf of a taxpayer.
B. Representing a taxpayer at an IRS examination.
C. Representing a taxpayer before the IRS appeals division.
D. Representing a taxpayer in the U.S. Tax Court.

18. Lamond's EA license was terminated by the Office of Professional Responsibility for disreputable conduct. Lamond disagrees with OPR's decision. What action should Lamond take if he chooses to appeal his termination from enrollment?

A. Call the Office of Professional Responsibility to request an appeal.
B. File a written protest within 30 days of the date of the notice of termination.
C. File a written protest within 60 days of the date of the notice of termination.
D. File a written protest within 90 days of the date of the notice of termination.

19. Enrolled agents who apply for renewal to practice before the IRS must retain information about continuing education hours completed. How long must this documentation be retained?

A. For one year following the enrollment renewal date.
B. For four years following the enrollment renewal date.
C. For five years if it is an initial enrollment.
D. The individual is not required to retain the documentation if the CE provider retains it.

20. An enrolled agent can represent a taxpayer _____.

A. Before any administrative level of the IRS.
B. Only if the EA prepared the return.
C. At all tax-related federal court proceedings.
D. Before collections, examinations, and the U.S. Tax Court.

21. Matias is an EA with a PTIN. What must he do to retain his existing PTIN?

A. Matias is allowed to retain his PTIN so long as he is current in his enrollment status.
B. Matias must renew his PTIN every three years when he renews his enrollment status.
C. Matias cannot retain his existing PTIN. He must apply for a new PTIN every year.
D. Matias must renew his existing PTIN each year.

Unit 2: Quiz Answers

1. The answer is C. Harold cannot represent Rose, because he is an unenrolled tax return preparer, and he did not prepare Rose's return. Even though Harold has an AFSP certificate, unenrolled tax preparers are not permitted to represent a taxpayer except in the examination of a tax return they prepared. According to current law, only unenrolled return preparers participating in the Annual Filing Season Record of Completion (AFSP) program may represent a taxpayer, and only with respect to returns prepared and signed by the preparer. The other persons listed would be able to represent Rose. Answer "A" is incorrect because Paula would be able to represent Rose because she is a licensed attorney. Answers "B" and "D" are incorrect, because Gary and Rosalie would both be permitted to represent Rose under the rules for limited practice (because of familial relationship).

2. The answer is C. Cameron will receive three hours of CE credit. Continuing education program credits are measured in terms of contact hours, which must be at least 50 minutes long. The class ran for 165 minutes, which counts as three contact hours. If the class had run continuously until 12:20 p.m., it would have lasted 200 minutes, so it would have been worth four CE hours.

3. The answer is D. Fernanda is not a tax return preparer and is not required to have a PTIN. An individual who provides only typing, reproduction, or other mechanical assistance but does not actually prepare returns is not considered a tax return preparer by the IRS.

4. The answer is A. Denise is not a close family member to Gabriela, so she may appear before the IRS only as a witness and communicate information. Simply appearing as a witness is not considered practice before the IRS. Individuals who are not practitioners may appear before the IRS as witnesses or communicate to the IRS on a taxpayer's behalf—but they may not advocate for the taxpayer.

5. The answer is B. The "enrollment cycle" means the three successive enrollment years preceding the effective date of renewal. After the initial enrollment period, regular renewal enrollments are required every three years. This is known as an enrollment cycle.

6. The answer is D. The Annual Filing Season Program is a voluntary certificate program to replace the registered tax return preparer program. Participants will be included in a public, searchable database of tax return preparers on the IRS website. The Directory of Federal Tax Return Preparers with Credentials and Select Qualifications includes the name, city, state, zip code, and credentials of all attorneys, CPAs, EAs, ERPAs, and enrolled actuaries with a valid PTIN, as well as all AFSP Record of Completion holders. An individual may opt-out of being listed in the directory. Unenrolled preparers with PTINs who are not Record of Completion holders are not listed in the directory.

7. The answer is B. All EAs are required to obtain PTINs as a condition of their licensing (the PTIN must be included on Form 23, which is the application form to become an enrolled agent). Attorneys and CPAs do not need to obtain a PTIN unless they prepare tax returns for compensation. Someone who prepares returns for free (or as a volunteer) is not considered a tax return preparer by the IRS and does not need a PTIN.

8. The answer is C. The registered tax return preparer designation is now defunct due to the IRS's loss in the *Loving v. Commissioner* case. An individual who passed the RTRP exam is considered an unenrolled preparer, not an enrolled practitioner. Currently, only Annual Filing Season Program participants have limited practice rights before the IRS as unenrolled preparers. An unenrolled preparer may only represent a taxpayer for the tax return or claim of refund he personally prepared and signed. This representation may occur only before revenue agents and similar employees of the IRS, and not before appeals or revenue officers. An unenrolled preparer also may not sign any document on behalf of a taxpayer.

9. The answer is C. Gabriela has not met her annual ethics requirement. The IRS requires a 16-hour minimum of CE per year and two hours of ethics per year, and Gabriela has only completed one hour of ethics CE. She has met her general CE requirement, but she has not met the ethics requirement for the year, so her minimum requirements have not been met.

10. The answer is B. Johnny must apply for enrollment by filing Form 23, and he must wait for his application to process. His enrollment becomes official on the date listed on his enrollment card.

11. The answer is A. Matthew is a full-time employee for Parkway Partnership, so in that capacity, he may represent his employer before the IRS. A regular full-time employee of an individual employer may represent the employer without any additional licensing.

12. The answer is C. A person who prepares tax returns for compensation is a tax return preparer, even if the activity is only part-time. A person who prepares and signs a tax return without compensation (such as for a family member or as a volunteer) is not considered a tax return preparer for purposes of preparer penalties. An employee who prepares a tax return for his employer or for another employee is not a preparer under Circular 230. The employer (or the individual with supervisory responsibility) is responsible for the accuracy of the return.

13. The answer is A. Barry is not considered to be practicing before the IRS. Simply appearing as a witness or communicating information to the IRS does not constitute practice before the IRS. Barry is merely assisting with the exchange of information and is not advocating on Jose's behalf. An example of an individual assisting with information exchange but not practicing would be a taxpayer's friend serving as a translator when the taxpayer does not speak English.

14. The answer is C. Lynne must obtain her own PTIN. Every individual who prepares or assists in the preparation of a tax return or claims for refund for compensation must have her own PTIN.

15. The answer is D. A minimum of 16 hours of continuing education credit, including two hours of ethics credits, must be completed in each year of the enrollment cycle. An EA must also complete a minimum of 72 hours of continuing education during each three-year period.

16. The answer is C. The minimum age for enrollment is 18, so an 18-year-old would not be denied enrollment based solely on his age. Failure to timely file tax returns or pay taxes, and felony convictions are all potential grounds for denying an enrollment application. The Return Preparer Office will review all of the facts and circumstances to determine whether a denial of enrollment is warranted.

17. The answer is D. "Practice before the IRS" does not include the representation of clients in the U.S. Tax Court. The Tax Court is independent of the IRS and has its own rules of practice and its own regulations regarding admission to practice.

18. The answer is B. Lamond should file a written protest within 30 days of the notice of termination, if he wants to appeal the termination of his enrollment. The protest must be filed with the Office of Professional Responsibility.

19. The answer is B. Each enrolled agent applying for renewal must retain information about CE hours completed for four years following the enrollment renewal date.

20. The answer is A. An enrolled agent can represent a taxpayer before any administrative level of the IRS, but not the U.S. Tax Court. Only enrolled agents, attorneys, and CPAs have unlimited practice rights before the IRS.

21. The answer is D. The IRS requires all paid preparers to have a preparer tax identification number (PTIN). Matias must renew his existing PTIN each year by the December 31 deadline to avoid any lapse in his active PTIN status. He may renew online at the IRS website or by mailing Form W-12.

Unit 3: Authorizations and Disclosures

> **More Reading:**
> Publication 947, Practice Before the IRS and Power of Attorney
> Instructions for Form 2848
> Publication 4019, Third Party Authorization, Levels of Authority
> Publication 4299, Privacy, Confidentiality, and Civil Rights

Power of Attorney

A power of attorney (POA) is a taxpayer's written authorization for an individual to act on the taxpayer's behalf in tax matters. A power of attorney gives an eligible individual, which includes all practitioners, the ability to represent a taxpayer before the IRS. Often, this occurs when a taxpayer wants to be represented at a conference with the IRS or to have a written response prepared and filed with the IRS.

When a taxpayer wishes to use a representative, he or she should fill out and sign Form 2848, *Power of Attorney and Declaration of Representative.* In doing so, the taxpayer authorizes a specific individual to receive confidential tax information and to perform the actions detailed on the form. Up to four representatives can be authorized per form.

> **Note:** The Taxpayer First Act (TFA) required the IRS to provide digital signature options for Form 2848, *Power of Attorney*, and Form 8821, *Tax Information Authorization.* On January 28, 2021, the IRS launched an online tool that allows the upload of Forms 2848 and 8821 with e-signatures. The practitioner must have a Secure Access account, including a current username and password, or create an account in advance of submitting an online authorization form. The taxpayer and the preparer must sign any uploaded Form 2848. Form 8821 needs only the taxpayer's signature. If using the new online tool, the taxpayer's signature can be handwritten or electronic.

A practitioner can also submit an authorization request directly to a taxpayer's online IRS account. It is an all-digital submission with a direct taxpayer electronic signature that allows for real-time processing of the Form 2848 or Form 8821.

On Form 2848, the representative must attest that he or she is subject to the regulations of Circular 230, governing practice before the IRS.[20] The Form 2848 must describe the tax matters the representative is authorized to handle, the time periods allowed, and the specific acts that are authorized or not authorized. A separate Form 2848 must be completed for each taxpayer who wishes representation; even joint filers must submit separate Forms 2848.

The types of tax and dates of a Form 2848 must be specific. The IRS will reject Forms 2848 with general references such as "all years" or "all taxes." In preparing the form, any tax years or periods that have already ended may be listed under "tax matters."

---

[20] This attestation gives the Office of Professional Responsibility the authority to regulate unenrolled tax preparers who use the form.

For future tax periods, the period specified is limited to no later than three years after the date the POA is received by the IRS. A representative must be eligible to practice before the IRS in order to sign Form 2848, and the duty may not be delegated to an employee.

A practitioner must provide his PTIN and use his own name as the representative, rather than the name of his business.

Example: Beatriz is an enrolled agent who owns and operates Remit Tax Service, Inc. She has multiple employees working for her, but she is the only enrolled practitioner in the office. When Beatriz prepares a Form 2848 for a client, she must represent her client as an individual. She must list her name on the Form 2848, not the name of her company or the name of another employee. Since Beatriz is the only enrolled practitioner in the firm, only she is granted permission to represent her client before the IRS. Her corporation and other employees of her firm are not.

In filling out Form 2848, a representative must enter the designation under which he or she is authorized to practice before the IRS, and list the applicable jurisdiction. For example, an enrolled agent must list the IRS as the licensing jurisdiction. If a tax practitioner is disbarred or suspended, his power of attorney will not be recognized by the IRS.

Unenrolled individuals may also be authorized to represent a taxpayer under Form 2848, if specifically permitted in very limited circumstances (such as a close family member representing a taxpayer, an executor representing an estate, or an unenrolled tax return preparer with an AFSP record of completion who prepared the specific tax return at issue).

Example: Christopher is an unenrolled tax preparer. He has a PTIN, but he does not participate in the IRS's Annual Filing Season Program, and only prepares about 25 tax returns every year for family and close friends. He does charge a nominal fee, so he is considered a tax return preparer for IRS purposes. In most circumstances, Christopher would not be able to represent a taxpayer before the IRS. However, his aunt Dorothea died in 2022, and Christopher is named as the executor of her estate in Dorothea's will. The estate received an audit notice in 2023. Christopher may file a Form 2848 and represent Dorothea's estate before all levels of the IRS. He will have full representation rights for the estate, because he is the estate's executor.

Example: Juana is a 25-year old accounting student in her senior year of college. She prepares the tax returns for herself and her parents, but she does not charge her parents a fee, so she does not have a PTIN. Juana's father, Rodrigo, receives an audit notice in 2022. Rodrigo does not speak English very well and does not want to deal with the IRS at all. Juana offers to help her father and fills out a Form 2848 to represent him. Rodrigo signs the form as the taxpayer, and Juana submits the Form 2848 to the IRS and lists herself as his representative. As an immediate family member, she is allowed to represent her father before all levels of the IRS.

Durable Power of Attorney

The IRS will accept a *non-IRS* power of attorney, such as a durable power of attorney, but it must contain all of the information included on a standard Form 2848. A non-IRS power of attorney must contain the following information:

1. The taxpayer's name, mailing address, and taxpayer identification number.
2. The name and mailing address of the representative.
3. The types of tax involved and the federal tax form number in question.
4. The specific periods or tax years involved.
5. For estate tax matters, the decedent's date of death.
6. A clear expression of the taxpayer's intention concerning the scope of authority granted to the representative.
7. The taxpayer's signature and date.

A signed and dated statement made by the representative should also be attached to the non-IRS power of attorney. The statement is signed under penalties of perjury. A non-IRS power of attorney may be rejected if the durable power of attorney does not contain all the required information.

> **Note:** An IRS power of attorney (Form 2848) is terminated if the taxpayer becomes incapacitated or incompetent. A *durable* power of attorney[21] is not subject to a time limit and will continue in force after the incapacitation or incompetency of the individual. An ordinary power of attorney is automatically revoked if the person who made it is found to be incompetent, but a durable power of attorney can only be revoked by the person who made it, and while that person is mentally competent. All POAs are terminated upon the death of the individual.

> **Example:** Eleanor has been ill for a long time. She signs a durable power of attorney that names her cousin, Jasper, as her representative. The durable power of attorney grants Jasper the authority to perform all acts on Eleanor's behalf. However, it does not list specific information, such as the types of tax covered. A year after Eleanor signs the power of attorney, she is declared incompetent due to Alzheimer's disease. Later, a tax matter arises concerning a prior year return filed by Eleanor. Jasper attempts to represent Eleanor before the IRS, but he is rejected because the durable power of attorney does not contain the required information. If Jasper attaches a statement that the durable power of attorney is valid under the laws of the governing jurisdiction, he can sign a completed Form 2848 and submit it on Eleanor's behalf. If Jasper is eligible to practice before the IRS, he can also name himself as the representative on Form 2848.

Unless a particular act is specifically not authorized by the taxpayer, a representative (with the exception of unenrolled tax return preparers) can generally perform the following acts:

- Represent a taxpayer before any office of the IRS.

---

[21] A *durable* power of attorney is one that either takes effect upon, or lasts after, the principal's incapacitation. Durable POAs are typically used in the event of a person's incapacity. However, a durable power of attorney can be drafted to take immediate effect.

- Record an interview or meeting with the IRS.
- Sign an offer or a waiver of restriction on assessment or collection of a tax deficiency, or a waiver of notice of disallowance of a claim for credit or refund.
- Sign consents to extend the statutory time period for assessment or collection of a tax
- Sign a closing agreement.
- Receive (but never endorse or cash) a tax refund check.

The rights of unenrolled tax return preparers (those with an AFSP certificate) are limited to representing taxpayers in examinations of the tax returns they prepared and signed. A qualified representative can represent a taxpayer before the IRS without the taxpayer present, so long as the proper power of attorney is signed and submitted to the IRS.

> **Example:** Geraldine is an enrolled agent with a signed Form 2848 for Hugo, who is being audited by the IRS. Geraldine did not prepare Hugo's tax return, but she is still eligible to represent him by virtue of her status as an EA. Hugo does not have to appear at the examination hearing. If Geraldine were an unenrolled preparer, her representation rights would be restricted to the particular tax returns she had prepared for Hugo that were under examination. She would be able to represent Hugo only before IRS revenue agents and not revenue officers or appeals officers.

Revocation or Withdrawal of a POA

A power of attorney is valid until revoked by the taxpayer or until the representative withdraws from representation. If the **taxpayer** is revoking a power of attorney, he must write "REVOKE" across the top of the first page with his signature and the date below it. If the **representative** is withdrawing from representation, he must write "WITHDRAW" across the top of the first page with his signature and the date below it. The revocation or withdrawal must be mailed or faxed to the IRS. It must clearly indicate the applicable tax matters and periods.

> **Example:** Karenna is an EA who had an IRS power of attorney for her former client, Lenny. Karenna fired Lenny for nonpayment, but she continued to receive IRS notices on his behalf. Karenna writes "WITHDRAW" on a copy of the POA and submits it to the IRS, notifying the IRS that she no longer represents Lenny.

If a taxpayer or representative does not have a copy of the power of attorney, a statement of revocation or withdrawal must be sent to the IRS.

A newly-filed power of attorney concerning the same matter will revoke a previously-filed power of attorney. For example, if a taxpayer switches their tax preparer, and the second preparer files a power of attorney on behalf of the taxpayer, the old power of attorney on file will be rescinded. However, the taxpayer can specifically request that the old power of attorney remains active when a newer power of attorney is filed.

Power of Attorney Not Required: If a third party is not representing a taxpayer before the IRS, a power of attorney is not required. This would include the preparation of a taxpayer's income tax return. The following situations also do not require a power of attorney:

- Providing information to the IRS.
- Authorizing the disclosure of tax return information through Form 8821, *Tax Information Authorization*, or other written or oral disclosure consent.
- Allowing the IRS to discuss return information with a third party via the checkbox provided on a tax return or other document.
- Allowing a tax matters partner to perform acts for a partnership.
- Allowing the IRS to discuss tax return information with a fiduciary or an executor.

Representative Signing in Lieu of the Taxpayer

A representative named under a power of attorney is generally not permitted to sign a personal income tax return unless both of the following conditions are met:

- The signature is permitted under the Internal Revenue Code and the related regulations, and;
- The taxpayer specifically grants signature authority on the power of attorney.

IRS regulations permit a representative to sign a taxpayer's return if the taxpayer is unable to sign for any of the following reasons:

- Disease or injury (such as a taxpayer who is completely paralyzed or who has a debilitating injury).
- Continuous absence from the United States (including Puerto Rico) for a period of at least 60 days prior to the date required by law for filing the return.
- Other good cause if specific permission is requested of and granted by the IRS.

> **Example:** Marcus is an EA with a client named Patsy who travels extensively for business. Patsy had signed Form 2848, specifically granting Marc the right to sign her tax returns in her absence. Patsy is currently traveling in Europe on business and will not return until six months after the due date of her returns. Marcus is allowed to sign Patsy's return. When Patsy's return is signed by Marcus, a copy of the Form 2848 must accompany the return.

When a tax return is signed by a representative, it must be accompanied by a copy of the power of attorney authorizing the representative to sign the return.

Tax Information Authorization, Form 8821

Form 8821, Tax Information Authorization, authorizes any individual, corporation, firm, organization, or partnership to inspect or receive confidential information for the type of tax and periods listed. Any third party may be designated to receive tax information.

Form 8821 is commonly used by tax preparers, employers, banks, and other institutions to receive financial information on behalf of an individual or a business. It is only a disclosure form, so it does not give an individual authority to represent a taxpayer before the IRS.

Example: Tasha is applying for a mortgage loan from her bank. She gives her bank her prior-year returns, but the bank also requires her to sign a Form 8821. The bank uses Form 8821 to request Tasha's official IRS transcripts, in order to verify the tax return information it received from Tasha is correct, and also to confirm that no outstanding tax liens or judgments are existent.

Similar to a POA form, Form 8821 requires the taxpayer to list the type of tax, the tax form number, the year or periods the authorization covers, and the specific tax matters that apply. Any prior tax years may be specified, but only future tax periods ending no later than three years after the date Form 8821 is received by the IRS are recognized.

Centralized Authorization File (CAF)

The centralized authorization file (CAF) is the IRS's computer database that contains information regarding the authorizations that taxpayers have given representatives for their accounts. When a power of attorney or disclosure authorization document is submitted to the IRS, it is processed for inclusion in the CAF. A CAF number is assigned to a tax practitioner or other authorized individual when either a Form 2848 or Form 8821 is filed. It is a unique nine-digit number that is not the same as an individual's SSN, PTIN, or enrollment number.

Example: Matilda works as a full-time bookkeeper for a small real estate company. She has an accounting background, but she does not prepare tax returns for compensation, but she does self-prepare her own return as well as her children's tax returns. In 2022, Matilda's 27-year-old son, Oscar, is audited by the IRS. Oscar does not wish to speak directly with the IRS. Matilda files Form 2848 on Oscar's behalf, and he signs the form since he is an adult. Matilda can be the authorized representative for her son. She is issued a CAF number. She does not need to obtain a PTIN, because she does not prepare tax returns for compensation.

Joint filers must complete and submit separate Forms 2848 to have a power of attorney recorded in the CAF. Alternative power of attorney forms, such as a durable power of attorney, will not be recorded in the CAF unless a Form 2848 is also attached.

The issuance of a CAF number does not indicate that a person is either recognized or authorized to practice before the IRS. It merely confirms that a centralized file has been established for the representative under that number.

Example: Salvador is an EA who recently submitted a Form 2848 to the IRS on behalf of his client, Tanesha. Tanesha's refund has been delayed for over 10 weeks and she does not know why. After waiting about 7-10 days for the Form 2848 to process, Salvador calls the IRS Practitioner Priority Line to check the status of Tanesha's tax refund. Mrs. Smith, the IRS employee who answers the call, requests Salvador's CAF number to verify his identity. Salvador provides his CAF number as well as his SSN to verify his identity to Mrs. Smith. Mrs. Smith finds Tanesha's power of attorney information in the CAF system and can now give Salvador the information about his client's refund over the phone.

Having a CAF number also enables the IRS to automatically send copies of notices and other IRS communications to a representative. A practitioner may list the current year and any tax years that have already ended. The practitioner may also list future tax years or periods. However, the IRS will not record on the CAF system future tax years listed that exceed <u>three years</u> from December 31 of the year that the IRS receives the power of attorney.

> **Note:** The Form 2848 instructions include an explanation of how practitioners can receive a list of their powers of attorney recorded on the CAF. A practitioner must make an FOIA request and ask the IRS to provide a copy of his CAF Representative/Client Listing. A sample letter and further instructions, including requirements to prove identity, are available on www.irs.gov by clicking on the "routine access to IRS records" link under the FOIA section.

Third-Party Authorizations

A third-party authorization is when a taxpayer authorizes an individual (usually his tax return preparer) to communicate with the IRS on his behalf. This authorization allows the IRS to discuss the processing of a taxpayer's current tax return, including the status of refunds, with whomever the taxpayer specifies. The authorization automatically expires on the due date of the next year's tax return.

A taxpayer can choose a third-party designee by checking the "yes" box on his tax return, which is why it is known as "Checkbox Authority." The taxpayer then enters the designee's name and phone number and a self-selected five-digit PIN, which the designee must confirm when requesting information from the IRS.

The designee can exchange verbal information with the IRS on return processing issues and on refunds and payments related to the return. The designee may also receive written account information, including transcripts, upon request. A designee cannot receive a tax refund check on a client's behalf.

The third-party designee authorization is more limited than the authority given by *Form 8821, Tax Information Authorization.* Form 8821 can be used to allow discussions with third parties and disclosures of information to third parties on matters other than a taxpayer's current return.

> **Example:** Tyler named his EA, Vicky, as his third-party designee on his tax return. A few months after filing his return, Tyler still had not received his refund. He asked Vicky if she could check the status of his refund. Vicky called the IRS and was given the information over the phone because she was listed as a third-party designee on Tyler's return. No further authorization was necessary for Vicky to receive this confidential taxpayer information. This third-party designee authorization is only temporary, and will expire automatically the following year.

Tax Return Copies and Transcripts

If a taxpayer needs an actual copy of his own tax return that has been filed and processed, he may use *Form 4506, Request for Copy of Tax Return.* Copies are generally available for the current year and the past six years. The IRS charges a fee for making the copy. Tax transcripts, on the other hand, are free.

Transcripts are available for the current year and the past three years. *Form 4506-T, Request for Transcript of Tax Return*, may be used when a taxpayer wants to authorize an individual or organization to receive or inspect confidential tax return information.

This form is often used by financial institutions to verify tax compliance or income, such as when a taxpayer is applying for a mortgage. Form 4506-T does not authorize an individual to represent a taxpayer before the IRS. The taxpayer must specify on the form what type of information is needed. If a "return transcript" is requested, the IRS will provide most of the line items of a filed tax return. A return transcript also includes items from any accompanying forms and schedules that were filed, but it does not reflect any changes made after the original return was filed.

If an "account transcript" is requested, the IRS will provide information on the financial status of the account, such as payments made and penalty assessments. Requesting a "record of account" produces the most detailed information as it combines the return transcript and account transcript information.

Privacy of Taxpayer Information

Section 7216 of the Internal Revenue Code (IRC) and a related provision, IRC section 6713, provide penalties[22] against tax return preparers who make unauthorized use or disclosure of tax return information. The regulations authorize two types of disclosures:

- Permissible disclosures without taxpayer consent
- Disclosures requiring taxpayer consent
- The following disclosures do not require prior consent from the taxpayer:
- Disclosures to the IRS
- Disclosures pursuant to a court order or subpoena issued by any court, whether at the federal, state, or local level. The required information must be clearly identified in the document (subpoena or court order) in order for a preparer to disclose information.
- An administrative order, demand, summons, or subpoena that is issued by any federal agency (such as the IRS or the FinCEN), a state agency, or commission charged under the laws of the state with licensing, registration, or regulation of tax return preparers.
- To report a crime to proper authorities. Even if the preparer is mistaken and no crime has occurred, he will not be subject to sanctions if he makes the disclosure in good faith.
- A preparer may disclose tax return information to a tax return processor. For example, if a preparer uses an electronic or tax return processing service, he or she may disclose tax return information to that service in order to prepare tax returns or compute tax liability.
- Tax preparers within the same firm in the United States may use or disclose information within the firm for purposes of assisting in the preparation of tax returns.[23]

---

[22] IRS Section 7216 and Section 6713 provide criminal and civil penalties against preparers who improperly disclose taxpayer information. Code §7216 is a criminal provision, while §6713 establishes civil penalties for improper disclosure.

[23] Generally, tax return preparers may not obtain consents to disclose social security numbers to tax return preparers located outside the United States. If social security numbers are included in documents for which the tax return preparer has obtained the consent of the taxpayer to disclose the tax return preparer must redact or mask any social security number before disclosing the tax return information to a return preparer outside the United States.

- A preparer may disclose private client information to his attorney or to an employee of the IRS, in connection with an IRS investigation of the preparer.
- For purposes of peer reviews.

Example: The IRS is investigating a CPA named Adam for possible misconduct. Adam has an attorney who is assisting in his defense. As it turns out, Adam was a victim of embezzlement because his bookkeeper was stealing client checks. He only discovered the embezzlement when the IRS contacted him about client complaints. Adam may disclose confidential client information to his attorney in order to assist with his own defense. Adam may also disclose confidential client information to the IRS during the course of its investigation.

Example: Della is an enrolled agent. Her client, Trevor, sends an email request to Della, asking her to send the past three years of his business tax returns to his attorney for purposes of preparing his estate plan. Della doesn't contact Trevor directly to confirm the request. She simply attaches Trevor's returns to an email and sends out copies of the returns to the attorney listed in the email, without realizing that the request didn't actually come from Trevor. Instead, the email came from Trevor's ex-wife, with whom Trevor is going through a contentious divorce. Trevor later discovers that his ex-wife obtained copies of his personal and business tax returns from Della, and he files a formal complaint with OPR. Della can be subject to fines as well as disciplinary sanctions for improperly disclosing Trevor's information to unauthorized parties.

Tax return preparers must generally obtain written consent from taxpayers before disclosing information to a third party or using the information for any purpose other than the preparation of tax returns. The consent form must meet the following guidelines:

- Identify the purpose of the disclosure.
- Identify the recipient and describe the authorized information.
- Include the name of the preparer and the name of the taxpayer.
- Include mandatory language that informs the taxpayer that he is not required to sign the consent, and if he does sign the consent, he can set a time period for the duration of the consent.
- Include mandatory language that refers the taxpayer to the Treasury Inspector General for Tax Administration if he believes that his tax return information has been disclosed or used improperly.
- If applicable, inform the taxpayer that his tax return information may be disclosed to a tax return preparer located outside the U.S.[24]
- Be signed and dated by the taxpayer. Electronic (online) consents must be in the same type as the website's standard text and contain the taxpayer's affirmative consent (as opposed to an opt-out clause).

Unless a specific time period is specified, a taxpayer's written consent is valid for one year.

---

[24] Disclosing tax return information to another tax return preparer located outside the United States is only permitted with a client's written consent, this is true even when the preparer works for the same accounting firm.

> **Note:** Internal Revenue Code §7216 is a *criminal* tax provision enacted by Congress that prohibits tax return preparers from knowingly or recklessly disclosing or using tax return information. A preparer may be fined up to $1,000, imprisoned up to one year, or both, for each violation of §7216.[25] There is also an additional civil penalty for improper disclosure or use of taxpayer information, outlined in IRC §6713. However, unlike §7216, this code section does not require that the disclosure be "knowing or reckless." This means that even an accidental disclosure of sensitive taxpayer information may cause the practitioner to be subject to a penalty.

These privacy regulations apply to paid preparers, electronic return originators, tax software developers, and other persons or entities engaged in tax preparation. The regulations also apply to most volunteer tax return preparers, such as Volunteer Income Tax Assistance (VITA) and Tax Counseling for the Elderly (TCE) volunteers, and to employees and contractors employed by tax preparation companies in a support role. These regulations pertain to the disclosure of "tax return information," which is defined by law and very broad in scope.

Tax return information is defined as:

"All the information tax return preparers obtain from taxpayers or other sources in any form or matter that is used to prepare tax returns or is obtained in connection with the preparation of returns. This includes personally identifiable information (PII) such as SSNs, address, bank account numbers, etc. It also includes all computations, worksheets, and printouts preparers create; correspondence from the IRS during the preparation, filing, and correction of returns; statistical compilations of tax return information; and tax return preparation software registration information."

"Tax return information" also includes the taxpayer's name, mailing address, and taxpayer identification number, including Social Security number or employer identification number; any information extracted from a return, including names of dependents or the location of a business; information on whether a return was, is being, or will be examined or subject to other investigation or processing; information contained on transcripts of accounts; the fact that a return was filed or examined; investigation or collection history; or tax balance due information.

Allowable Disclosures

A preparer may disclose information to a second taxpayer from another person's tax return in certain circumstances. The preparer may disclose return information obtained from the first taxpayer if:

- The information obtained from the first taxpayer appears on the first person's tax return;
- The information is used for the purpose of preparing the second person's tax return;
- The second taxpayer is related to the first taxpayer;
- The first taxpayer's interest is not adverse to the second taxpayer's interest; and
- The first taxpayer has not prohibited the disclosure.

---

[25] A violation of IRC 7216 is a misdemeanor, with a maximum penalty of up to one year imprisonment or a fine of not more than $1,000, or both, together with the cost of prosecution.

> **Example:** Cherise is an enrolled agent. She prepares tax returns for Gary and his son, Timothy, who is 17 years old and still a minor. Gary claims his son, Timothy, on his tax return, but Timothy also has a part-time job after school, so he also has a filing requirement. Since Gary and Timothy are a parent and minor child, Cherise can share information between them.

> **Example:** Xiang is an EA with two married clients, Wendy and Stewart, who file jointly. Wendy works long hours, so she is unavailable when Stewart meets with Xiang to prepare their joint tax return. Later, Wendy comes in alone to sign the return. She also has a question regarding the mortgage interest on the joint tax return. Xiang is allowed to disclose return information to Wendy because it is a joint return. Stewart has not prohibited any disclosures, and both Wendy and Stewart's names are on the return.

> **Example:** Felipe is an enrolled agent. His client, Gustavo, has a 19-year-old daughter named Lydia. Gustavo has always claimed Lydia on his tax returns, but in January 2022, Lydia gets into a big fight with her father, and she moves out of the home. Lydia gets a job and moves into a shared apartment with some roommates. Lydia wants Felipe to help her prepare her own return, and asks him not to share any of her information with her estranged father. Felipe assures Lydia of the privacy of her information and agrees to prepare her return. A few weeks later, Gustavo comes into Felipe's office and demands information about his daughter's return, because he still wants to claim her as a dependent. Gustavo also wants to see a copy of his daughter's Form W-2 so he can obtain her new address and contact information. Felipe refuses to share any of this information with Gustavo, because even though Gustavo and Lydia are related persons, (1) Lydia has specifically requested that her information not be shared, and (2) Lydia's interest is adverse to Gustavo's interest. Therefore, any disclosure that Felipe makes about Lydia's tax information would be prohibited by law.

A taxpayer is considered "related" to another taxpayer in any of the following relationships:

- A spouse
- Child and parent
- Grandparent and grandchild
- A partner and a partnership
- A trust or estate, and the beneficiary of the trust or estate
- A corporation and shareholder
- Members of a controlled group of corporations

A tax return preparer may also disclose tax return information that was obtained from a first taxpayer in preparing a tax return of the second taxpayer, if the preparer has obtained written consent from the first taxpayer. For example, if an unmarried couple lives together and splits the mortgage interest, the preparer may use or disclose information from the first taxpayer to the second so long as the preparer has written consent.

If a taxpayer dies or becomes incompetent, insolvent, or bankrupt, or the taxpayer's assets are placed in conservatorship, a tax preparer may disclose the information to the duly appointed fiduciary of the taxpayer or his estate, or to the duly authorized agent of the fiduciary.

> **Example:** Tonya is an enrolled agent. She has always prepared the tax returns for her long-time client, Larry Jones. On February 16, 2022, Larry Jones dies. Larry's daughter, Mariah, is named the executor of her late father's estate. Mariah has a certified copy of her letters testamentary[26] from the courts, which allows her to perform the necessary actions to gather and assess all the assets of the estate. Mariah asks Tonya for copies of her late father's tax returns, because she needs the information to prepare his final return as well as the tax return for the estate. After reviewing the letters testamentary and verifying that Mariah is the fiduciary of Larry's estate, Tonya may share information regarding Larry's tax returns.

Affordable Care Act Disclosures

§7216 prohibits tax return preparers, including those who offer services related to the Affordable Care Act, from using tax return information for unauthorized purposes. In addition to criminal penalties, a civil penalty for each unauthorized disclosure or use of tax return information by a tax return preparer is imposed by §6713.

Current regulations allow preparers to use a list of client names, addresses, email addresses, and phone numbers to provide them general educational information, such as that related to the Affordable Care Act. However, a tax preparer must first obtain taxpayer consent before using tax return information to directly solicit clients for health care enrollment services or other services.

> **Example:** Sherry is an enrolled agent who is also a health care facilitator that helps enroll people in the Healthcare Marketplace insurance plans. She wants to contact clients to let them know that she is offering these services. Under the terms of §7216, she must first obtain written consent from her clients before she can solicit them.

This mandate also applies to VITA and Low-Income Taxpayer Clinic (LITC) volunteers. Solicitation to offer health care enrollment services by all tax return preparers, including volunteer preparers, requires prior taxpayer consent.

Tax Practitioner Confidentiality Privilege

Under IRC §7525, enrolled practitioners and their clients are granted limited rights of confidentiality protection. This Federally Authorized Tax Practitioner Confidentiality Privilege (FATP) applies to attorneys, CPAs, enrolled agents, enrolled actuaries, and certain other individuals allowed to practice before the IRS.[27] This limited confidentiality protection applies to communications that would be considered privileged if they were between the taxpayer and an attorney and that relate to:

- Noncriminal tax matters before the IRS, or
- Noncriminal tax proceedings brought in federal court by or against the United States.

---

[26] A "Letter of Testamentary" is a document granted to the Executor of an estate by the probate court. This document gives the executor (or administrator) the legal ability to reach out to a financial institution like banks, mortgage lenders, creditors, and other relevant parties in order to act on behalf of an estate.

[27] The "federally authorized tax practitioner privilege" is an amendment to the Internal Revenue Code made by the Internal Revenue Service Restructuring and Reform Act of 1998.

This confidentiality privilege cannot be used with any agency other than the IRS. For example, an enrolled agent cannot assert the federal confidentiality privilege with any state taxing agency. The confidentiality privilege does not apply:

- In any criminal tax matter.
- To any written communications regarding the promotion of a tax shelter.
- In any state tax proceedings.
- To the general preparation of tax returns.

There is a long history of court decisions that deny confidentiality of information disclosed to an attorney for purposes of preparing tax returns. In a key court ruling, the court stated that "information transmitted for the purpose of preparation of a tax return," though transmitted to an attorney, is not privileged information.[28]

> **Example:** Daniel and Jasmine Bernstein filed a joint tax return that was selected for audit. The IRS revenue agent assigned to the case suspected that the Bernsteins may have had foreign bank accounts and tax shelter activities that were not properly reported. The IRS issued an administrative summons to the couple's accountant, Isana, who was a licensed CPA. Isana responded to the summons, but refused to answer specific questions at her IRS interview, claiming tax practitioner privilege. Isana also made no showing that she performed any work for the Bernsteins beyond tax preparation. The IRS took Isana to court in order to force her to comply with the summonses. Isana asserted in court that she had prepared the couple's tax return, but did not mention any specific tax advice she gave that would qualify as privileged information. The court ruled that Isana could not assert the tax practitioner privilege, and ordered her to comply with the IRS summons (based on the case of *United States of America v. Radchik*).

When information is transmitted to a third party (in this case, on a tax return), such information is not confidential. This restriction on the confidentiality privilege related to tax preparation applies to other practitioners besides attorneys, including enrolled agents and CPAs.

Certified Acceptance Agents (CAA)

A Certified Acceptance Agent (CAA) is a person or an entity who, pursuant to a written agreement with the IRS, is authorized to assist individuals and other foreign persons who do not qualify for a Social Security Number but who still need a Taxpayer Identification Number to file a Form 1040. Certified Acceptance agents can authenticate a passport and birth certificate for dependents. There are four steps that need to be taken by all new and renewing applicants.

- Complete Form 13551, Application to Participate in the IRS Acceptance Agent Program, and attach the fingerprint card.
- Complete the Mandatory Acceptance Agent training, print, sign, and submit the certification form. Attach the certification form for each authorized representative to Form 13551.

---

[28] *United States v. Lawless*, (7th Cir. 1983).

- Complete forensic training and submit the certificate of completion to the IRS.

ITIN Expirations: ITINs that have not been used on a federal tax return at least once in the last three consecutive years will expire. For example, if a taxpayer's ITIN wasn't included on a U.S. federal tax return at least once for tax years 2020, 2021, and 2022, the ITIN will expire on December 31, 2023. To renew an ITIN, the taxpayer must complete a Form W-7 and submit all required documentation.

(Test yourself and then check the correct answers at the end of this chapter.)

1. Which authorization form gives the appointed person the greatest rights to represent a taxpayer?

A. Third-party designee, also known as "Checkbox" authority.
B. Form 8821, *Tax Information Authorization.*
C. Form 2848, *Power of Attorney and Declaration of Representative.*
D. Form 4506-T, *Request for Transcript of Tax Return.*

2. Esteban is an enrolled agent. He fires his client, Jackie, for nonpayment. Esteban had submitted a power of attorney for Jackie several months ago, but now Esteban does not want to represent Jackie anymore, or receive any notices regarding her account. What should Esteban do?

A. Esteban should write the word "DELETE" on the POA form and mail or fax it to the IRS.
B. Esteban should write the word "REVOKE" on the POA form and mail or fax it to the IRS.
C. Esteban should write the word "REMOVE" on the POA form and mail or fax it to the IRS.
D. Esteban should write the word "WITHDRAW" on the POA form and mail or fax it to the IRS.

3. The Centralized Authorization File (CAF) is:

A. An IRS computer database with information regarding the authority of individuals appointed under powers of attorney or designated under tax information authorizations.
B. A public, searchable database of federally authorized practitioners and certain other tax preparers with professional credentials.
C. An automated list of disbarred practitioners.
D. An automated file of taxpayer delinquencies.

4. Wyatt is an enrolled agent. In which of the following situations is he allowed to disclose information <u>without</u> first obtaining written permission from his client?

A. When Wyatt is contacted by a newspaper reporter investigating a possible crime committed by his client.
B. When he is issued a subpoena by a U.S. court.
C. When the information is requested by his client's adult child, who helps support the client financially.
D. Disclosing tax return information to another tax return preparer outside the United States, as long as both preparers are working for the same accounting firm.

5. Which of the following statements regarding the §7525 tax practitioner confidentiality privilege is <u>correct</u>?

A. Advice on non-criminal tax matters from a federally authorized practitioner has the same confidentiality protection as communication with an attorney.
B. Advice on criminal tax matters from a federally authorized practitioner has the same confidentiality protection as communication with an attorney.
C. Advice on tax shelter activities from a federally authorized practitioner has the same confidentiality protection as communication with an attorney.
D. Advice on any type of federal tax matter from a federally authorized practitioner has the same confidentiality protection as communication with an attorney.

6. Bellamy self-prepared his own tax return in 2022. He later received an audit notice for that return, but he does not want to deal with the IRS. Bellamy wants to hire someone to represent him at the examination. In order to have someone else represent him during the audit, all the following statements are correct <u>except</u>:

A. Bellamy must furnish that representative with written authorization on Form 2848, Power of Attorney and Declaration of Representative.
B. His paid representative must be an attorney, CPA, or EA.
C. In order to save some money, Bellamy can potentially hire an unenrolled preparer, as long as that person has an AFSP certificate.
D. Even if Bellamy appoints a representative, he may choose to attend the examination or appeals conference if he wishes.

7. Form 8821, *Tax Information Authorization,* may be used to authorize the following:

A. Any individual, corporation, firm, organization, or partnership to receive confidential information for the type of tax and periods listed on Form 8821.
B. Any designated third party to receive tax information.
C. For unenrolled tax return preparers to indicate a representative relationship with a taxpayer and to authorize practice before the IRS.
D. Both A and B.

8. Which of the following is not required for a properly-completed Form 2848?

A. The signatures must be notarized.
B. The form must be faxed or mailed to the IRS.
C. Every enrolled practitioner must include their PTIN on the form.
D. A valid CAF number must be listed on the form.

9. How long is an IRS power of attorney authorization valid?

A. One year.
B. Three years.
C. Until the due date of the next tax return.
D. Until it is revoked, withdrawn, or superseded.

10. Axford is an unenrolled tax return preparer for a married couple. He is also licensed to sell securities. After preparing the couple's joint return, he was concerned that they were not saving adequately for retirement. Using information from their tax return, Axford created a custom retirement plan for the couple and solicited them both for retirement planning. He had not obtained their prior consent. Which of the following statements is correct?

A. Because he is not a practitioner, Axford is not subject to the rules of §7216.
B. Axford is in violation of §7216.
C. Axford is not in violation of §7216 because he used information from current clients; therefore, he was not required to obtain their consent.
D. Axford is not in violation of §7216 because retirement planning is one of the exceptions listed as an allowable use of information.

11. Taxpayers are granted a limited confidentiality privilege with any federally-authorized tax practitioner. Confidential communications include all of the following except:

A. Written tax advice.
B. A noncriminal tax proceeding in Federal court.
C. Participation in a tax shelter.
D. Noncriminal tax matters before the IRS.

12. How many representatives can a taxpayer appoint using a single Form 2848?

A. One
B. Two
C. Three
D. Four

13. A durable power of attorney remains in effect until an individual:

A. Gets divorced.
B. Becomes mentally incompetent or incapacitated.
C. Dies.
D. A durable power of attorney never expires.

14. How many years in the future can an authorization on a Form 2848 be recorded to the Centralized Authorization File (CAF)?

A. Current year + 1 year.
B. Current year + 2 years.
C. Current year + 3 years.
D. Current year + 4 years.

Unit 3: Quiz Answers

1. The answer is C. Only Form 2848, Power of Attorney and Declaration of Representative, allows a third party to represent a taxpayer before the IRS. The other consents are much more limited and only allow the third party to receive or inspect tax account information.

2. The answer is D. Esteban should write the word "WITHDRAW" on the first page of the POA form, include his signature and the date, and **mail** or **fax** the form to the IRS. Email is not an acceptable means of contact. The form must clearly indicate the applicable tax matters and periods. In contrast, if a taxpayer chooses to end a previously authorized power of attorney, he must write the word "REVOKE" on the form, include his signature and the date, and mail or fax the form to the IRS.

3. The answer is A. The Centralized Authorization File, or "CAF," contains information on third parties authorized to represent taxpayers before the IRS and receive and inspect confidential tax information on active tax accounts or those accounts currently under collection or examination by the IRS.

4. The answer is B. Wyatt can disclose a client's tax return information in response to a lawful subpoena. A tax return preparer who is issued a subpoena or court order, whether at the federal, state, or local level, is not required to obtain disclosure permission from a client. In all the other cases, disclosure is not allowed unless there has been prior written consent from the client.

5. The answer is A. Advice on *non-criminal* tax matters from a federally authorized practitioner has the same confidentiality protection as communication with an attorney. The Federally Authorized Tax Practitioner Confidentiality Privilege (FATP) is limited to:
- *Noncriminal* tax matters before the IRS, or
- *Noncriminal* tax proceedings brought in federal court by or against the United States.

6. The answer is C. Bellamy cannot hire an unenrolled preparer to represent him. AFSP certificate holders can only represent clients with respect to returns that they have prepared. Since Bellamy self-prepared the return under audit, he must hire an enrolled practitioner (EA, CPA or attorney). An unenrolled preparer who did not prepare and sign the specific tax return under examination would not be allowed to represent Bellamy.

7. The answer is D. *Form 8821, Tax Information Authorization*, authorizes any individual, corporation, firm, organization, or partnership to receive confidential information for the type of tax and periods listed on the form. Any third party may be designated by the taxpayer to receive confidential tax information. Form 8821 is only a disclosure form, so it will not give an individual any power to represent a taxpayer before the IRS. It may be used only to obtain information, such as copies of tax returns or tax return transcripts.

8. The answer is A. The signatures on Form 2848 are not required to be notarized. Answer "B" is incorrect because the form may be submitted by fax or uploaded on the IRS website. Answer "C" is incorrect because not all enrolled practitioners are required to have PTINs; only those who prepare tax returns for compensation. Answer "D" is incorrect because a Form 2848 will not be rejected if it does not have a CAF number. If a CAF number is not already established, one will be issued with first recorded submission.

9. The answer is D. A power of attorney obtained via Form 2848 is valid until revoked, withdrawn, or superseded. It may be revoked by the taxpayer or withdrawn by the representative, or it may be superseded by the filing of a new power of attorney for the same tax and tax period. An IRS power of attorney also terminates automatically upon a taxpayer's death or incompetency.

10. The answer is B. Axford is in violation of §7216 because he did not obtain written consent from his clients prior to using their private information. All paid tax return preparers are subject to the rules of §7216, a criminal statute. A tax return preparer must generally obtain written consent from taxpayers before he can disclose information to a third party or use the information for any purpose other than the preparation of tax returns. Each violation of §7216 could mean a fine of up to $1,000, a prison term of up to one year, or both. There is also a separate civil penalty for improper disclosure or use of taxpayer information, as outlined in IRC §6713. However, unlike §7216, this code section does not require that the disclosure be "knowing or reckless."

11. The answer is C. The confidentiality privilege does not apply in the case of communications regarding the promotion of or participation in a tax shelter. A tax shelter is any entity, plan, or arrangement whose significant purpose is to avoid or evade income tax. Unlike the attorney-client privilege, the federally-authorized tax practitioner privilege does not apply in criminal tax matters and does not apply in state tax proceedings. The privilege may be asserted only in a "noncriminal tax matter before the Internal Revenue Service" and a "noncriminal tax proceeding in Federal court brought by or against the United States." The confidentiality privilege is also not extended to matters related to the general preparation of tax returns.

12. The answer is D. Up to four representatives can be authorized per form, an increase from the previous Form 2848 that allowed only three representatives to be designated.

13. The answer is C. A durable power of attorney is not subject to a time limit. It remains in effect until the death of the individual, or until the individual revokes it.

14. The answer is C. An authorization on Form 2848 can be recorded to the Centralized Authorization File (CAF) for the current year, plus up to 3 future years (this question is based on an example from the most recently released EA exam sample questions).

Unit 4: Circular 230 and Best Practices

> **More Reading:**
> **Publication 947, Practice Before the IRS and Power of Attorney**
> **Publication 4687, Paid Preparer Due Diligence**
> **Publication 4019, Third Party Authorization, Levels of Authority**

The Treasury Department's Circular 230 sets forth regulations that govern all tax practitioners, including enrolled agents, CPAs, attorneys, and others who practice before the IRS. Circular 230 imposes professional standards and codes of conduct for practitioners and tax advisors. It prohibits certain actions, requires other actions, and details penalties for ethical violations and other misconduct by practitioners. Circular 230 is broken into four subparts:

- **Authority to practice**
- **Duties and restrictions relating to practice**
- **Sanctions for violations**
- **Disciplinary procedures**

In the next two units, we will look closely at subpart 2 of Circular 230, which describes practitioner responsibilities and standards.

Diligence as to Accuracy §10.22

Central to the Circular 230 regulations is the mandate for practitioners to exercise due diligence when performing the following duties:

- Preparing or assisting in preparing, approving, and filing of returns, documents, affidavits, and other papers relating to IRS matters.

- Determining the correctness of oral or written representations made to the Department of the Treasury, including documents that are filed and submitted to the IRS on the taxpayer's behalf.

- Determining the correctness of oral or written representations made to clients related to any matter administered by the IRS.

§10.22 does not state what due diligence entails, but there is more specific guidance in Circular 230 sections related to standards for written advice.[29]

Reliance on Others: A practitioner will be presumed to have exercised due diligence if he relies on the work product of another person. That is assuming that the practitioner used "reasonable care" when he hired, supervised, trained, and evaluated that person or the information provided.

---

[29] Publication 4687, *Paid Preparer Due Diligence*, is a more recent IRS publication that specifically discusses the due diligence rules for preparing tax returns that include refundable credits.

> **Example:** Blanca is an enrolled agent. A new client, Clayton, comes to her during the year to prepare his tax return. Clayton is self-employed and files a Schedule C. Blanca asks to see his prior year return, which she examines for accuracy. Another tax practitioner prepared the return, and it includes a depreciation schedule for Clayton's business assets. The schedule appears correct, and the listed items are reasonable. Blanca may use the depreciation schedule as a reference, even though she did not prepare it herself.

Best Practices §10.33

Circular 230 explains the broad concept of best practices. Practitioners must provide clients with the highest quality representation concerning federal tax matters by adhering to best practices in providing advice and in preparing documents or information for the IRS.

Practitioners who oversee a firm's practice should take reasonable steps to ensure that the firm's procedures for all employees are consistent with best practices. Best practices include the following:

- Communicating clearly with the client regarding the terms of the engagement.
- Establishing the facts, determining which facts are relevant, evaluating the reasonableness of any assumptions, relating the applicable law to the relevant facts, and arriving at a conclusion supported by the law and the facts.
- Advising the client of the conclusions reached and the impact of the advice rendered; for example, advising whether a taxpayer may avoid accuracy-related penalties if he relies on the advice provided.
- Acting fairly and with integrity in practice before the IRS.

Competence §10.35

This provision states that a practitioner must be competent to engage in practice before the IRS. "Competence" is defined as having the appropriate level of knowledge, skill, thoroughness, and preparation for the specific matter related to a client's engagement.

Circular 230 says a practitioner can become competent in various ways, including consulting with experts in the relevant area or studying the relevant law.

> **Example:** Chantelle is an enrolled agent who has many years of experience in preparing partnership tax returns. In 2022, she takes continuing education classes related to changes in partnership law, and consults with another tax professional in her office on a particularly complex partnership return. Also, during the year, a longtime client whose mother has died asks Chantelle to handle the estate tax returns for him. Chantelle rarely handles estate tax matters and does not have time to research the law sufficiently to handle this case, so she refers the estate return to a tax attorney who specializes in estate tax law. Chantelle has fulfilled her Circular 230 obligations related to §10.35.

Knowledge of Client's Omission §10.21

A practitioner who knows that a client has not complied with the revenue laws or who has made an error or omission on his tax return has the responsibility to advise the client promptly of the noncompliance, error, or omission, as well as its consequences.

The practitioner is not responsible for correcting the noncompliance once he has notified the client of the issue, or for notifying the IRS of a client's noncompliance.

> **Example:** Daniel is an EA with a new client, Laura, who has self-prepared her own returns in the past. Daniel notices that Laura has been claiming head of household status on her tax returns, but she does not qualify for this status, because she does not have a qualifying dependent. Daniel is required to promptly notify Laura of the error and tell her the consequences of not correcting the error. However, Daniel is not required to amend Laura's prior-year tax returns to correct the error. Nor is he required to notify the IRS of her claim of incorrect status.

The §10.21 obligations are not limited to practitioners preparing returns, so the discovery of an error in the course of a tax consulting or advisory engagement will also trigger its requirements.

> **Example:** Cynthia is an EA who takes over another tax return preparer's practice. She discovers that the previous preparer has been taking section 179 deductions on assets that do not qualify for this treatment. Cynthia must notify her clients of the errors and the consequences of not correcting the errors. She is not required to correct the errors.

Conflicts of Interest §10.29

Conflicts of interest are common, especially when it comes to divorce. There are special rules that apply to tax practitioners with regard to conflicts of interest between two clients. If there is a potential conflict of interest, the practitioner must disclose the conflict and be given the opportunity to disclose all material facts. A practitioner will have a conflict of interest if:

- The representation of one client will be directly adverse to another client; or

- There is a significant risk that the representation of one or more clients will be materially limited by the practitioner's responsibilities to another client, a former client, a third person, or by a personal interest of the practitioner.

A practitioner may still represent a client when a conflict of interest exists if:

- The practitioner reasonably believes that he or she will be able to provide competent and diligent representation to each affected client;

- The representation is not prohibited by law; and

- Each affected client waives the conflict of interest and gives informed consent, confirmed in writing, within 30 days after giving any non-written informed consent to the tax practitioner.

Regulations allow the written consent to be made within a reasonable period after the informed consent, but not later than 30 days after the date on which the conflict is known by the practitioner.

> **Example:** Artie and Damian are business partners in Bloomfield Brokerage, LLP. Kristen is an enrolled agent who prepares both their partnership return and their individual returns. In 2022, Artie and Damian have a major argument about the direction of the business. Artie calls Kristen and tells her that he is going to dissolve the partnership. Kristen must prepare a conflict-of-interest waiver for Artie and Damian, as well as the partnership itself, if she plans to keep them both as her clients.

The written consent must be retained for at least 36 months from the date representation ends, and must be given to any officer or employee of the IRS, if requested. At a minimum, the consent should adequately describe the nature of the conflict and the parties the practitioner represents.

> **Example:** Janessa is an EA who prepares tax returns for Bernadette and Elmer Smith, a married couple. In 2022, Bernadette and Elmer go through a contentious divorce, and Janessa believes there is potential for conflict of interest relating to the services she would provide each of them. She prepares a written statement explaining the potential conflict of interest and reviews it with her clients. Bernadette and Elmer still want Janessa to prepare their returns, and Janessa determines that she will be able to represent each fairly and competently. She has both Bernadette and Elmer sign the statement that waives the conflict and gives their consent for her to prepare their individual tax returns. Janessa must retain the record of their consent for at least 36 months after she last represents either party.

IRS Information Requests §10.20

Under Circular 230, §10.20, when the IRS requests information, a practitioner must comply and submit records promptly. If the requested information or records are not in the practitioner's possession, the preparer must promptly advise the requesting IRS officer and provide any information the practitioner may have, regarding the identity of the person who may have possession or control of the requested information or records. The practitioner must also make a "reasonable inquiry" of the client, regarding the location of the requested records.

However, a practitioner is not required to make an inquiry of any other person or to verify any information furnished by a client. Further, the practitioner is not required to contact any third party who might have possession of the records.

A practitioner may not interfere with any lawful effort by the IRS to obtain any record or information unless he or she believes in good faith and on reasonable grounds that the record or information is privileged under IRC §7525 or if the practitioner believes, in good faith, that the request is of doubtful legality. If the IRS's Office of Professional Responsibility requests information concerning possible violations of the regulations by other parties, such as other preparers, the practitioner must furnish the information and be prepared to testify in disbarment or suspension proceedings.

> **Example:** Mrs. Jones is an IRS revenue agent. She submitted a lawful records request to Howell, an enrolled agent, for accounting records relating to a former client who is currently under IRS investigation. However, earlier in the year, Howell had fired his client for nonpayment and also returned his client's records. Howell contacts Mrs. Jones, promptly notifying the IRS officer that he no longer has possession of his former client's records. Howell tells Mrs. Jones that he attempted to contact his former client, but the phone number was disconnected. Howell is not required to contact any third parties to discover the location of the requested records. Therefore, Howell has fulfilled his obligations under §10.20.

Return of Client Records §10.28

A practitioner is required to return a client's original records upon request, whether or not the practitioner's fees have been paid. Client records include:

- All documents a client provided to a practitioner that pre-existed their business engagement.
- Any materials that were prepared by the client or a third party that were provided to the practitioner relating to the subject matter of the representation.
- Any document prepared by the practitioner that was presented to the client relating to a prior representation if such a document is necessary for the taxpayer to comply with his current federal tax obligations.

At the request of a client, the practitioner must promptly return any and all records necessary for the client to comply with his federal tax obligations. Client records generally do not include the practitioner's work product. However, they may include any work product that the client has already paid for, such as a completed copy of a tax return.

Client records do not include any return, claim for refund, schedule, affidavit, appraisal, or any document prepared by the practitioner if he withholds these documents pending the client's payment of fees. A client must be given reasonable access to review and copy any additional records retained by the practitioner that are necessary for the client to comply with his federal tax obligations. The practitioner may retain copies of all the records returned to a client.

> **Example:** Carol's business client, Alpine Snow Resort, Inc., has been slow to pay in the past, so Carol asks the owner of the business to pay for the tax returns when he picks them up. The president of Alpine Snow becomes furious and refuses to pay Carol's invoice. He demands the tax returns anyway. Carol must return the corporation's original records, but she is not required to give away any work product that the owner has not yet paid for.

> **Example:** Jamison is an EA with a client, Samantha, who becomes upset after he tells her she owes money to the IRS. Samantha wants to get a second opinion, and she refuses to pay Jamison for his time. Jamison is required to hand over Samantha's original tax records, including copies of her W-2 forms and any other information she brought to his office. Jamison is not forced to give her a copy of the tax return he prepared, since she did not pay his fee for the return.

Copies of Tax Returns

Under IRC §6107, tax return preparers are required to give a completed copy of a tax return or claim for refund no later than the time the return or claim is presented for the taxpayer's signature. The copy can be in any media, including electronic media. Preparers are required to keep copies of all returns they have prepared or retain a list of clients and tax returns prepared. At a minimum, the list must contain the taxpayer's name, taxpayer identification number, tax year, and the type of return prepared. The copies of tax returns or the lists must be retained for at least three years after the close of the return period.[30]

Note: This provision has existed for decades, before scanners and copy machines were commonplace. Long ago, tax professionals would often just keep a list of returns prepared. In modern times, most preparers keep scanned, digital, or hard copies of client tax returns rather than simply a list of the returns prepared.

Tax Return Preparer Employer Records (IRC §6060): An employer of tax return preparers must keep a record of all those employed and make it available for IRS inspection upon request.

The records must include the name, taxpayer identification number, and workplace of each tax return preparer employed. In general, business-related records must be retained for at least three years following the close of the return period, but payroll records must be retained for a minimum of four years.

Example: Starla is an enrolled agent that owns three separate tax franchises in three different cities. Between the three tax offices, Starla employs a total of 35 full-time and part-time employees. Starla must keep detailed employment records for all of her employees, including their names, Social Security numbers, and which franchise location the employee works at. She must also retain payroll records for each location for a minimum of four years.

Practitioner Fees §10.27

The IRS prohibits practitioners from charging "unconscionable fees." Although that term has not been defined, it is generally believed to refer to fees that the courts would consider grossly disproportionate in relation to the services provided, or fees retained for services not provided.

The IRS has traditionally held that a practitioner may not charge a contingent fee (for example, a fee determined as a percentage of the taxpayer's refund) for preparing an original tax return pursuant to Circular 230.

A contingent fee might also include a fee that is based on a percentage of the taxes saved or one that depends on a specific result. However, in July 2014, a U.S. district court ruled that the IRS lacked statutory authority to regulate contingent fee arrangements for a certified public

---

[30] Under section 6060(c) the term "return period" means the 12-month period beginning on July 1 of each year. The close of the return period is defined as June 30, meaning the three-year period to retain records begins July 1 of each year.

accountant for the preparation and filing of ordinary refund claims (refund claims after the taxpayer has filed a return but before the IRS has started an audit of the return).[31]

> **Note:** At the time of this book's printing, the IRS had not issued a public comment on the issue of contingent fees specifically, so test-takers should be aware that if they encounter an exam question about the topic of contingent fees, they should proceed with caution.

It should also be noted that certain practitioners, such as licensed attorneys and certified public accountants, may still be subject to prohibitions against charging contingent fees under applicable state regulations.

> **Example:** Gavin is a CPA licensed in the state of California. A California Board of Accountancy licensee is prohibited from preparing an original tax return for a contingent fee. Irrespective of Circular 230 requirements, Gavin would not be able to prepare original tax returns on a contingent fee basis, because his state board of accountancy prohibits it.

Notwithstanding the general limitation that applies to contingent fees, a practitioner is allowed to charge a contingent fee in limited circumstances under Circular 230, including:

- Representation during the examination of an original tax return, or
- During the examination of an amended return or claim for refund, if the amended return or claim for refund was filed within 120 days of the taxpayer receiving a written notice of examination or a written challenge to the original tax return.
- Services rendered in connection with a refund claim for credit or a refund filed in conjunction with a penalty or interest charge assessed by the IRS.
- Services rendered in connection with any judicial proceeding arising under the IRC.

Advertising Restrictions §10.30

A practitioner may not use any form of advertising that contains false, deceptive, or coercive information or that violates IRS regulations. In describing their professional designation, enrolled agents may not use the term "certified" or imply any type of employment relationship with the IRS. Examples of acceptable descriptions for EAs are "enrolled to represent taxpayers before the Internal Revenue Service," "enrolled to practice before the Internal Revenue Service," and "admitted to practice before the Internal Revenue Service."[32]

Solicitation Restrictions: A practitioner may, in certain circumstances, solicit his or her professional services. The solicitation may not violate federal or state law, or other applicable rules (such as attorneys who are bound to conduct guidelines in their particular states). A practitioner may not continue to contact a prospective client who has communicated that he does not wish to be solicited.

---

[31] The relevant case is *Ridgely v Lew*, where the U.S. District Court for the District of Columbia found Section 10.27 (b) of Circular 230 invalid as it pertains to refund claims and permanently enjoined the IRS from enforcing the regulation with respect to fees for preparing refund claims. The IRS Advisory Council (IRSAC) issued a public report recommending that legislation be enacted to overturn the results in Loving and Ridgely by expressly affirming the Treasury Department's authority under 31 U.S.C. §330 to regulate paid tax return preparers. At the time of this book's printing, no such legislation had been passed. The IRS did not appeal the Ridgely decision, but they have not acquiesced to the case.

[32] Enrolled agents and enrolled actuaries may abbreviate their professional designation to either EA or E.A.

Mail Advertising: Mail advertising is allowed, but a solicitation must be clearly labeled as such and, if applicable, the source of information used in choosing the recipient must be identified. In the case of direct mail and e-commerce communications, the practitioner must retain a copy of the communication, along with a list of persons to whom the communication was mailed or distributed, for at least 36 months.

Practitioners may also send solicitations to other practitioners indicating their availability to provide professional services (such as bookkeeping or payroll services). The advertising and communications must not be misleading, deceptive, or violate IRS regulations.

Example: Juliana is a newly-licensed enrolled agent that wants to attract as many new clients as possible. She runs a flashy commercial ad on a local news station that she can settle any client's back tax debt for "pennies on the dollar" and she also states that every new client has a chance to win a lavish Hawaiian Cruise. In reality, there is no cruise, and Juliana's commercial also misleadingly inflated the chances of tax relief. Her commercial was merely a fabricated incentive to get new clients. This is false advertising that is purposely misleading. Juliana can be subject to penalties as well as potential suspension or even disbarment.

Fee Information: A practitioner may publish and advertise a fee schedule. A practitioner must adhere to the published fee schedule for at least 30 calendar days after it is last published. Fee information may be published in newspapers, mailings, websites, email, or by any other method. A practitioner may charge based on the following:

- Fixed fees for specific routine services.
- Hourly rates.
- A range of fees for particular services.
- A fee for an initial consultation.

Example: Lorene is an EA who publishes an advertisement in her local newspaper. The ad includes a published fee schedule for preparing certain tax return forms at deeply discounted rates. Lorene is inundated with calls and decides that the ad was a mistake. Regardless, she must adhere to the published fee schedule for at least 30 days after it was published.

Example: Jermaine is an EA who pays for a radio commercial about his tax services business. He also includes average prices for tax preparation and an hourly rate for his bookkeeping services. The advertisement plays on various radio stations for four months during the tax season. Jermaine must keep a copy of the radio commercial for at least 36 months from the last date that the commercial aired.

When advertising fees on radio or television, the broadcast must be recorded, and the practitioner must retain a copy of the recording for at least 36 months from the date of the last transmission or use. Practitioners who are authorized e-Service providers may use the IRS e-file logo. Tax practitioners are *specifically prohibited* from using official IRS insignia or U.S. Treasury seals in their advertising.

Advertising Standards: Permissible Logos	
Permitted	**Not Permitted**

Negotiation of Taxpayer Refund Checks §10.31

A practitioner must not endorse, negotiate, or cash a refund check issued to the taxpayer. For example, a practitioner cannot use *Form 8888, Allocation of Refund (Including Savings Bond Purchases)*, to enter his own bank account in order to obtain payment for his tax preparation fee. Form 8888 instructions state that entering an account in someone else's name, such as a preparer's, will cause the direct deposit request to be rejected and the taxpayer to be sent a paper check instead. A preparer could also be subject to a penalty under IRC §6695(f).

In the most recent Circular 230 revision, §10.31 clarifies that this provision applies to any practitioner, not just to one who prepares tax returns. It also expands the scope of "endorse or otherwise negotiate any check" to state that negotiation of a taxpayer check includes accepting or directing payment by any method, including electronically or via direct deposit or wire transfer.

> **Example:** McKinley is an enrolled agent with a new client, Donna, who will receive a $600 refund on her tax return. Donna has not yet paid McKinley's tax return preparation fee, and she doesn't have the money to pay the fee up-front, so McKinley enters his own bank account number, rather than Donna's, on Form 8888. McKinley plans to take his $200 fee from the refund and give Donna the remaining $400. However, directing a taxpayer's refund into the preparer's bank account is expressly forbidden, and McKinley could be subject to a preparer penalty for improper negotiation of Donna's refund.

Other Duties and Prohibited Acts in Circular 230

No Delay Tactics Allowed §10.23: A practitioner must not unreasonably delay the prompt disposition of any matter before the IRS.

> **Example:** Pablo is an enrolled agent who is representing his client, Melissa, in an IRS examination. Melissa owes a lot of money to the IRS but has no intention of paying her bill. She tells Pablo to delay the IRS as much as possible so she can transfer assets to her family members in order to escape any garnishments or levies. Pablo agrees, and he repeatedly rescheduled appointments with an IRS revenue agent in an attempt to delay proceedings. Pablo also delays furnishing certain documents that the IRS has requested, and when he does provide them, the records are incomplete. Not only Pablo's actions are in violation of Circular 230, but there could be criminal exposure for such actions.

No Employment of Disbarred or Suspended Persons §10.24: A practitioner may not knowingly employ a person or accept assistance from a person who has been disbarred or suspended from practice. This restriction applies even if the duties of the disbarred or suspended person would not include actual preparation of tax returns. In addition, a practitioner may not accept assistance from a former government employee in matters in which the former employee personally and substantially participated in the particular matter while employed by the government.

> **Example:** Yanni is an enrolled agent who owns a popular tax franchise, Tax Busters, Inc. Yanni has several tax preparers working for him, including an enrolled agent named Maribelle. During the year, Maribelle is caught forging checks, and she is convicted of a felony. She is later disbarred by the Office of Professional Responsibility. Yanni must immediately terminate Maribelle's employment, because he cannot knowingly employ a person who has been disbarred or suspended from practice.

Practice by Former Government Employees §10.25: A former government employee (and his partners and associates) cannot represent or knowingly assist a taxpayer if the representation would violate any law of the United States. A government employee who personally and substantially participated in a particular matter cannot represent or assist a taxpayer in the same particular matter after leaving his government position. §10.25 also places other restrictions on former government employees, including former IRS workers, in order to avoid conflicts of interest during representation.

Performance as a Notary §10.26: A practitioner who is a notary public and is employed as counsel, attorney, or agent in a matter before the IRS or who has a material interest in the matter cannot engage in any notary activities related to that matter.

> **Note:** This does not mean that an enrolled practitioner is prohibited from being a notary. An enrolled practitioner cannot notarize a document for a taxpayer if he is *representing* the same taxpayer before the IRS. This follows the laws for most states, where a notary public generally cannot notarize a document that he is a party to in some way.

Signature Requirements for Tax Returns

Signature requirements for the preparation of tax returns are not spelled out in Circular 230, but instead, are based on Treasury regulations. The requirements are as follows:

Preparer Signature and PTIN: A preparer is required by law to sign the tax return and fill out the preparer areas of the form, which must include the preparer's PTIN. The preparer's declaration statement is signed under penalties of perjury. The preparer must sign the return <u>after</u> it is completed but <u>before</u> it is presented to the taxpayer for signature. The preparer can sign original returns, amended returns, or requests for filing extensions by rubber stamp, mechanical device (such as a signature pen), or computer software program.[33]

Taxpayer Signature: Regardless of whether a paid preparer or someone else has prepared a return, a taxpayer must sign his own return, affirming it is correct under penalties of perjury. A taxpayer is legally responsible for the accuracy of every item on the return. A paper-filed return is required to have a "wet signature" or an original signature.[34]

Example: Henry is 75 years old and prefers to prepare his own return on paper in order to save on the cost of software. His return is very simple, as he only has Social Security income and some interest income from a certificate of deposit. Henry downloads the Form 1040-SR directly from the IRS website and prints it out, then fills out the form with a ballpoint pen. He signs the return with an original "wet signature" and mails it in.

More Than One Preparer: If the original preparer is unavailable for signature, another preparer must review the entire preparation of the return or claim and then must manually sign it. For purposes of the signature requirement, the preparer with primary responsibility for the overall accuracy of the return or claim is considered the preparer, if more than one preparer is involved. The other preparers do not have to be disclosed on the return.

Note that a preparer may sign on behalf of the taxpayer in the client's signature area only if certain standards are met (see previous unit, under the section: *Representative Signing in Lieu of the Taxpayer*).

---

[33] Use of electronic signatures is optional for tax professionals. For e-filed returns, a taxpayer may always choose to sign their return or e-file forms using a handwritten signature, instead of an electronic one, if they so choose. For paper-filed returns, a client must provide a handwritten signature.

[34] Although the taxpayer is ultimately responsible for the items reported on the tax return, when a preparer e-files a taxpayer's return, the Form 8879 (IRS e-file Signature Authorization) must be completed by the preparer and signed by both the preparer and the taxpayer. The Form 8897 is signed under penalty of perjury by both parties.

(Test yourself and then check the correct answers at the end of this chapter.)

1. Oliver is an enrolled agent. He has a new client named Minnie, who asks him to prepare her business tax return. When he presents the return to Minnie for signature, she gets upset about the amount that she owes, and refuses to pay for the return or sign it. She demands her original records back. Which of the following statements is correct regarding Minnie's request for her original records?

A. Oliver may choose to withhold the client's records if there is a fee dispute.
B. A legal case relieves Oliver of his responsibility to return a client's records.
C. Oliver must, at the request of his client, promptly return her records, regardless of fee disputes.
D. Oliver must, at the request of the client, return client records within 24 hours of payment.

2. Under IRC §6107, what is a tax return preparer required to keep for at least three years after the close of the return period?

A. A list of clients/tax returns prepared.
B. Copies of all tax returns prepared.
C. Both a list of clients/tax returns prepared and copies of all tax returns prepared.
D. Either A or B.

3. Drake is an enrolled agent. He has a new client, Alexia, who has self-prepared her own returns in the past. Drake notices several errors on Alexia's prior-year return. What is Drake required to do?

A. Drake must correct the errors by preparing an amended return for Alexia.
B. Drake must advise Alexia about the errors and the consequences of not correcting the errors.
C. Drake did not prepare the return with the errors, so he is not required to do anything.
D. Drake is required to inform the IRS about the errors.

4. Constanza is an enrolled agent. Her client, Aaron, is a wealthy businessman who frequently travels on extended business trips. Aaron is planning to be outside of the United States on business for at least 9 months this year. Constanza has a properly signed power of attorney from Aaron. Which of the following actions is she permitted to do on Aaron's behalf?

A. Receive Aaron's refund check, but not endorse or cash the check.
B. Sign Aaron's signature on his refund check, but only to deposit it into his account.
C. Receive a taxpayer's refund check and endorse it, but only to pay tax preparation fees.
D. Use her own bank account to receive Aaron's refund, then transfer the entire amount to him via a wire transfer.

5. Deangelo is an enrolled agent in the process of representing Arthur, his client, before the Internal Revenue Service for an old tax matter on a jointly-filed return. Arthur's ex-wife, Michelle, also asked Deangelo to represent her for the same matter. Which of the following is required for Deangelo to represent them both?

A. Both taxpayers must sit down together and discuss the matter before a mediator.
B. Both taxpayers must waive the conflict of interest with written informed consent
C. Deangelo must charge both parties the same amount.
D. This representation is prohibited by law.

6. Dennis, an enrolled agent, wants to hire his friend, Brandon, who is an attorney. Brandon has been disbarred from practice by his state bar association for gross misconduct. Brandon has appealed the disbarment, and it is currently under review. Which of the following statements is correct?

A. Dennis can still hire Brandon as a tax return preparer, provided Brandon does not represent any taxpayers.
B. Dennis can still hire Brandon, provided Brandon does not prepare or sign any tax returns.
C. Dennis cannot hire Brandon.
D. Dennis can hire Brandon while his appeal is pending.

7. Grace, an enrolled agent, represented Marley and his former business partner before the Internal Revenue Service with regard to a specific tax matter. Due to the potential conflict of interest, Grace obtained written consent from each of her clients, waiving the conflict of interest and giving informed consent. Grace must keep those written consents for how long after the conclusion of representation?

A. 24 Months.
B. 36 Months.
C. 48 Months.
D. 72 Months.

8. If more than one tax return preparer is involved in preparing a return, which preparer is required to sign?

A. All preparers involved in the preparation of the return.
B. Only the preparer with primary responsibility for the accuracy of the return; however, the other preparers must be disclosed on the return.
C. Only the preparer with primary responsibility for the accuracy of the return; the other preparers do not need to be disclosed on the return.
D. Only the taxpayer must sign the return.

9. Whitman is an EA who decides to advertise his fee schedule in the local newspaper. Which of the following fee arrangements is likely prohibited under the language contained in Circular 230?

A. Hourly fee rates.
B. Fixed fees for tax preparation.
C. Unconscionable fees for representing a taxpayer before the IRS.
D. Flat fees for initial consultations.

10. Sarah, an enrolled agent, buys a practice owned by Kellan, a tax preparer who is retiring. As she reviews the records from Kellan's practice, she learns he has been incorrectly claiming dependents for certain clients. What should Sarah do?

A. Notify the clients of the error and the consequences of not correcting the error.
B. Inform the clients that she will refuse to prepare their taxes if they do not file amended returns.
C. Contact the IRS to alert agents about the error and to request audits of those clients' prior year returns.
D. Inform Kellan that he made mistakes on his clients' returns and advise him to notify them.

11. Circular 230 §10.35 states that a practitioner must be _____ to engage in practice before the IRS.

A. Honest
B. Diligent
C. Ethical
D. Competent

12. Keagan is a CPA and an owner of his own tax practice. Keagan has spent hours finishing the year-end bookkeeping for a client. The client has yet to pay Keagan for fees charged in connection with the bookkeeping, but the client demands a copy of the back-up file, because he cannot prepare his tax return without it. Which of the following best describes Keagan's responsibility regarding the client's request for a copy of the spreadsheet?

A. The firm is under no obligation to hand over the bookkeeping file the client has not paid for, but must return the client's original records.
B. The firm is required to hand over the bookkeeping file, regardless of any fee dispute.
C. The firm is required to allow the client to copy the file.
D. The firm is required to hand over the bookkeeping as well as prepare the taxpayer's return, as long as the client signed an engagement letter.

13. Which of the following is not listed as a "best practice" for practitioners in Circular 230?

A. Acting fairly and with integrity in practice before the IRS.
B. Communicating clearly with the client regarding the terms of the engagement.
C. Advising the client regarding the consequences of advice rendered.
D. Consulting other professionals when questions arise about a particular tax issue.

14. All of the following statements regarding a practitioner's responsibility to provide information requested by the IRS are correct except:

A. If the records are not in his possession, he must make a "reasonable inquiry" of his client about their whereabouts.
B. He must promptly turn over all records relating to the IRS request, no matter what the circumstances.
C. He is not legally obligated to contact any third party who might possess the requested records.
D. If he believes in good faith and on reasonable grounds that the requested material is legally privileged information, a practitioner may choose to decline a records request.

15. Zoe is an enrolled agent who is also a notary public. Which of the following statements is correct?

A. Zoe cannot notarize documents for IRS matters for clients she represents before the IRS.
B. Zoe must resign her notary commission, EAs cannot be notaries.
C. Zoe is prohibited from performing notary services for her tax clients.
D. Zoe is permitted to notarize any documents of the clients she represents before the IRS.

16. Which of the following statements is correct?

A. Conflicts of interest apply only to attorneys and not to other tax professionals.
B. A practitioner may represent clients who have a conflict of interest under certain circumstances, but waivers to the conflict must be signed by both parties.
C. A practitioner may represent clients who have a conflict of interest if the practitioner receives a written conflict of interest waiver from the clients within 45 days of receiving any non-written, informed consent from the clients.
D. A practitioner may not represent clients who have a conflict of interest.

17. Arthur is an enrolled agent. He must, at all times, exercise due diligence when:

A. Renewing his PTIN.
B. When making comments on social media about taxation topics.
C. Preparing the FAFSA for his own family members.
D. Preparing any document involving IRS matters.

18. Melanie is an EA who submits her clients' returns via IRS e-file. In order to save paper, she does not give a copy of the prepared tax return to her clients if they do not request it. Melanie allows her clients to have a copy of the return, so long as they pay a small fee. Which of the following statements is correct?

A. Melanie is not in violation of IRC §6107.
B. Melanie is in violation of IRC §6107.
C. Melanie is not in violation of IRC §6107 if she gives clients the option of receiving a copy of their return for a small fee.
D. Melanie cannot offer a copy of the return to a client unless the client requests it.

Unit 4: Quiz Answers

1. The answer is C. Oliver must, at the request of his client, promptly return her records, regardless of fee disputes. Client records must generally be returned promptly upon client demand, regardless of fee disputes. Client records are defined as any original records belonging to the client, including any work product that he has already paid for, such as a completed copy of a tax return. However, the practitioner is allowed to withhold the return of his own work papers or work product until the client has resolved any outstanding payment issues.

2. The answer is D. Under IRC §6107, a tax return preparer must keep copies of all returns he or she has prepared or a list of clients and tax returns prepared. The list must include the taxpayer's name, taxpayer identification number, tax year, and the type of tax return prepared. The copies or list must be kept for at least three years after the close of the return period.

3. The answer is B. Drake must advise Alexia about the error and the consequences of not correcting the error. Drake is not required to amend the return, but he must advise the client about the error and the consequences of not fixing the error. He is not required to notify the IRS about his client's error.

4. The answer is A. Constanza may receive Aaron's refund check, but she <u>cannot endorse or cash</u> the check. With proper authorization, an enrolled practitioner may receive a refund check issued to the taxpayer. A practitioner is not allowed to negotiate taxpayer refunds under any circumstances, regardless of whether the client has given permission.

5. The answer is B. In order for Deangelo to represent Arthur and Michelle, *both* taxpayers must waive the conflict of interest and give informed consent in writing to the EA.

6. The answer is C. Dennis cannot knowingly hire a disbarred practitioner, regardless of whether that person would prepare tax returns. A practitioner may not knowingly employ a person or accept employment from a person who has been disbarred or suspended by the Office of Professional Responsibility, even if that person's case is under appeal.

7. The answer is B. Grace must retain the records related to the conflict of interest for at least 36 months (three years) from the date the representation ends.

8. The answer is C. Only the preparer with primary responsibility for the accuracy of the return is considered the preparer and is thus required to sign the return under penalties of perjury. The other preparers do not need to be disclosed on the return. The taxpayer is also required to sign the return, whether prepared by a preparer or not. The taxpayer is legally responsible for the accuracy of every item on his tax return.

9. The answer is C. Under Section 10.27 of Circular 230, an EA may not charge "unconscionable" fees in connection with any matter before the IRS.

10. The answer is A. Sarah must notify the clients of the error and the consequences of not correcting the error. Under the rules of Circular 230, a practitioner *must* advise a client about issues of noncompliance, errors, or omissions, in addition to the consequences of the errors. However, the practitioner is not obligated to correct the error, inform the IRS of the error, or insist the client file an amended return. The duty to advise also applies when a practitioner discovers an error or omission in the course of tax consulting or an advisory engagement.

11. The answer is D. Circular 230 §10.35 replaces the previous section detailing the covered opinion rules. It states that a practitioner must be competent to engage in practice before the IRS. "Competence" is defined as having the appropriate level of knowledge, skill, thoroughness, and preparation for the specific matter related to a client's engagement.

12. The answer is A. Keagan is under no obligation to hand over its own work product to a client who has not paid his fees. Keagan is required to return his client's original records, regardless of any fee dispute.

13. The answer is D. Although it may be advisable to consult with other tax professionals when particular tax questions arise, this is not listed as one of the "best practices" in Circular 230.

14. The answer is B. Although Circular 230 dictates that a practitioner comply promptly with information and record requests, there are limited circumstances when records do not have to be turned over. A practitioner may decline to do so if he believes in good faith that the request is not legal or that the information is privileged. A practitioner also does not have to contact any third party to inquire about the records; he must simply make a reasonable inquiry of his client.

15. The answer is A. Zoe cannot notarize documents of the clients she represents before the IRS if the document relates to a matter administered by the IRS. However, she is not prohibited from performing notary services for clients in connection with other financial or personal matters.

16. The answer is B. Under certain circumstances, a practitioner can represent clients who have a conflict of interest. The practitioner must reasonably believe he will be able to provide competent and diligent representation to each affected client; the representation cannot be prohibited by law, and each affected client must be fully notified and sign a consent waiving the conflict of interest in writing. A practitioner must receive written confirmation of a waiver of the conflict of interest from the clients within 30 days of receiving any non-written, informed consent from the clients.

17. The answer is D. As an enrolled agent, Arthur must at all times exercise due diligence when preparing any document involving IRS matters.

18. The answer is B. Melanie is in violation of IRC §6107. Tax return preparers must furnish copies of completed returns and claims for refund to all their clients, and this must be done no later than when clients sign the original documents. The copy can be a paper copy or a digital copy, but a complete copy of the return must be provided to the client.

Unit 5: Practitioner Standards and Tax Advice

> **More Reading:**
> **Circular 230, Regulations Governing Practice Before the Internal Revenue Service**

Circular 230 outlines broad standards for practitioners when it comes to tax positions taken on income tax returns, as well as other forms of written advice they provide clients. Practitioners who fail to meet these standards are subject to penalties and other sanctions.

Requirements for Written Advice §10.37

§10.37 was extensively revised in the most recent version of Circular 230. It presents the due diligence requirements for practitioners to exercise when issuing written advice. The definition of "written advice" has been expanded to encompass almost anything in writing, including email, text, or any other type of electronic communication, on any federal tax matter.[35] A practitioner must:

- Base the written advice on reasonable factual and legal assumptions.
- Consider all relevant facts and circumstances that he knows or reasonably should know.
- Use reasonable efforts to identify and ascertain the facts relevant to written advice on each federal tax matter.
- Not rely upon representations, statements, findings, or agreements of the taxpayer or any other person if reliance on them would be unreasonable.
- Relate applicable law and authority to facts.

In addition, when issuing written advice, a practitioner cannot take into consideration the chances that a tax return may or may not be audited, or that a particular matter may or may not be raised during an audit.

> **Example:** Randy is an enrolled agent. Randy's client, Paulette, asks him what the odds are that the IRS will audit certain deductions she wants to claim on her Schedule C. Randy's response is that the IRS audits only about 2% of these types of tax returns, so the risk is worth taking, although the law is unsettled about whether the deductions are allowable. In the tax return he prepares, Randy includes the questionable deductions. Randy is playing the "audit lottery," which is in violation of Circular 230. This type of practitioner advice is specifically prohibited by the IRS.

Similar to the provisions in §10.22, §10.37 has a paragraph that allows a practitioner to rely on the advice of another person, so long as the advice is reasonable and the reliance is in good faith. However, the section specifies that reliance is not reasonable when the practitioner knows or reasonably should know that:

- The opinion of the other person should not be relied on;

---

[35] There are two exceptions to what is considered "written advice" under §10.37: (1) continuing education presentations on federal tax matters and (2) government submissions on general policy are excluded.

- The other person is not competent or lacks the necessary qualifications to provide the advice; or
- The other person has a conflict of interest in violation of the rules described in this part.

A "standard of review" paragraph was added that establishes the basis by which the IRS will evaluate whether a practitioner has complied with the written advice rules of §10.37. It applies a "reasonable practitioner" standard, with all facts and circumstances taken into account. The scope of the engagement and the type and specificity of the advice sought by the client are also to be considered.

Standards for Tax Returns and Documents (§10.34)

In addition to §10.37, Circular 230's §10.34 is vital to understanding a practitioner's responsibilities when providing written advice to a client.

The section directly relates to IRC §6694,[36] which describes tax return preparer penalties. §10.34 has four parts: (1) positions taken on tax returns, (2) positions taken on other documents or affidavits submitted to the IRS, (3) advising clients on potential penalties, and (4) relying on information furnished by clients.

Standards for Tax Returns: A practitioner may not willfully sign a tax return or claim for refund that he knows (or reasonably should know) contains a position that:

- Lacks a reasonable basis.
- Is an unreasonable position, as described in IRC §6694(a)(2).
- Is a willful attempt by the practitioner to understate the liability for tax or reflects a reckless or intentional disregard of rules or regulations.

In determining potential penalties, the IRS will take into account a pattern of conduct to assess whether a practitioner acted willfully, recklessly, or through gross incompetence. In addition to civil penalties, criminal penalties may also apply to tax return preparers who file fraudulent returns with unreasonable positions.

Tax Position Definitions

1. **More Likely Than Not:** There is a greater-than-50% likelihood that the tax treatment will be upheld if the IRS challenges it. If a preparer is unsure that a position meets this standard, he may generally avoid penalties by disclosing the position on the return. However, a disclosure statement will not protect the preparer if the position is patently frivolous—the "more likely than not" standard must be used for tax shelters and reportable transactions.

2. **Substantial Authority:** The weight of authorities in support of a position is substantial in relation to the weight of authorities in opposition to the position; this is a higher level of certainty than a "reasonable basis."

---

[36] Section 6694(a) imposes penalties on paid preparers who prepare returns reflecting an understatement of liability due to an unreasonable position if the preparer knew (or reasonably should have known) of the position. No penalty is imposed, however, if it is shown that there is reasonable cause for the understatement and the preparer acted in good faith.

3. **Reasonable Basis:** This is the minimum standard for all tax advice and preparation of tax returns. Reasonable basis is a relatively high standard of tax reporting, that is, significantly higher than not frivolous or not patently improper. The reasonable basis standard is not satisfied by a return position that is merely "arguable," or that is merely a colorable claim. If a return position is reasonably based on one or more of the tax authorities, taking into account the relevance and persuasiveness of the authorities, and subsequent developments, the return position will generally satisfy the reasonable basis standard. For purposes of avoiding §6694 penalties, the reasonable-basis standard applies only if the relevant tax position is disclosed on the return or document so that the IRS is aware of a potential issue.

4. **Unreasonable Position:** In general, this is either a position without substantial authority or an undisclosed position without a reasonable basis.

5. **Frivolous position:** A position that is patently improper with no reasonable basis.[37]

Adequate and appropriate disclosure can be normally made by using Form 8275, *Disclosure Statement*, which allows a preparer to disclose positions that do not have substantial authority, but still have a reasonable basis, assuming the position is not otherwise already disclosed on the return.

> **Example:** Vicente is a nonresident alien and a citizen of Spain. He earns substantial royalties from a passive U.S. investment that he owns. Vicente would be subject to U.S. tax on the income "effectively connected" with the U.S. on this investment. The United States and Spain do have an income tax treaty in place. However, Vicente's accountant is unsure if the royalties are subject to a special, lower tax rate based on the treaty. Vicente and the accountant decide that they have a reasonable basis to take a treaty-based return position, but it will be disclosed on Vicente's return. The accountant prepares Vicente's Form 1040-NR and attaches the Form 8275, explaining the position. No accuracy-related penalty will be imposed on any portion of an underpayment if Vicente can show that there was reasonable cause and that he acted in good faith.

Disclosure Statements

Circular 230 §10.34 specifies the use of disclosure statements in certain instances. A tax return that requires a disclosure to the IRS must include *Form 8275, Disclosure Statement*, or *Form 8275-R, Regulation Disclosure Statement.*

Form 8275 is used by taxpayers and preparers to disclose certain items or positions on a tax return. It is primarily used to avoid accuracy-related penalties so long as the return position has a reasonable basis, and the taxpayer (and the preparer) acted in good faith when taking the position. If the disclosure is made in good faith, the penalty for a substantial understatement of income tax or negligent disregard of rules or regulations may be avoided, even if the IRS later

---

[37] A frivolous tax position is a way to delay the taxation process. Taxpayers may not rely on frivolous arguments to avoid or evade taxes. See the document, *Truth About Frivolous Tax Arguments,* available at: https://www.irs.gov/pub/irs-utl/2022-the-truth-about-frivolous-tax-arguments.pdf.

disallows the deduction or disagrees with the position. However, Form 8275 *cannot* be used to avoid the portion of the accuracy-related penalty attributable to certain types of misconduct, including the following:

- Negligence.
- Disregard of regulations.
- Any substantial understatement of income tax on a tax shelter item.

A disclosure statement cannot be used by a preparer to avoid penalties if the position has no reasonable basis. Form 8275 is used for most disclosure matters. Form 8275-R is only used in limited circumstances when a taxpayer takes a position that runs contrary to Treasury regulations.

Example: Rochelle is an enrolled agent. She prepares a tax return for her client, Pavel, who is a self-employed carpenter. Pavel would like to take an aggressive tax position in order to deduct a large travel expense, which may not have been deductible as a business expense. This large deduction on the return did not have a reasonable basis and was not disclosed. Pavel's return is later selected for audit, and the entire deduction is disallowed. Rochelle may be liable for a preparer penalty, and Pavel may be liable for an accuracy-related penalty.

Example: Hazel is an EA with a client who has a very complex tax situation. She notices that the IRS publications reflect one position, but there is a recent court case that may allow a more favorable position for her client. There are also two other similar cases being litigated, but the outcome of those cases is currently unknown. Hazel believes that the position has a 35% chance of prevailing on its merits. Hazel thinks that the client's position has a reasonable basis and decides to disclose the position on the tax return. Even though the position is contrary to the IRS's current position, Hazel may take the position on the return, so long as it is disclosed. She must file Form 8275 along with the tax return stating the position and referencing the court case or any other basis she has for the position.

Example: Frank, a CPA, is hired to prepare a final tax return for a deceased individual. He receives a question from the executor about the deductibility of a particular expense. The IRS has no applicable guidance for the deduction, but there has been a recent court case where the taxpayer was allowed to claim a similar deduction. Thus, prior law supports a position favorable to the taxpayer. However, Frank's client is now deceased, and the executor's records are incomplete. The executor is certain that the expense can be ultimately deducted, but Frank believes that the deductibility of the expense is uncertain. Frank uses Form 8275, *Disclosure Statement,* to properly disclose the taxpayer's position. By filing Form 8275, Frank and his client can avoid the accuracy-related penalty if the IRS later disallows the expense.

Standards for Submission of Documents to the IRS: A practitioner may not advise a client to submit a document, affidavit, or other paper to the IRS:

- The purpose of which is to delay or impede the administration of the federal tax laws,
- That is frivolous, or

- That contains or omits information in a manner that demonstrates an intentional disregard of a rule or regulation, unless the practitioner also advises the client to submit a document that evidences a good faith challenge to the rule or regulation (such as a disclosure statement).

A practitioner may sign a return with a tax position that meets at least one of two standards:

- The position has a "reasonable basis" for most positions, or
- The position is "more likely than not" to be sustained on its merits for tax shelters and other uncommon types of positions.

A practitioner must not knowingly sign a frivolous return. A frivolous position is defined as one that the practitioner knows is in bad faith and is improper.

> **Example:** Heidi is a tax preparer who prepares a Form 1040 for her client, Herman, showing $95,000 of wages and the appropriate tax due. Six months later, on behalf of the same client, she files an amended return, showing zero income, and requesting a full refund of the income taxes paid. Herman attaches a signed statement to the return saying that "filing taxes is completely voluntary, and that he is a sovereign citizen and not subject to income tax." The amended return is considered frivolous. Heidi signs the return as the preparer, because Herman offered her a nice fee if she would prepare the return for him and sign it, believing it would add legitimacy to his frivolous tax position. The IRS flags the return and sends a notice, advising that the position reflected on the amended return was frivolous. The IRS can assert a penalty against Herman, as well as Heidi, for the frivolous tax position (based on the U.S. Tax Court case: *Kestin, 153 T.C. No. 2*).

Advising Clients on Potential Penalties

A practitioner is required to inform a client of any penalties that are reasonably likely to apply to a position taken on a tax return if:

- The practitioner advised the client concerning the position, or
- The practitioner prepared or signed the tax return.

The practitioner must also inform the client of any opportunity to avoid penalties by disclosing the position and the requirements for adequate disclosure. This rule applies even if the practitioner is not subject to an IRC penalty related to the position, or the document or tax return submitted.

Reliance on Information from Clients: When preparing income tax returns, a practitioner is not required to verify all the information furnished by his clients. In general, a practitioner:

- May rely on, in good faith, the information that a client provides.
- Should not ignore the implications of the information.
- Should make reasonable inquiries if the information appears to be incorrect, inconsistent, or incomplete.

Example: Shayne is an EA who conducts an interview with his new client, Tameka. She states she made a $50,000 charitable contribution of valuable artwork during 2022. However, this is not true, and Shayne fails to make reasonable inquiries to Tameka about the contribution. He does not ask about the existence of a qualified appraisal, and he does not complete an IRS-required substantiation form. Shayne includes the deduction for the charitable contribution on Tameka's tax return, which results in an understatement of tax liability. Tameka's return is later audited, and the charitable deduction is disallowed. Shayne is in violation of §10.34 and, in addition, would be subject to a preparer penalty for his negligence.

Example: Jennie is an EA, whose client, Emilio, says he paid $19,000 of deductible alimony during the year. However, from Emilio's statement alone, Jennie cannot know whether the $19,000 is indeed deductible alimony. All or a portion of payments to a former spouse may be child support or family support, which are treated differently than alimony for federal tax purposes. It is Jennie's responsibility to ask pertinent questions of her client in order to make the correct determination of whether or not the payment is actually alimony.

Example: Oleg is an enrolled agent, and his client's name is Carmen. Carmen wants to claim her 5-year-old niece, Sofia, on her tax return, and claim EITC and the CTC. Carmen tells Oleg that Sofia lived with her all year. However, Oleg prepared the return for Sofia's parents last week, and he knows that Sofia lived with her parents all year. In preparing Carmen's return, Oleg cannot ignore what he knows about Sofia's residency.

Reporting Requirements for Tax Shelter Activities

Certain types of tax shelter activities must be reported to the IRS. A reportable transaction, also sometimes called a listed transaction, is one that the IRS has determined has the potential for tax avoidance or evasion.

The rules for reportable transactions apply to all individuals and entities (including trusts, estates, partnerships, and corporations). Form 8886, *Reportable Transaction Disclosure Statement,* must be attached to a taxpayer's return for any year that he participates in this type of tax shelter.[38]

A separate statement must be filed for each reportable transaction. A taxpayer may request a ruling from the IRS to determine whether a transaction must be disclosed. The fact that a tax shelter transaction must be reported on this form does not necessarily mean the IRS will disallow its tax benefits.

If a reportable transaction is not disclosed and results in an understatement of tax, an additional penalty equal to 30% of the understatement may be assessed. In addition to the 30% understatement of tax penalty, a civil penalty of 75% of the reduction of tax associated with the reportable transaction may be imposed, with a minimum penalty of $10,000 ($5,000 if the taxpayer is an individual) and a maximum penalty as high as $200,000 ($100,000 if the taxpayer

---

[38] Abusive tax shelters and abusive trust schemes will try to hide the true ownership of assets and income or to disguise the substance of transactions. When the IRS identifies a promoter of an abusive trust or an abusive tax shelter, the IRS will request a list of the promoter's clients through legal means, such as a judicial subpoena.

is an individual), pursuant to IRC section 6707A(b). Even with proper disclosure, taxpayers may still be subject to a 20% penalty on the understatement of tax.

> **Example:** Alexander participated in a Guam Trust that was aggressively marketed primarily to wealthy individuals. The IRS later audited the promoter of this scheme and deemed it to be an abusive tax shelter transaction. Alexander did not disclose his participation in the tax shelter on his individual tax return. Alexander may be liable for a penalty of 75% of the tax he underpaid as a result of the tax scheme. In addition, he may also be liable for criminal penalties.

Note about Covered Opinions: One of the most significant changes in the latest revision to Circular 230 was the elimination of the complex "covered opinion" rules in §10.35.[39]

These rules led many practitioners to use blanket disclaimer statements on almost every piece of written communication, including emails. With the deletion of the covered opinion requirements, the IRS stated that practitioners must remove all such references in these disclaimers to the IRS, OPR, or Circular 230.

Firm Compliance Procedures §10.36

Circular 230 §10.36 was rewritten to address the measures a firm must take to ensure compliance with all provisions of Circular 230. A practitioner (or practitioners, if the duty is shared) who oversees a firm's practice must ensure adequate procedures are in place for every member, associate, or employee to comply with the requirements specified in Circular 230.

If a firm has not identified an individual with principal authority over the practice, the IRS may identify one or more practitioners who will be considered responsible for the §10.36 compliance requirements.

A practitioner who does not take reasonable steps to ensure the firm has adequate procedures in place to comply with Circular 230 requirements may face disciplinary action. The practitioner may also be subject to sanctions if they know of other firm members who are engaging in a pattern of noncompliance and fail to take prompt action to correct the noncompliance.

> **Example:** Blaine and William are both CPAs, and they are partners in an accounting practice and prepare hundreds of tax returns every year. After reviewing a few business returns that William has prepared, Blaine thinks that his business partner, William, might be advising his clients to take credits for which they do not qualify. Blaine decides to say nothing, and does not confront William about his suspicions. If the firm is later audited by the IRS, Blaine may be sanctioned by the IRS for William's negligent or reckless actions.

> **Example:** Catherine is an enrolled agent working for a tax practice. Catherine knows that her coworker is filing fraudulent EITC claims, but does nothing. Catherine can be subject to sanctions because she knew that other members of the firm were committing EITC fraud, and she did not report the illegal activity.

---

[39] Now replaced by the general "competence" standard.

Unit 5: Study Questions

(Test yourself and then check the correct answers at the end of this chapter.)

1. A penalty may be assessed on any preparer who:

A. Gives advice (written or oral) to a taxpayer or to a preparer not associated with the same firm.
B. Signs a return with an undisclosed position without a reasonable basis.
C. Prepares and signs a tax return or claim for refund for a nonresident alien.
D. Represents a member of their own family before the IRS.

2. A practitioner cannot sign:

A. A tax return for a family member.
B. A tax return that he prepares for free.
C. A tax return with a properly disclosed tax shelter position.
D. A tax return with a frivolous position.

3. When should a practitioner <u>not</u> rely on the advice of another person?

A. When the advice is reasonable, and the reliance is in good faith.
B. When the person is competent in providing the advice.
C. When the person has a conflict of interest in the tax matter.
D. When the practitioner has a professional relationship with the other person.

4. Under Circular 230, what is the responsibility of a practitioner who oversees a firm's tax practice?

A. To ensure the firm has adequate procedures in place to ensure compliance with all provisions of Circular 230.
B. To appoint another practitioner in the firm to monitor the compliance of other employees.
C. To review the personal tax filings of all employees of the firm to make sure they comply with Circular 230.
D. All of the above.

5. Which type of transaction must always be reported to the IRS?

A. Listed transaction.
B. Reliance opinion.
C. A loss from a Ponzi scheme.
D. A position with a more likely than not chance of being upheld.

6. In the "standard of review" section of Circular 230, the IRS will evaluate whether a practitioner has complied with the written advice rules of §10.37 by applying a _____ standard.

A. "Substantial authority"
B. "More likely than not"
C. "Reasonable authority"
D. "Reasonable practitioner"

7. Violeta is an EA with a client, Maximo, who wishes to claim a deduction for a large business expense. However, there is a question about whether the expense is "ordinary and necessary" for his business. If the deduction were later disallowed, there would be a substantial understatement of tax. Violeta believes the position has a reasonable basis, but not substantial authority. Maximo does not want to disclose the position on the return, because he is afraid that the IRS will disallow it. What are the repercussions for Violeta if the position is not disclosed and she signs the tax return?

A. Violeta has no repercussions, as all the penalties would apply to the client.
B. Violeta may be liable for IRC §6694 preparer penalties.
C. Violeta will not be liable for preparer penalties so long as she explains the potential penalties to the client.
D. Violeta may be liable for a failure-to-file penalty for filing a false return.

8. Glenn is an EA who prepares income tax returns for his clients. One of his clients submits a list of expenses to be claimed on Schedule C of the return. Glenn is required to do which one of the following?

A. Glenn is required to independently verify the client's information.
B. Glenn can ignore the implications of information known by him.
C. Glenn must audit the client's financial statements.
D. Glenn must make appropriate inquiries to determine whether the deductions are correct.

9. All of the following statements are correct about section §10.37 of Circular 230 on written advice except:

A. An email to a client about a tax matter would be included in the definition of written advice.
B. A practitioner should advise a client of the chances his tax return will be chosen for audit.
C. A practitioner should base his written advice on reasonable factual and legal assumptions.
D. A practitioner should relate the applicable law and authority to the facts relevant to written advice issued on a federal tax matter.

10. A practitioner is required to inform a client of penalties that are reasonably likely to apply to a position taken on a tax return if:

A. The taxpayer decides to self-prepare a return.
B. The practitioner gave the client advice on the position.
C. The IRS has the taxpayer under examination.
D. The taxpayer is deceased.

11. Ryan is an EA with a client named Hannah, who has had significant income from a partnership for the past five years. However, Ryan did not see a Schedule K-1 from the partnership among the information Hannah provided to him this year. What do Circular 230 due diligence provisions require Ryan to do?

A. Attempt to estimate the taxable amount that would be reported as income on Schedule K-1 based on last year's Schedule K-1 and include that amount on Hannah's return.
B. Call Hannah's financial advisor and ask him about Hannah's investments.
C. Nothing, because Ryan is required to rely only on the information provided by his client, even if he has reason to believe the information may not be accurate.
D. Ask Hannah why she did not provide him with the partnership's Schedule K-1, as she had in previous years.

Unit 5: Quiz Answers

1. The answer is B. A penalty may be assessed on any preparer who signs a return with an undisclosed position without a reasonable basis. No penalty will be imposed if the preparer can show that there is reasonable cause for the understatement and the position was adequately disclosed.

2. The answer is D. A tax return preparer cannot sign a frivolous tax return, even if the return has a disclosure A frivolous position is defined as one that the preparer knows is in bad faith or is improper.

3. The answer is C. The revised §10.37 of Circular 230 details the current standards for written tax advice. Similar to the provisions in §10.22, §10.37 says a practitioner may rely on the advice of another person, so long as the advice is reasonable and the reliance is in good faith. However, reliance is not reasonable when the practitioner knows, (or reasonably should know), that:

- The opinion of the other person should not be relied on,
- The other person is not competent, or lacks the necessary qualifications to provide the advice, or
- The other person has a conflict of interest in violation of the rules.

4. The answer is A. Under §10.36, a practitioner (or practitioners, if the duty is shared) who oversees a firm's practice must ensure adequate procedures are in place for every member, associate, or employee to comply with the requirements specified in Circular 230. A practitioner who does not take reasonable steps to ensure the firm has adequate procedures in place may face disciplinary action or sanctions if he knows of other members of the firm who are engaging in a pattern of noncompliance, and he fails to take prompt action to correct the noncompliance.

5. The answer is A. A listed transaction, also called a reportable transaction, is a type of tax shelter activity that must be reported to the IRS. Form 8886, Reportable Transaction Disclosure Statement, must be attached to a taxpayer's return for any year he participates in this type of tax shelter.

6. The answer is D. In the most recent revision of Circular 230, a "standard of review" paragraph was added that establishes the basis that the IRS will use to evaluate whether a practitioner has complied with the written advice rules of §10.37. It applies a "reasonable practitioner" standard, with all facts and circumstances taken into account. The scope of the engagement and the type and specificity of the advice sought by the client will also be considered.

7. The answer is B. If the return does not adequately disclose the position and the IRS later examines the return, Violeta may be subject to a preparer penalty. The disclosure form is filed to avoid the potential for penalties due to disregard of rules regarding the substantial understatement of income tax.

8. The answer is D. Glenn must make appropriate inquiries to determine whether the deductions are correct. A practitioner is not required to independently examine evidence of deductions. He may rely in good faith, without verification, upon information furnished by the taxpayer if it does not appear to be incorrect or incomplete. However, the practitioner must make reasonable inquiries about the validity of the information.

9. The answer is B. §10.37 has been expanded to define written advice as almost anything in writing, including electronic communications, on any federal tax matter. When issuing written advice, a practitioner is expressly prohibited from taking into consideration the chances that a tax return may or may not be audited, or that a particular matter may or may not be raised during an audit. A practitioner must:

- Base the written advice on reasonable factual and legal assumptions.
- Consider all relevant facts and circumstances that he knows or reasonably should know.
- Use reasonable efforts to identify and ascertain the facts relevant to written advice on each federal tax matter.
- Not rely upon representations, statements, findings, or agreements of the taxpayer or any other person if reliance on them would be unreasonable.
- Relate applicable law and authority to facts.

10. The answer is B. A practitioner is required to inform a client of any penalties that are reasonably likely to apply to a position taken on a tax return if:

- The practitioner advised the client with respect to the position, or
- The practitioner prepared or signed the tax return.

11. The answer is D. Ryan must ask Hannah about the missing Schedule K-1 and ask pertinent questions to understand the facts of the situation. A practitioner who has reason to believe his client has not complied with the revenue laws or has made an error in or omission from any return, document, affidavit, or other required paper has the responsibility to advise the client promptly of the noncompliance, error, or omission.

Unit 6: Due Diligence for Refundable Credits

More Reading:
www.eitc.irs.gov
Publication 596, Earned Income Credit
Publication 4687, Refundable Credits Due Diligence
Publication 5713, Due Diligence Interviews

Each year, tax preparers complete more than half of the tax returns claiming the Child Tax Credit (CTC), Additional Child Tax Credit (ACTC), Earned Income Credit (EITC), and/or the American Opportunity Tax Credit (AOTC). The IRS estimates that one in four of these claims is incorrect, which results in billions of dollars paid out in erroneous refunds each year.

The IRS has expansive due diligence requirements for the Child Tax Credit as well as the American Opportunity Credit. Under the *Tax Cuts and Jobs Act,* comprehensive due diligence requirements were expanded to include Head of Household filing status and the Credit for Other Dependents (ODC).

The due diligence rules for these credits are more stringent than they were in previous years. This is because both the number of individuals claiming these refundable credits and the number of erroneous claims is high. Paid preparers must meet four additional due diligence requirements on returns with these claims or face possible penalties. Employers may also be penalized for an employee's failure to exercise due diligence.

There are four due diligence requirements for each EITC, CTC/ACTC/ODC, AOTC, and/or HOH filing status claim prepared. The due diligence requirements apply to individual income tax returns claiming the head of household filing status. A preparer is required to:

1. **Complete and Submit Form 8867:** The *Paid Preparer's Due Diligence Checklist,* must be included for each EITC, CTC, ACTC, ODC, AOTC, and/or HOH filing status claim prepared.

2. **Compute the Credit on Required Worksheets:** The preparer must complete and keep all worksheets used to compute the credit, or complete the computations using similar worksheets and make sure to keep records showing the information used and how the computations were made.

3. **The Knowledge Requirement:** Preparers must apply the "knowledge requirement"— the preparer must be knowledgeable and not know (or have reason to know) any information used to determine a client's eligibility for, or the amount of the refundable credit is incorrect.

4. **Keep Records for Three Years:** a preparer must keep required records for each claim in either a paper or electronic format.

Requirement #1: Form 8867, Paid Preparer's Due Diligence Checklist

Form 8867, Paid Preparer's Due Diligence Checklist, includes several mandatory questions that preparers must ask taxpayers in order to comply with due diligence requirements.

A Form 8867 must be completed for each EITC, CTC/ACTC/ODC, AOTC, and/or HOH filing status claim prepared, every year, *without exception.*

Form 8867 is also used by a preparer to identify the documents that the taxpayer provided and that the preparer used to determine credit eligibility. In determining the residency of qualifying children, a preparer must specify whether he relied upon documents such as school, medical, or social service records. In determining the disability of a qualifying child, a preparer must indicate whether he relied upon documents such as a statement from a doctor, other health care provider, or social services agency.

> **Note:** For the EA exam, you should memorize the four "due diligence" compliance requirements that apply to tax preparers with regards to refundable claims. You may be asked several questions about this topic.

> **Example:** Collin is an EA. His new client, Delia, 62, wants to take a dependency exemption for her son, Ernest, who is 32. She also wants to claim the Earned Income Tax Credit and the Child and Dependent Care Credit for her son. Since Ernest is beyond the normal age limit for these credits, Collin makes reasonable inquiries, and Delia produces a doctor's statement that says Ernest is severely disabled and incapable of self-care. Therefore, Delia may claim her son as a dependent, and the credits will be allowed regardless of Ernest's age. Collin has fulfilled his due diligence requirements by conducting a thorough interview with his client, including asking enough questions to understand an individual tax situation, documenting the answers, and seeking appropriate supporting evidence. He completes his due diligence requirements by submitting Form 8867 to the IRS.

If a Schedule C is included with the tax return, the preparer must specify whether he determined credit eligibility by relying upon any documents the taxpayer provided in connection with the business. These documents may include a business license, Forms 1099, records of gross receipts and expenses, or bank statements.

There are certain types of errors that the IRS commonly sees on refund claims. Errors can delay the taxpayer's refund or can lead to a rejection of the credits listed on the return.

> **Note:** Preparers are not always required to ask for documents to prove the relationship and residency of a qualifying child before completing a claim for a refundable credit, although a paid preparer may request those documents if the information provided by the client appears to be incorrect, inconsistent, or incomplete.

Requirement #2: Compute the Credits on the Required Worksheets

Most tax preparation software will compute these credits automatically on worksheets within the actual software program. Still, the IRS emphasizes that using software is not a substitute for knowledge of the law.

A tax preparer must complete the appropriate refundable credit worksheets from the instructions for Form 1040 (or complete documents with the same information). The worksheets show what to consider in the computation. The preparer must retain the records showing how he or she did the computations.

Requirement #3: Apply the Knowledge Requirement

IRS regulations specify due diligence requirements and set a "performance standard" for the knowledge requirement for all EITC, CTC, ACTC, ODC, AOTC, and HOH returns: what a reasonable and well-informed tax return preparer, knowledgeable in the law, would do.[40]

The IRS assesses more than 90% of all due diligence penalties for failure to comply with the knowledge requirement of IRC §6695. Under the "knowledge requirement," a preparer must:

- Apply a common-sense standard to the information provided by the client.
- Evaluate whether the information is complete and gather any missing facts.
- Determine if the information is consistent; recognize contradictory statements and statements the preparer knows are not true.
- Conduct a thorough, in-depth interview with every client every year.
- Ask enough questions to reasonably know the return is correct and complete.
- Document in the file any questions he asked and his client's responses.

Example: Norman is an EA. His client, Ayanna, states that she is separated from her spouse. Her dependent son is 12 years old and lives with her. Ayanna wants to claim the EITC and file as head of household. In reviewing his client's records, Norman notes that Ayanna earns a minimal income, which appears insufficient to support a household. As the preparer, Norman must ask appropriate questions to determine Ayanna's correct filing status, determine how long the child lived with each parent during the year, and probe for any additional sources of income. He must interview her thoroughly and document her answers. He must also fill out *Form 8867, Paid Preparer's Earned Income Credit Checklist,* and complete the EITC worksheet. After asking various questions, Ayanna discloses that she receives substantial child support, which is not taxable or reportable on the return. She also receives food stamps and other public benefits, which also help support her son. Food stamps are also not taxable. Norman notes this information in his work papers and is now more confident that he can prepare Ayanna's return accurately.

Example: Ezekiel is an EA. Geneva is his new client. Geneva wants to claim the EITC as well as the AOTC. She has two qualifying children who both attend a local community college. Geneva tells Ezekiel she had a Schedule C business and earned $12,500 in income, but had no expenses. This information appears incomplete because it would be unusual that someone who is self-employed has no business expenses. Ezekiel is required to ask reasonable questions to determine if the business exists and if the information about Geneva's income and expenses is correct. Ezekiel must submit Form 8867 to the IRS and keep copies of any documents Geneva provides for at least three years.

---

[40] Treasury Regulations give more examples of the application of the knowledge requirement.

> **Example:** Amanda is an EA. A new 28-year-old client, Bernie, wants to claim two sons, ages 14 and 15, as qualifying children for the EITC and the Child Tax Credit. Amanda is concerned about the age of the children since Bernie's age seems inconsistent with the ages of the children. Amanda asks additional questions and discovers the boys are both adopted, which explains the age inconsistency. She completes the EITC Worksheet and Form 8867, and submits Form 8867 to the IRS. She retains copies of these records, as well as the adoption records that Bernie provides her and notes of her client interview, for a period of three years. Amanda has complied with her due diligence requirements.

Requirement #4: Preparer Recordkeeping Compliance Requirements

A preparer must retain the following records for each claim:

- Form 8867, Paid Preparer's Due Diligence Checklist.
- The applicable worksheet(s) for EITC, CTC/ACTC, and AOTC claimed on the return.
- Any documents or other written proof relied on to complete the Form 8867 or to determine eligibility for any refundable credit or, if applicable, to the taxpayer's eligibility for Head of Household filing status.
- A record of how, when, and from whom the information the preparer obtained to prepare the tax return as well as a record of any additional questions the preparer asked to determine eligibility for and the amount of the credits and the client's answers.

All records should be kept for three years from the latest of:

- The due date of the tax return.
- The date the tax return was electronically filed.
- For a paper return, the date the return was presented to the client for signature.
- The date you gave the part of the return for which you are responsible to the signing tax return preparer (if you are a non-signing tax return preparer).

The records must be retained in either paper or electronic format, and they must be produced on-demand if an IRS field auditor asks for them.

Most Common EITC Errors

The three issues that account for most EITC errors are:

- Claiming EITC for a child who does not meet the qualifying child requirements.
- **Filing status errors:** Filing as single or head of household when married. A taxpayer cannot file as Married Filing Separately (MFS) and receive the EITC or the AOTC. The EITC and the AOTC can only be claimed with four filing statuses:
    - Married filing jointly (MFJ).
    - Qualifying surviving spouse (QSS).
    - Single.
    - Head of household (HOH).

- **Misreported income and expenses:** misreported income is the most common error found on returns claiming EITC. Be aware of these potential problem areas in reporting income:
    - Questionable Schedule C or F income to qualify for the EITC, specifically income that is not reported on a Form 1099.
    - Insufficient income to support the client and their children.
    - A Schedule C or F when the client has no records for income or expenses.
    - Schedule C or F businesses with no expenses, particularly when similar businesses routinely have expenses.

Another common method of EITC fraud is the "borrowing" or "selling" of dependents. Unscrupulous tax preparers will "share" one taxpayer's qualifying child or children with another taxpayer in order to allow both to claim the EITC. Any taxpayer who is claiming the EITC must have a Social Security number that is valid for employment purposes.

> **Example:** Herbert has four children, but he only needs the first three children to receive the maximum EITC amount. The preparer lists the first three children on Herbert's return and lists the other child on another return. The preparer and Herbert are "selling" the dependents and will then split a fee or split the refund. This is an example of tax fraud that involves both the preparer and the taxpayer.

> **Example:** Susan is an enrolled agent. New clients, Ivan and Mila, come into Susan's office. They are married and both are 27 years old. Their seven-month-old son, Erik, was born in the U.S. and has lived with them since birth. Mila does not work because she is caring for their newborn. Ivan's Form W-2 shows earnings of $21,000. Peter and Mila's social security cards bear the legend "VALID FOR WORK ONLY WITH INS AUTHORIZATION." Ivan and Mila state that they obtained their green cards in the previous year. Their cards are valid social security cards. Therefore, Ivan and Mila would be eligible to claim the EITC if they meet the other eligibility requirements.

Most Common AOTC Errors

The AOTC is a refundable credit available for clients who pay post-secondary education expenses. To qualify for the AOTC, a student must meet the following requirements:

Attend an eligible educational institution. The AOTC is for post-secondary education only, which may include education at a college, university, or technical school. The AOTC can only be claimed for the first four years of post-secondary education. The school must be eligible to participate in a student aid program administered by the U.S. Department of Education.

> **Example:** Loren is a student at a nontraditional college, studying alternative medicine and astrology. Although she is enrolled in a degree program, the college is not accredited and therefore ineligible to participate in the U.S. Department of Education student aid program. Since the college is not a qualifying institution, Loren's tuition is not a qualifying educational expense for the purposes of the AOTC.

Have qualifying college expenses. Educational expenses must be paid or considered paid by the client, the client's spouse or the dependent student claimed on the tax return. Allowable expenses include: college tuition, required enrollment fees, and course materials. Nonqualifying expenses for the AOTC include:

- Health insurance, car insurance, or any other type of insurance,
- Medical expenses (including student health fees, even if the fees are mandatory),
- Room and board,
- Transportation,
- Personal, living, or family expenses.

Only Available for Four Years: The AOTC is only available for four years of post-secondary education, and a taxpayer can only claim the credit for four tax years.

> **Example:** Ariella is an enrolled agent. She interviews Harley, a 27-year-old client who states that he's a full-time college student and would like to claim the AOTC. He provides a Form 1098-T, Tuition Statement, showing $6,000 paid for tuition at a qualifying institution. The Form 1098-T is a good indicator that Harley is eligible for the AOTC, but Ariella must ask more questions to determine eligibility. Harley states that he does not have a bachelor's degree yet, because he switched majors last year. He has been an undergraduate student for five years. Since a taxpayer can only claim the AOTC for four tax years, Harley is likely *ineligible* to take the American Opportunity Credit on his current year return. He may be eligible for the Lifetime Learning Credit.

The Most Common Child Tax Credit Errors

Since tax professionals prepare more than half of all returns claiming refundable credits, the quality of their work has a significant impact on reducing erroneous claims. Preparers who file high percentages of questionable claims or returns with a high risk of error may be subject to on-site audits. IRS agents will review preparer records to verify due diligence compliance, including whether they are meeting the knowledge requirement. Penalties may be assessed when noncompliance is identified. The most common errors for this credit are:

- **Claiming a child who does not meet the age requirement:** The child must be under the age of 17 at the end of 2022. There are no exceptions to this rule.
- **Claiming a child who does not meet dependency requirements:** The child must be claimed as a dependent on the client's return and meet all the eligibility rules for a dependent.
- **Claiming the credit for a child who does not meet the residency requirement:** The child must be a U.S. citizen, U.S. national or a U.S. resident alien, and the child must have lived with your client for more than half the year.
- **Children with an ITIN:** If the qualifying child uses an ITIN, Individual Taxpayer Identification Number, the child does not qualify for the Child Tax Credit.

The IRS says many incorrect claims are prepared using "do-it-yourself" tax software rather than professional tax software that requires Form 8867 to be submitted along with each applicable refund claim.

Credit for Other Dependents (ODC)

The credit for other dependents (ODC) is a $500 nonrefundable tax credit. The credit is worth $500 for each qualifying dependent. Unlike the Child Tax Credit, the dependent does not have to have an SSN for the taxpayer to claim the ODC. The maximum amount of the credit is $500 for each dependent who qualifies. A taxpayer cannot use the same child to claim both the CTC (or ACTC) and ODC. A qualifying dependent is a person who meets all of the following conditions.

- The person is claimed as a dependent on the taxpayer's return.
- The same dependent cannot be used to claim the CTC or ACTC.
- The person was a U.S. citizen, U.S. national, or U.S. resident alien.

Example: Alejandro supports his elderly mother and his 10-year-old niece. His niece and mother both live in Mexico and qualify as his dependents. However, his niece and his mother are not U.S. citizens, U.S. nationals, or U.S. resident aliens. Alejandro cannot use his mother or his niece to claim ODC, because they do not meet the residency requirement for the ODC.

Penalties for Failure to Exercise Due Diligence

The penalties for preparers failing to exercise due diligence with refund claims can be severe. Taxpayers also face consequences for not complying with the due diligence rules. If the IRS examines a taxpayer's return and disallows all or part of an EITC, AOTC, CTC/ACTC, ODC or Head of Household claim on a return, the taxpayer:

- Must pay back the amount in error with interest,
- May need to file *Form 8862, Information to Claim Certain Credits After Disallowance*
- Cannot claim the credit for the next two years if the IRS determines the error is because of reckless or intentional disregard of the rules, or
- Cannot claim the credits for the next ten years if the IRS determines the error is because of fraud.

For tax year 2022, tax preparers face a penalty of $560 for each failure to comply with due diligence requirements. This penalty applies per credit. There is no maximum dollar penalty amount. Further, if the IRS examines a taxpayer's claim and it is determined that the preparer did not meet all four due diligence requirements, the preparer can be subject to penalties even beyond the usual penalty for each failure to comply. If a preparer receives a return-related penalty, he or she may also face:

- Disciplinary action by the OPR.
- Suspension or expulsion from the IRS e-file program.
- Injunctions barring the practitioner from preparing tax returns in the future.

The IRS has streamlined procedures for faster referrals to the U.S. Department of Justice to prevent preparers from making fraudulent refund claims. These preparers could be permanently or temporarily barred from all types of federal tax preparation.

Unit 6: Study Questions

(Test yourself and then check the correct answers at the end of this chapter.)

1. When must a tax preparer complete a client checklist for a client claiming the AOTC?

A. Every year.
B. For the first year preparing a return for a new client.
C. Every other year.
D. The client checklist is recommended, but is not required.

2. Roger is a tax preparer, and he has a new client named Samantha. Samantha tells Roger:

- She has no Form 1099-NEC.
- She was self-employed cleaning houses.
- She earned $13,000.
- She had no expenses related to the cleaning business.
- She has three children who live with her; all three are under the age of 10.

Samantha says she would like to claim the Earned Income Tax Credit and the Child Tax Credit. What is the best course of action for Roger in this case?

A. Refuse to prepare the return based on Samantha's information.
B. Ask questions to determine the facts and ask for proof of income or any expenses.
C. Accept Samantha's word, so long as she fills out a legal liability release form.
D. Make Samantha swear to the truthfulness of her statements before an IRS officer.

3. All of the following are potential penalties for a preparer who files fraudulent refund claims except:

A. Suspension or expulsion from IRS e-file.
B. Criminal prosecution by the OPR.
C. A ban from preparing tax returns.
D. A preparer penalty.

4. All of the following are due diligence requirements except:

A. To evaluate the information received from the client.
B. To apply a consistency and reasonableness standard to the information.
C. To verify the taxpayer's information with the appropriate third parties.
D. To make additional reasonable inquiries when the information appears to be incorrect, inconsistent, or incomplete.

5. Austin is an EA who submits a return for his client on March 1, 2023 for the 2022 tax year. The return claims the Earned Income Tax Credit, but Austin fails to submit Form 8867 for the return, because he did not purchase professional software, and the Form 8867 isn't available in the consumer software he is using. What penalty does Austin potentially face?

A. $0
B. $400
C. $560
D. $1,000

6. The IRS can impose the following ban related to the AOTC, EITC, and/or CTC:

A. Ten-year ban for fraud.
B. Two-year ban for fraud.
C. Permanent ban for fraud.
D. The IRS cannot ban a taxpayer from claiming credits on future returns if the taxpayer otherwise qualifies for them.

7. Andreas and Briseis both have valid ITINs. They have two children, both of whom have valid SSNs. Can Andreas and Briseis claim the EITC on their tax return, if they meet the income requirements?

A. They can claim the EITC for themselves and their children.
B. They can claim the EITC for their children, but not for themselves.
C. They cannot claim the EITC, regardless of whether their children have valid SSNs.
D. Their children can claim the EITC, but only if they file separate returns.

8. All of the following are common errors taxpayers make in claiming the EITC except:

A. Incorrectly reporting income or expenses.
B. Incorrectly claiming a child who does not meet the specific EITC requirements.
C. Filing as head of household when married.
D. Listing earned income for the year.

9. All of the following are common errors taxpayers make in claiming the Child Tax Credit or Additional Child Tax Credit except:

A. Claiming the CTC/ACTC for a child who does not meet the age requirement.
B. Claiming the CTC/ACTC for a child who does not meet the dependency requirements.
C. Claiming the CTC/ACTC for a child who does not meet the educational requirements.
D. Claiming the CTC/ACTC for a child who does not meet the residency requirement.

10. Which of the following is not one of the requirements for AOTC claims?

A. Reviewing the client's Social Security Card.
B. Making sure the client has qualifying educational expenses.
C. Completing and submitting the Form 8867.
D. Following the knowledge requirement.

11. In preparing a Form 8867, *Paid Preparer's Due Diligence Checklist,* how long should a return preparer retain copies?

A. One year from the filing of the return.
B. Two years from the filing of the return.
C. Three years from the filing of the return.
D. Six years from the filing of the return.

Unit 6: Quiz Answers

1. The answer is A. For any client claiming the AOTC, a preparer must complete *Form 8867, Paid Preparer's Due Diligence Checklist,* every year, even if the client is an existing client who has claimed the credit in the past. The preparer is required to keep a copy of the form in his records for at least three years.

2. The answer is B. The best course of action would be to ask probing questions and ask for proof of income and expenses. Roger must document Samantha's answers as part of his due diligence requirements. During the interview, a preparer must ask additional questions if the information appears incorrect, inconsistent, or incomplete.

3. The answer is B. The OPR may take disciplinary action against tax return preparers who violate rules related to fraudulent claims. However, the OPR never prosecutes criminal cases. Criminal cases are referred out to the proper authorities (the U.S. Justice Department or the IRS Criminal Division).

4. The answer is C. A tax return preparer is not required to verify a taxpayer's answers with third parties. Due diligence requires a preparer to:

- Evaluate the information received from the client,
- Apply a consistency and reasonableness standard to the information,
- Make additional reasonable inquiries when the information appears to be incorrect, inconsistent, or incomplete, and
- Document additional inquiries and the client's response.

5. The answer is C. Form 8867, *Paid Preparer's Earned Income Credit Checklist*, must be submitted for each client's return that claims the Earned Income Tax Credit, Child Tax Credit, American Opportunity Credit, Other Dependent Credit, or HOH filing status, or the preparer will be in violation of his due diligence requirements. For tax year 2022, each failure can result in a penalty of $560.

6. The answer is A. The IRS can impose the following types of bans related to refund claims of the AOTC, EITC, or CTC:

- Two-year ban for reckless or intentional disregard of due diligence rules, or
- Ten-year ban for fraud.

7. The answer is C. Andreas and Briseis do not qualify for EITC. If a primary taxpayer, the spouse, or both have ITINs, they are ineligible to claim the Earned Income Tax Credit, even if their dependents have valid SSNs. A taxpayer (and his or her spouse, if married) must have valid Social Security numbers in order to claim the EITC. Qualifying children also must have valid SSNs.

8. The answer is D. To qualify for the EITC, a taxpayer must have earned income during the tax period. Assuming it is reported correctly, listing earned income is not an error made in claiming the EITC. The IRS cites the other three errors as common issues it sees with EITC claims.

9. The answer is C. The Child Tax Credit does not have an "educational" requirement. The IRS cites the other three errors as common issues with CTC/AOTC claims. For more information on this subject, see detailed instructions in Publication 4687, *Refundable Credits Due Diligence*.

10. The answer is A. Reviewing a client's Social Security cards is not a legal requirement, but is a "best practice," and recommended by the IRS.

11. The answer is C. In preparing a Form 8867, *Paid Preparer's Due Diligence Checklist*, the tax preparer should retain copies for at least three years from the filing of the return.

Unit 7: Recordkeeping Requirements and Penalties

More Reading:
Publication 583, Starting a Business and Keeping Records
Publication 535, Business Expenses

There are basic recordkeeping requirements for U.S. taxpayers that tax professionals need to be familiar with and make sure their clients understand. Recordkeeping requirements may be tested on all three parts of the EA exam, with Part 3 focusing primarily on substantiation and record retention for preparers.

Records that *clearly demonstrate* income, expenses, and basis should be retained, but tax law generally does not require that specific types of records be kept. Taxpayers may scan records and retain them electronically, as the IRS does not require a taxpayer to keep original paper records. A taxpayer must be able to store, preserve, retrieve, and reproduce electronic records when needed.

Supporting Documents

As an essential part of due diligence, it is a preparer's responsibility to request appropriate documentation from clients in order to prepare an accurate tax return. A preparer should review prior-year tax returns to identify relevant issues, such as items that need to be carried forward to the current year and tax years going forward.

In addition, depending on the type of tax return being prepared, a preparer may need to see the following types of supporting documentation:

- **Personal Financial documents:** Canceled checks, bank statements, credit card statements, receipts, brokerage records.

- **Legal documents:** Birth certificates, divorce decrees, lawsuit settlements.

- **Business entity supporting documents:** Partnership agreements, corporate bylaws, corporate minutes. In addition, business records should include supporting documents such as: sales slips, paid bills, invoices, receipts, deposit slips, and canceled checks.

- **Expense records:** Mileage logs; receipts for business expenses such as travel, meals, and lodging; and receipts and written acknowledgments from charitable organizations, particularly for non-cash contributions and expenses of $250 or more.

For a taxpayer to deduct travel, gift, transportation, charitable, employee business expenses,[41] and other expenses, the taxpayer must be able to substantiate those expenses.

---

[41] Miscellaneous itemized deductions were eliminated for most taxpayers under the Tax Cuts and Jobs Act starting in 2018, so employee business expenses are only deductible for certain professions (Armed Forces reservists, qualified performing artists, fee-basis state or local government officials, or employees with impairment-related work expenses).

Example: Jasmine is a teacher. She tells her tax return preparer, Liam, that she had $23,000 in charitable gifts during the tax year. Jasmine provides no documentation, and Liam does not ask to verify any of her receipts. The IRS audits her return and disallows most of Jasmine's itemized deductions, which include an improper deduction for an $8,000 Mediterranean cruise. Liam's failure to request receipts from his client shows a lack of due diligence. Liam and Jasmine can both be liable for penalties.

Example: Ursula claims numerous deductions for her volunteer work in caring for feral cats. Her tax return is later chosen for examination, and she receives a notice of deficiency. Ursula takes her case to the U.S. Tax Court. The U.S. Tax Court disallows any expenses that were $250 or more because she failed to meet the substantiation requirement that required acknowledgment from the charitable organization. Even though the cat rescue organization is a qualifying charity, Ursula did not obtain a contemporaneous, written acknowledgment from the organization, so her deduction was disallowed, even though she had proof of her expenses.

Business expenses claimed on a taxpayer's Schedule C must be both "ordinary and necessary." An "ordinary" expense is one that is common in the taxpayer's particular trade or business.

A "necessary" expense is one that is helpful and appropriate in the taxpayer's trade or business. An expense does not have to be indispensable for it to be deductible. A taxpayer generally cannot deduct personal, family, or living expenses. If an asset is used partly for business and partly for personal purposes, only the business portion is deductible.

Example: Salma is a self-employed architect who uses her personal minivan to visit clients and meet with suppliers and other subcontractors. She and her family also use the minivan for personal purposes. Salma keeps a mileage log that shows the business purpose, her business destination, and the date of each use of the vehicle. Her records are adequate to substantiate that 75% of the car's use is for business purposes and 25% is for personal purposes, so she may deduct 75% of her auto expenses on her Schedule C. This is true whether she decides to deduct actual costs, or use the standard milage rate.

A taxpayer generally cannot deduct amounts that are estimates, although there are exceptions in the law for taxpayers who are victims of a casualty or a disaster. In that case, taxpayers are permitted to use a good-faith estimate based on records they do have.

Example: Nathaniel owns an auto repair business which he runs as a sole proprietorship. He only accepts cash payments from customers and refuses to keep proper books and records. He simply estimates his income and expenses every year. In 2023, the IRS audits Nathaniel's 2022 tax return and disallows most of the expenses claimed on his Schedule C. In addition to assessing additional tax, the IRS assesses an accuracy-related penalty. This penalty can be asserted for the understatement of income tax because of negligent acts or a disregard of the rules or regulations. "Negligent acts" includes the failure to keep adequate books and records.

> **Example:** Babette is a self-employed therapist that works out of a home office. During the year, her house burns down. The house is completely destroyed, including her home office, her computer and all of her client records. She is able to reconstruct a portion of her records by using bank statements she requests from her bank, but the rest of her records are lost. The IRS will permit Babette to use a good-faith estimate of her expenses for the year because she was the victim of a casualty. Babette should disclose the use of estimates on her return by attaching a disclosure statement.

The Statute of Limitations for Records Retention

A taxpayer should keep all relevant records as long as they may be needed for the administration of any provision of the Internal Revenue Code.[42] As a practical matter, this means a taxpayer must retain relevant records until the assessment statute of limitations for each tax return expires.

The responsibility to prove entries, deductions, and statements made on a taxpayer's tax return is known as the "burden of proof." The taxpayers must meet their burden of proof by having the information and receipts for the expenses and deductions taken on the return. For assessment of tax owed, the statute of limitations period is *generally* three years from the filing date or unextended due date, whichever is later.

There is also a statute of limitations on refunds being claimed on amended returns. In general, if a refund is expected on an amended return, taxpayers must file the return within three years of the filing date of the original return, or within two years after the date they paid the tax, whichever is later.

> **Example:** Magdalena is a delinquent filer and has not filed a tax return for many years. On January 30, 2023, she hires Timothy, an enrolled agent, to prepare her delinquent tax returns, for tax years 2017 through 2021. Timothy will also prepare Magdalena's 2022 tax return, which is not delinquent. With Magdalena's authorization, Timothy prepares and files all of these returns before April 18, 2023. Each of Magdalena's returns show an overpayment of taxes, because Magdalena always had enough withheld from her paychecks to cover her income tax. However, she will receive refunds only for tax years 2019 through 2022, because those are the years still open under the three-year refund statute. Magdalena will not receive refunds for her older tax returns, because the refund statute has expired for those years (unless an exception to the refund statute applies).

If the return was filed *prior* to the original due date, the refund statute of limitations starts as of the original due date of the return (usually, this is April 15). If the return is filed on extension, the three-year period starts when the IRS receives the return.

---

[42] Treasury Regulation 1.6001–1(e) provides that all books and records must be maintained as long as they remain "material" to the computation of any tax. The books or records required by this section should be available for inspection by authorized internal revenue officers or employees.

Example: Alyssa always files her tax returns on extension. She files a valid extension every year. On October 15, 2019, Alyssa e-filed her 2018 return, exactly on the extended due date. The return was accepted and considered timely-filed. Alyssa later finds an error on the return that would result in a refund. Alyssa would have until October 15, 2022 (three years from the filing date), to file the claim for a refund because the extension period is added to the three-year refund statute time period.

There are exceptions to this "three-year rule" for net operating losses, capital loss carrybacks (for C corporations), foreign tax credits, worthless securities, and exceptions for Armed Forces personnel (covered in more detail later). For amended returns filed within 60 days of the limitations date, (Form 1040-X) the IRS has only 60 days after it receives the amended return to assess the additional income tax on the amended return.[43]

Example: Devon usually files his tax return on extension. On October 15, 2019, Devon filed his 2018 return, exactly on the extended due date. The return was accepted, and he received a refund. Devon later discovers an error on the return. The error *increases* his tax. Devon files an amended return on October 15, 2022, to correct this error. The IRS has 60 days to review his return and assess additional income tax if necessary.

Property Records: Records relating to the basis of property should be retained as long as they may be material to any tax return involving the property.

The basis of property is material until the statute of limitations expires for the tax year an asset is sold or otherwise disposed of. A taxpayer must keep these records to figure the asset's basis, as well as any depreciation, amortization, or depletion deductions.

Example: Reynold sells a vacation home he has owned for eight years. He uses records relating to the purchase of the property and improvements made on it to compute the basis and his gain. He reports the sale on his 2022 tax return. He must retain the records relating to the sale until the statute of limitations for the tax return expires, usually three years from the original due date of the return.

Employment Tax Records: A business must retain payroll and employment tax records for at least four years after the tax becomes due or is paid, whichever is later. This rule also applies to businesses that employ tax preparers.

Example: Shantel is an EA who employs five other tax preparers in her tax preparation franchise. Shantel has six employees working for the franchise. One employee is a full-time receptionist, and does not prepare tax returns, but does collect taxpayer information when clients come into the office. The other five employees are full-time preparers. Shantel is required to keep the employment tax records relating to her employees for at least four years.

---

[43] IRC Section 6501(c)(7) extends the assessment statute of limitations 60 days from the filing of an amended return for the IRS to assess the additional income tax on the amended return.

Applicable employer tax records must be made available for IRS review upon request. These include:

- Employer identification numbers,
- Amounts and dates of wages, annuity, and pension payments,
- Amounts of tips reported,
- Names, addresses, Social Security numbers, and occupations of employees,
- Dates of active employment and sick leave,
- Records of fringe benefits provided,
- Forms W-4,
- Dates and amounts of tax deposits.

All copies of employment returns must also be retained for at least four years (this refers to payroll tax returns and applicable employment records related to wages paid, such as Forms 940 and 941).

Other Retention Periods

Longer record retention periods may apply in some cases. For example, if a taxpayer files a claim from a loss of worthless securities, the period to retain records related to the transaction is seven years. If a taxpayer fails to report income that exceeds 25% of the gross income shown on his return, the assessment statute of limitations is six years from when the return is filed.

Statute of Limitations	
Type of Record/Return	**Applicable Statute or Retention Period**
Normal tax return	Three years after a return is due or filed, whichever is later
Omitted income that exceeds 25% of the gross income shown on the return	Six years from the filing date
Fraudulent return	No limit
No return filed	No limit
A claim for credit or amended return	The later of: three years from the filing date of the original return, or two years after the tax was paid
A claim for a loss from worthless securities	Seven years
Employment and payroll tax records	Four years after the tax becomes due, or is paid
Fixed assets, real estate	Until the statute of limitations expires for the tax year in which the asset is disposed

> **Example:** Many years ago, Racine purchased stock in a corporation that went bankrupt. The stock was delisted from the New York Stock Exchange and became worthless in 2017, but Racine didn't pay much attention to her brokerage account and didn't realize that her stock had become worthless. Even though the normal statute of limitations for refund claims has passed, Racine may file an amended return in 2022 and claim the loss from the worthless securities and still receive a refund. This is because a loss for worthless securities is subject to special rules.

Note that there is no time limit for the IRS to assess additional tax if a taxpayer never files a return or if a taxpayer files a fraudulent return.

Tax Avoidance vs. Tax Evasion

The U.S. system of federal taxation operates on the concept of voluntary compliance; it is the taxpayer's responsibility to report all income. When a taxpayer fails to pay what officials say he owes, the IRS can collect back taxes and assess penalties.

The Internal Revenue Code imposes many different kinds of penalties, ranging from civil fines to imprisonment for criminal tax evasion.

The term "tax avoidance" is not defined by the IRS, but it is commonly used to describe the legal reduction of taxable income, such as through deductions, credits, and adjustments to income. Avoidance of tax is not a criminal offense. Taxpayers have the right to reduce, avoid, or minimize their taxes by legitimate means. Most taxpayers use at least a few methods of tax avoidance in order to reduce their taxable income and therefore lower their tax liability.

> **Example:** Tamera contributes to her employer-sponsored 401(k) retirement plan with pre-tax funds. She also uses an employer-based flexible spending account for her medical expenses, which reduces her taxable income by making all of her medical expenses pre-tax. She owns a home and claims a deduction for mortgage interest. All of these strategies lower her taxable income by using legal tax avoidance.

On the other hand, *tax evasion* is an illegal practice in which individuals or businesses intentionally avoid paying their true tax liabilities. Evasion involves some affirmative act to evade or defeat a tax, or payment of tax. Examples of affirmative acts are deceit, subterfuge, camouflage, concealment, attempts to obscure events, or make things seem other than they are.

IRS auditors are trained to spot common types of deception and fraud on tax returns. These acts are known as "badges of fraud" and include deducting personal items as business expenses, the overstatement of deductions, and the understatement of income. Other common tax evasion schemes include:

- Intentional omission of income, especially cash payments;
- Claiming fictitious deductions;
- False allocation of income;
- Improper claims, credits, or exemptions; and/or
- Concealment of assets.

Although most Americans comply with their tax obligations, the U.S. government estimates that 3% of taxpayers do not file tax returns at all. Tax evasion is a felony, and those caught evading taxes are subject to criminal charges and substantial penalties.

Note: For each year a taxpayer willfully does not file a tax return, the penalty can include a fine of up to $25,000 and a prison sentence of up to one year. If it can be demonstrated that the taxpayer deliberately did not file in an attempt to evade taxation, the IRS can pursue a felony conviction, which can include an additional fine of up to $100,000 ($500,000 for corporations) and a maximum prison sentence of five years (IRC §7201).

Example: Victor owns a jewelry store. For several years, he failed to report the cash he received from his stores. He often accepted large cash payments from his customers but did not report the income. He also kept a separate accounting system for the cash receivables as a second set of books. In addition, Victor broke cash receipts greater than $10,000 into smaller receipts in order to evade federal cash reporting requirements. When he filed his tax return, Victor reported income of $27,000 on his Schedule C, while his actual taxable income was nearly $195,000. Victor was convicted of committing tax evasion, a felony.

Penalties Imposed Upon Taxpayers

The IRS can assess penalties on individual taxpayers who fail to file, fail to pay, or both. The failure-to-file penalty is generally greater than the failure-to-pay penalty. If someone is unable to pay all the taxes he owes, he is better off filing on time and paying as much as he can, as the IRS will consider payment options with individual taxpayers.

A taxpayer will not have to pay either penalty if he shows he failed to file or pay on time because of reasonable cause and not willful neglect.

Penalties are payable upon notice and demand. They are generally assessed, collected, and paid in the same manner as taxes. The taxpayer will receive a notice that contains:

- The name of the penalty,
- The applicable code section, and
- How the penalty was computed.

Failure-to-File Penalty: The penalty for filing late is usually 5% of the unpaid taxes for each month or part of a month that a return is late, up to a maximum of 25% of the amount due. The penalty is based on the tax that is not paid by the due date, without regard to extensions.

If both the failure-to-file penalty and the failure-to-pay penalty apply in any month, the 5% failure-to-file penalty is reduced by the failure-to-pay penalty. However, if a taxpayer files their tax return more than 60 days after the due date or extended due date, for the 2022 tax year, the minimum penalty is the smaller of: $450, or 100% of the unpaid tax. Taxpayers who are owed a refund, will not be assessed a failure-to-file penalty.[44] The late filing penalties can be higher for business returns.

---

[44] The penalty for fraudulent failure-to-file is higher; 15% of the unpaid balance per month, up to a maximum of 75%

Example: Bautista does not bother to file his tax return on time, or file an extension, because he thought he was getting a refund like he usually does every year. However, he forgot that he had taken a retirement plan distribution at the beginning of the year that increased his tax liability. He eventually files his 2022 return on July 30, 2023 (over 60 days late) and discovers that he owes $134. His failure-to-file penalty is equal to 100% of the amount he owes, or $134. He will also owe a small amount of interest on the unpaid amount as well.

Failure-to-Pay Penalty: Taxpayers that do not pay their taxes by the due date will be subject to a failure-to-pay penalty of ½ of 1% (0.5%) of unpaid taxes for each month or part of a month after the due date that the taxes are not paid. This penalty can be as much as 25% of a taxpayer's unpaid taxes.

The failure-to-pay penalty rate increases to a full 1% per month for any tax that remains unpaid the day after a demand for immediate payment is issued, or ten days after notice of intent to levy certain assets is issued. For taxpayers who filed on time but are unable to pay their tax liabilities, the failure-to-pay penalty rate is reduced to ¼ of 1% (0.25%) per month during any month in which the taxpayer has a valid installment agreement with the IRS.[45]

The taxpayer will also owe interest on the amount due. Interest accrues daily on any unpaid tax from the due date of the return until the taxpayer pays in full. The IRS may abate a taxpayer's penalties for filing and paying late if the taxpayer can show reasonable cause. There are exceptions in the law benefiting individuals for the following situations:

- A member of the Armed Forces serving in a combat zone or contingency operation,
- A citizen or resident alien working abroad,
- Victims in certain disaster situations. In those situations, the IRS has the legal authority to extend filing and payment deadlines.[46]

Example: Stephen is an active-duty member of the Armed Forces. He serves in a combat zone from April 30, 2022, to March 1, 2023. Stephen has additional time to <u>file and pay</u> his tax return and any amounts due, following his exit date from the combat zone. He has at least 180 additional days to file his 2022 tax return <u>and pay</u> his 2022 tax. Stephen is married. His wife, Daniella, is not in the miliary, but she also has a filing requirement. Daniella also gets additional time to file, because this additional extension also applies to the spouses of those serving in the combat zone.

Note: If a taxpayer is affected by a natural disaster in a presidentially declared disaster area, and the taxpayer receives a late filing or late payment penalty notice from the IRS that has an original or extended filing payment or deposit due date that falls within the postponement period, the taxpayer should call the disaster assistance telephone number on the notice to have the IRS abate the penalty.

---

[45] Regardless of whether or not the taxpayer has the ability to pay, it is always better to file and pay what you can. The IRS will normally work with a taxpayer who makes the attempt to be compliant with their tax obligations.

[46] The IRS automatically identifies taxpayers located in the covered disaster area (based on the taxpayer's zip code) and applies automatic filing and payment relief. But affected taxpayers who reside or have a business located outside the covered disaster area must call the IRS disaster hotline to request tax relief.

Example: Yuliana was affected by a hurricane that took place on September 1, 2022, in Texas. Yuliana's business was flooded and severely damaged by the storm. The President declared the entire region a FEMA disaster area. The IRS postponed the filing deadlines as well as deposit deadlines for employment taxes for people who were living in the affected region. Yuliana later receives a notice from the IRS because the payroll tax returns for her business are delinquent. She calls the IRS disaster hotline to request tax relief, which is granted. Yuliana will receive additional time to file her payroll returns and make any applicable tax deposits.

Accuracy-Related Penalty on Underpayments

IRC §6662 describes penalties for accuracy-related violations of underpaying income tax, including penalties for substantial understatement, substantial valuation misstatement, and negligence or disregard of rules or regulations. This section imposes an accuracy-related penalty equal to 20% of the underpayment to which Section 6662 applies. These penalties are calculated as a flat 20% of the net understatement of tax. However, this penalty does not apply to any portion of an underpayment where the taxpayer acted with reasonable cause and in good faith.

Penalty for Substantial Understatement: For **individual** taxpayers, an understatement is considered **substantial** if it is more than the *larger* of:

- 10% of the correct tax, or $5,000.
- If a taxpayer's return claims a Section 199A deduction, then the 10% threshold is reduced to 5%.

Example: Jennifer is self-employed and has a SEP-IRA retirement plan for her business. She prepares her own tax return using online software. She makes a mistake and claims a large adjustment to income for a self-employed retirement contribution to her SEP-IRA, but she forgot to make the contribution by the deadline. The correct amount of tax on Jennifer's return should have been $9,700, but Jennifer's return only reported tax of $3,000. The IRS disallows the erroneous contribution deduction. The substantial understatement penalty would apply to Jennifer's return, because the $6,700 shortfall is more than $5,000, which is the greater of the two thresholds.

Example: Jermaine self-prepares his own tax return. He makes a math error when he is calculating his itemized deductions and accidentally claims a much larger deduction for medical expenses than he actually is entitled to. Jermaine's tax return is later chosen for audit, and the medical deduction is disallowed. The correct amount of tax on his return should have been $10,000. The tax shown on Jermaine's originally filed return was only $6,000. Jermaine would owe the underreported tax ($4,000), the failure-to-pay penalty, as well as interest back to the original due date of the return. However, the substantial underpayment penalty under IRC §6662(b)(2) would not apply, because although the $4,000 shortfall is *more* than 10% of the correct tax that he should have paid, it is less than the fixed $5,000 threshold.

This means that, if the understatement shown on the return is more than (1) 10% of the correct tax or (2) greater than $5,000 for individuals, it is considered a **"substantial"** understatement.

> **Example:** Crystal is a self-employed interior designer. In 2022, Crystal's tax returns were audited by the IRS. Crystal provided her accounting records and bank statements to the IRS. However, while her documents reflected the expenses allegedly incurred by the taxpayer, the records did not show why the alleged expenses were ordinary and necessary expenses that were deductible. Crystal claimed numerous large deductions for expensive furniture, cruises, and airline trips. Crystal could not provide a reasonable explanation for the deductions she claimed on her Schedule C. The IRS issued Crystal a notice of deficiency for $42,000 and an additional accuracy-related penalty of $8,400 under IRC §6662(a).

For **corporations** (other than an S-corporation or personal holding company), an understatement is "substantial" if it exceeds the lesser of:

- 10% of the tax required to be shown on the return for the tax year (or if greater, $10,000), or
- $10,000,000.[47]

If the taxpayer can show that they made a reasonable attempt to report the correct tax, or if the taxpayer's position was adequately disclosed,[48] this penalty may not apply.

> **Example:** The IRS issued an audit notice to Harvest Foods Corporation, a family farming business. The business was audited, and a large deduction was disallowed under examination. Disallowance of the deduction created a substantial understatement of 25% of the correct tax shown on the return. However, the company included a proper disclosure on Form 8275, which was attached to the corporation's tax return, disclosing their position for the deduction. Harvest Foods Corporation was issued a notice of deficiency for $15,800, disallowing the deduction, but an accuracy-related penalty was not assessed, because the company adequately disclosed their position, even if the deduction was later disallowed.

Penalty for Valuation Misstatement

A valuation misstatement can be either **"Substantial"** [IRC §6662(e)] or **"Gross"** [IRC §6662(h)].

1. **"Substantial"** valuation misstatements are subject to a 20% penalty.
2. **"Gross"** valuation misstatements are subject to a 40% penalty.

The **substantial** valuation misstatement penalty generally applies when a taxpayer incorrectly reports an asset's value or its adjusted basis on a tax return; the value or basis is overstated by at least 150% of the correct value; and which results in an underpayment of tax of at least $5,000 (the threshold is $10,000 for most C corporations).

---

[47] See IRC §6662(d)(1).

[48] A way to avoid the penalty is to adequately disclose the position, typically on Form 8275, Disclosure Statement, Form 8275-R, Regulation Disclosure Statement. The adequate disclosure exception only applies if the taxpayer has a "reasonable basis" for the position and keeps adequate records. However, the adequate disclosure exceptions do not apply to understatements resulting from a tax shelter.

Example: Walter donated a large parcel of land to a charitable foundation. He valued the donation at $9 million on his tax return and claimed a $3 million charitable deduction. The IRS examined his return and discovered that the land was significantly overvalued. The IRS adjusted the value of the land downward to $5 million, making Walter's true charitable deduction worth only $1.5 million. Walter is assessed a **substantial valuation misstatement** penalty for overvaluing his property in order to receive an inflated deduction and pay less tax. The penalty rate would be 20% since the overstated amount of the land was greater than 150% of the land's correct value.

This penalty jumps to 40% of the net understatement of tax if the taxpayer claims a value for property on a tax return that is 200% or more of the correct amount. This is known as a **gross valuation misstatement.**

Example: Gary donated a large plot of farmland to his church. On his federal income tax return for that year, Gary valued his donation at $900,000 and claimed a large charitable contribution deduction. Gary claimed a carryover of charitable contribution deductions related to the land donation for the next three years. The IRS later audited Gary's tax returns and determined that he did not meet the legal requirements for his charitable contribution. Gary cannot produce a qualified appraisal of the farmland that he donated. The IRS deems that the actual value of Gary's donation was $45,000. The actual value of the donation was far less than what was reported, and in Gary's case, the error is more than 200% of the land's actual value. The IRS disallows the deduction, and assesses a 40% penalty against Gary for the **gross valuation misstatement**.

The valuation misstatement penalty also may apply if the price or valuation for any property or service claimed on a return is substantially less than the correct valuation. In the previous examples, the taxpayer attempted to claim larger deductions than they were legally entitled to claim. However, there are times when a taxpayer will attempt to "undervalue" an asset in order to escape tax, as well. This happens most often with the valuation of an estate. Since an estate is taxed on the value of its assets, a lower value could result in a lower tax.

Example: After a Pennsylvania woman died, her executor initially valued her estate's assets at $7.9 million when he filed Form 706, the estate tax return. The executor did not hire an appraiser to help determine the correct value, and he used cost basis for many of the decedent's assets, even those that had substantially increased in value over time. The IRS disputed the valuation, putting the estate's assets at $18.2 million. The IRS assessed a 40% "gross valuation misstatement" penalty against the estate. The executor fought this determination by appealing to the courts, and the U.S. Tax Court ultimately ruled that $12 million was the correct value of the estate. Since the correct value of the estate was over 150% of what the executor originally reported, the IRS then imposed a 20% substantial valuation misstatement penalty upon the estate, which the Tax Court upheld.

A taxpayer may avoid both the substantial understatement and the substantial overvaluation penalties if he has substantial authority for his position or the position has a reasonable basis and is adequately disclosed. If the understatement is due to *fraud*, the penalty jumps to 75% of understatement.

140

Information Return Penalties, §6723

IRC §6723 establishes a penalty for failing to timely comply with information return reporting requirements. Information returns are year-end forms issued by businesses or employers to employees, vendors, or contractors. Examples of common information returns include: Form W-2, Form W-2G, Form 1099-MISC, Form 1099-R, and Form 1099-NEC. If a business unknowingly fails to file or files incomplete or incorrect returns, there is a penalty of $50 per failure. If a business does not include a Social Security number, (or other TIN, if applicable) the issuer may be subject to a penalty of $50 for each failure.

Late filing penalties vary, depending on how late the forms are submitted. The penalties per form are as follows:

Penalties for Each Unfiled Information Return				
Year Due	Up to 30 Days Late	More than 30 days past the deadline, but by August 1	Filing after August 1	Intentionally neglecting to file the forms
2023	$50	$110	$290	$580
2022	$50	$110	$280	$570

For most 1099 forms, the deadline for issuers to send the forms to the recipients is January 31. If this date falls on a weekend, the deadline will be extended to the next business day. Issuers must remit 1099 forms to the IRS by February 28, (if filed on paper) or by March 31 if filing electronically.

> **Example:** David is a private consultant who files a Schedule C. David hires several independent contractors during the year. David does not wish to file 1099-NEC forms for his contractors because he doesn't want to pay his accountant the additional expense of filing them. Instead, he lies to his accountant and says that he filed the forms using an online service. In 2022, his tax return is chosen for examination. The IRS examiner discovers that David failed to file 10 required 1099 forms. David is assessed a penalty of $570 per unfiled form because the lack of filing of these returns was intentional.

Penalties for Negligence and Intentional Disregard

IRC §6662 defines **negligence** as any failure to make a reasonable attempt to comply with the internal revenue laws. **Disregard** means a taxpayer carelessly, recklessly or intentionally ignored the tax rules or regulations. Examples of **negligence** include:

- Not keeping records to prove deductions claimed on a return
- Not including income on a tax return that was shown in an information return, like income reported on Form 1099 or a Form W-2.
- Not checking the accuracy of a deduction or credit that seems too good to be true.

> **Example:** Rosalie self-prepares her own tax return, claiming the EITC, and the CTC for her niece, who she claims on her return. However, her niece was not Rosalie's qualifying child because the child did not live with Rosalie at all during the year. Rosalie doesn't bother to look up any of the rules for claiming a dependent, and she also ignores the e-file warnings that she receives from the software. The IRS later audits Rosalie's return and disallows all the credits on the return. The IRS also imposes a §6662 penalty for negligence.

Note that negligence occurs when someone acts in a careless, reckless, or negligent manner, but it is an unintentional mistake. The difference between negligence and fraud is **willfulness**. Simple ignorance of the law does not constitute fraud.

Civil Fraud Penalty (§6663): Fraud, as distinguished from negligence, is always intentional. Fraud cannot be a mistake or an accident, carelessness, or reliance on others. If the IRS does impose a fraud penalty, the burden of proof switches to the IRS to prove that the taxpayer committed fraud by "clear and convincing" evidence.

If there is any underpayment of tax due to **fraud**, a penalty of 75% of the underpayment will be assessed against the taxpayer. In the case of a joint return, the penalty will apply to both spouses <u>only</u> if some part of the underpayment is due to the fraud of each spouse.[49] Indicators of tax fraud include:

- Filing a false tax return,
- Hiding or transferring assets or income,
- Claiming false deductions,
- Keeping a second set of books,
- Failure to deposit receipts to business accounts,
- Covering up sources of receipts or deliberately omitting income.

> **Note:** The IRS characterizes fraud as a *deliberate* action for the purpose of "deceit, subterfuge, camouflage, concealment, some attempt to color or obscure events, or make things seem other than what they are."

In addition to being a *civil offense*, fraud may also be a criminal offense. A criminal offense must generally include an element of willfulness, meaning a voluntary and intentional violation of a known legal duty.

> **Note: Civil fraud** cases are corrective actions taken by the government such as assessing the correct tax and imposing civil penalties as an addition to tax. **Criminal fraud** cases are punitive actions with penalties consisting of fines and/or imprisonment.[50]

If IRS examiners find evidence of criminal fraud in the course of an audit, they will refer the case to the IRS Criminal Investigation Division. In tax fraud cases, the burden of proof switches to the government.

---

[49] IRC §6663(c) states, the fraud penalty is imposed on each spouse separately: "In the case of a joint return, this section shall not apply with respect to a spouse unless some part of the underpayment is due to the fraud of such spouse."
[50] The IRS Fraud Handbook is located in IRM 25.1

Example: Hussain self-prepared his own tax return using an online software program. The return contained numerous gross errors and was later audited. Hussain could not afford representation, so when he met with the IRS auditor, Ms. Smith, he admits that he made several mistakes on the return that resulted in an underpayment of tax of more than $13,000, but he says it was an unintentional error. The IRS auditor doesn't believe Hussain's arguments, and she imposes a 75% civil fraud penalty. Hussain fights the fraud penalty by appealing his audit results by filing a petition in the U.S. Tax Court. Hussain admits that he made mistakes on his tax return, but argues that he did not clearly understand the law and that he did not intend to commit tax fraud. The Tax Court finds Hussain's testimony convincing, and although he is responsible for the additional tax on the return, as well as an accuracy-related penalty of 20%, Hussain will not be responsible for the more severe 75% fraud penalty.

Frivolous Tax Return Penalty (IRC §6702): Frivolous submissions include tax protester arguments. Tax protester arguments are taxpayers who contend that various tax laws are unconstitutional or otherwise invalid. For example, they may make arguments that filing of a tax return is voluntary; that only foreign-source income is taxable; or that a taxpayer is not a citizen of the United States and thus not subject to federal income tax.

A frivolous tax return is one that does not include enough information to figure the correct tax, or that contains information clearly showing that the tax reported is substantially incorrect.

A taxpayer faces a penalty of $5,000 for filing a frivolous tax return or other frivolous submissions. This penalty is *in addition* to any other penalties allowed by law. A taxpayer may face a penalty of up to $25,000 if the taxpayer makes frivolous arguments in the U.S. Tax Court.

Example: Anson is a tax protestor. While employed by an airline company, Anson filed a Form W-4 form claiming 60 withholding allowances. He also filed a frivolous tax return, reporting zero income and striking out the jurat. The IRS audits his return in 2022 and assesses a $5,000 frivolous return penalty, an accuracy-related penalty, and a civil fraud penalty. Anson is incensed. Rather than paying the penalties and filing a correct return, he files a petition with the U.S. Tax Court. If Anson takes his case to court, and attempts to make a frivolous argument before the court, the Tax Court can assess an additional penalty of $25,000.[51]

Example: Elizabeth refused to file any income tax returns for over a decade. The IRS sent her dozens of letters. Elizabeth refuses to file because she believes that the income tax laws are invalid, and she responded to one of the IRS letters with a tax protestor argument. She eventually is convicted for failure to file income tax returns. She appeals to the courts, stating in open court that she was not subject to federal tax laws because she was "an absolute, freeborn, and natural individual". The court rejected Elizabeth's contention as a frivolous tax protestor argument, and her conviction was upheld.[52]

---

[51] Example based on a real "tax protestor" case, *United States of America v. John L. Cheek.*
[52] United States v. Studley, 783 F.2d 934, 937, 937 n.3 (9th Cir. 1986).

Alteration of a Jurat

Frivolous submissions also include taxpayers who alter or strike out the preprinted language above the space provided for a signature. This declaration is called the jurat. Civil penalties for altering a jurat may include:

- A $5,000 penalty imposed under IRC §6702;
- Additional penalties for failure to file a return, failure to pay the tax owed, and fraudulent failure to file a return under IRC §6651.

Alteration of the jurat is prohibited

Example: Jude is self-employed. He self-prepares his own Form 1040 using commercial software, and then prints it out, intending to mail his return. Jude signs the form, but crosses out the jurat on the return and writes the word "void" across it. This is a deliberate act. Jude's return is now considered frivolous and is subject to penalties. The return is also considered unfiled, so a failure-to-file penalty will also apply.[53]

Trust Fund Recovery Penalty (TFRP)

Authorized by IRC §6672, the trust fund recovery penalty involves the income and Social Security taxes an employer withholds from the wages of employees. These taxes are called trust fund taxes because they are held in trust on behalf of employees until they are remitted to the government. Sometimes, business owners neglect to remit these taxes to the IRS. A trust fund recovery penalty equal to 100% of the amount of unpaid trust fund taxes can be assessed against anyone who is considered a "responsible person" in the business.

This may include corporate officers, directors, stockholders, and rank-and-file employees. The IRS has assessed the penalty against accountants, bookkeepers, and even clerical staff, if they have the authority to sign checks.

A person must be both "responsible" and "willful" to be liable for an employer's failure to collect or pay trust fund taxes. This means that the person knew (or should have known) that the payroll taxes were not being remitted to the IRS, and that he or she also had the power to correct the problem.

---

[53] See IRS Rev. Rul. 2005-18 for examples of striking or otherwise invalidating the written declaration (the jurat) on a tax return.

> **Example:** Thelma works for Smithy Construction as a full-time bookkeeper and processes all the payroll tax forms. She also has check-signing authority to pay the bills when her boss is working off-site. In 2022, her boss has a heart attack, and his wife, Sheri, takes over the business in his absence. Sheri cannot manage the business properly, and Smithy Construction is unable to meet its financial commitments. Sheri tells Thelma to pay vendors first. The business continues to withhold payroll taxes from employee paychecks, but does not remit the amounts to the IRS. Eventually, the business declares bankruptcy. Sheri disappears, and the IRS contacts Thelma. Even though Thelma was "just an employee," the IRS can assess the trust fund recovery penalty against her because she had check-signing authority, and she knew that the business was not remitting payroll taxes to the IRS as required.

Penalties Imposed on Tax Preparers

Just like taxpayers, tax professionals are also subject to penalties on improperly filed or fraudulent returns. Preparer fraud typically involves preparing and filing false income tax returns for clients. The returns may have inflated personal or business expenses, false deductions, unallowable credits, or excessive exemptions.

Preparers may also manipulate income figures to obtain fraudulent tax credits, such as the Earned Income Tax Credit, for clients who are not eligible. Sometimes a tax preparer will prepare a fraudulent return without the taxpayer being aware of the fraud.

A preparer's clients may or may not know about the fraudulent items on their tax returns. Fraud may benefit preparers financially by:

- Diverting a portion of taxpayers' refunds for their own personal benefit,
- Increasing clientele by developing a reputation for obtaining large refunds; and/or
- Charging inflated fees for return preparation.

In some cases, an unethical tax preparer might steal the client's whole refund by changing direct deposit information to a different bank account that they control. This is a criminal act.

> **Example:** Sylvester is a tax preparer. He prepares a return for his client, Margaux. He gives Margaux a complete copy of her return, and she goes home. After Margaux leaves his office, Sylvester adds fraudulent credits to her return, then adds his personal bank account to Margaux's Form 8888, funneling a portion of her refund to himself. Sylvester has committed tax fraud. A preparer can never use Form 8888 to divert a portion of a taxpayer's refund into their own bank account.[54]

In the case of a tax professional who has committed tax fraud, or filed fraudulent returns, the IRS' Criminal Investigation Division works closely with the US Justice Department to prosecute the tax professionals who commit financial fraud.

---

[54] Example based on an actual criminal case. Criminal Case No. 14CR3658-JM (U.S. District Court, Southern California District).

Preparer Penalties for Substantial Understatement

If a tax return preparer willfully understates a client's tax liability, the preparer can be subject to penalties for understatement, just like a taxpayer can. Under IRS regulations, understatement of liability means:

- Understating net tax payable.
- Overstating the net amount creditable or refundable.

Under IRC §6694, there are two specific penalties when a tax preparer understates a taxpayer's liability. The first penalty, under §6694(a), is for a *nonwillful* act. The second penalty, under §6694(b), is much harsher, and is imposed for a *willful* act. According to the IRS, the test is whether there was an intentional violation of the law. "Willfulness" is defined as a voluntary, intentional violation of a known legal duty.[55] The two penalties under this section are as follows:

IRC §6694(a)–Understatement due to unreasonable position: If there is an understatement on a tax return due to an unreasonable position, the penalty is the greater of:

- $1,000 per tax return, or
- 50% of the income the preparer received (or would have received) in income for preparing the tax return with the understatement.

IRC §6694(b) – Understatement due to willful or reckless conduct: If a tax return preparer shows negligent or willful disregard of IRS rules and regulations, and makes a willful or reckless attempt to understate tax liability, the penalty is the greater of:

- $5,000 per tax return, or
- 75% of the income the preparer received (or would have received) in income for preparing the tax return with the understatement.

> **Example:** Samuel is a tax preparer. His client, Kamila, states that she had made a charitable contribution of $70,000 in cash to her church, when in fact she had not made this contribution. Kamila's income was only $65,000 for the year. In addition, Kamila has significant debts and very little assets (which Samuel is aware of), so it was unlikely that she would have been able to make such a large cash contribution based on her level of income and overall financial situation. However, Samuel did not ask any further questions about the contribution or ask for any proof that Kamila actually made it. He merely reports the deduction on the tax return. Later, the return is audited, and the charitable deduction is entirely disallowed when Kamila cannot produce any proof. Samuel would likely be subject to an IRC §6694 penalty.

The IRC §6694 penalty applies when a preparer knows, or "reasonably should have known," that the position was unreasonable and would not have been sustained on its merits. However, a preparer may be excused from the penalty if he or she acted in good faith, or there was reasonable cause for the understatement.[56]

---

[55] Internal Revenue Manual, Part 25. Special Topics, Chapter 1. Fraud Handbook.
[56] Examples based on the examples in IRS Notice 2008-13, Guidance Under the Preparer Penalty Provisions of The Small Business and Work Opportunity Tax Act Of 2007.

Example: Jenny is an enrolled agent. Her new client, Ahmad, provided a depreciation schedule prepared by another tax advisor. The depreciation schedule is for an office building that Ahmad owns and rents to commercial tenants. The depreciation schedule did not appear to be incorrect or incomplete. On the basis of this information, Jenny completed Ahmad's tax return. Ahmad's return is later audited, and the depreciation schedule was called into question, because the basis of the building was significantly overstated, resulting in a larger depreciation deduction than Ahmad was actually entitled to. This creates a large understatement of liability on Ahmad's tax return that is directly related to the erroneous information on the depreciation schedule. Since Jenny reasonably believed the information on the schedule was correct when Ahmad provided the schedule to her, she is not subject to a penalty under section 6694.

If a tax return preparer is subject to a penalty for understatement of liability and this includes a change to the Earned Income Tax Credit, the preparer may be subject to additional penalties for failure to exercise due diligence while claiming the EITC.

IRC §6694 specifies that the understatement penalty will be abated if, under final judicial decision, it is found that there is no actual understatement of liability. Sometimes this occurs when a Tax Court case is decided in favor of the taxpayer.

Example: In 2022, Denny was audited, and a large deduction was disallowed on his return. Cassandra is Denny's tax attorney, and she prepared the return under examination. In addition to assessing penalties against Denny himself, the IRS also assesses the IRC §6694(b) understatement penalty against Cassandra, his tax preparer. The position had not been disclosed, but Denny and Cassandra both believe that the tax position on the return is correct, and Denny takes his case all the way to the U.S. Tax Court, where Cassandra represents him. The U.S. Tax Court decides in Denny's favor. The court victory allows Denny to claim the previously disallowed deduction in full. Denny's understatement penalty is abated, and Cassandra's preparer penalty is abated, as well.

Listing of Preparer Penalties

Study Tip: Specific penalties that may be imposed on both preparers and taxpayers are frequently tested on Part 3 of the EA exam. Although it is not generally necessary to memorize the IRC section numbers, test-takers should be familiar with each of the penalties and the penalty amounts listed in this PassKey study guide. Most of these penalties are now adjusted for inflation every year.[57]

IRC §6694 – Understatement of taxpayer's liability by tax return preparer.

- **IRC §6694(a)** – Understatement due to unreasonable position. The penalty is the greater of $1,000 or 50% of the income derived by the tax return preparer with respect to the return or claim for refund.

---

[57] To see a full list of preparer penalties on the IRS website, see the official detail page here: https://www.irs.gov/payments/tax-preparer-penalties.

- **IRC §6694(b)** – Understatement due to willful or reckless conduct. The penalty is the greater of $5,000 or 75% of the income derived by the tax return preparer with respect to the return or claim for refund.

IRC §6695 – Other penalties with respect to the preparation of tax returns: these penalties are adjusted for inflation. For returns filed in calendar year 2023, (for the 2022 tax year)

- **IRC §6695(a)–Failure to furnish a copy to the taxpayer:** The penalty is $55 for each failure to furnish a copy of a completed return to a taxpayer. The maximum penalty cannot be greater than $28,000.

- **IRC §6695(b)–Failure to sign return:** The penalty is $55 for each failure to sign a return. The maximum penalty cannot be greater than $28,000.

- **IRC §6695(c)–Failure to furnish an identifying number:** The penalty is $55 for each failure to furnish an identifying number (an SSN, ATIN, or ITIN) on a tax return. The maximum penalty cannot be greater than $28,000.

- **IRC §6695(d)–Failure to retain a copy of the return (or list):** The penalty is $55 for each failure to retain a copy (or list) of each completed return or claim. The maximum penalty cannot be greater than $28,000.

- **IRC §6695(e)–Failure to file correct information returns.** The penalty is $55 for each failure to file correct information returns for a client. The maximum penalty cannot be greater than $28,000.

- **IRC §6695(f)–Negotiation of a taxpayer's refund check:** The penalty is $560 in 2023 (for 2022 tax filings) for a tax return preparer who endorses or negotiates any check made in respect of taxes imposed by Title 26 which is issued to a taxpayer.

- **IRC §6695(g)–Failure to exercise due diligence in determining eligibility for EITC, AOTC, CTC/ ACTC/ODC or Head of Household filing status:** The penalty is $560 in 2023 (for 2022 tax filings) for each failure to comply with the EITC, AOTC, or CTC due diligence requirements. This penalty is adjusted for inflation, and there is no annual maximum.

Example: Juliana is a tax preparer that owns a tax franchise. In 2022, Juliana institutes a policy at her office that clients will not be able to obtain copies of tax returns unless they pay an additional fee. This includes the preparation of an original return. Some clients decline the fee, and leave her office without a complete copy of the return, even after they have paid a preparation fee and Juliana has filed their return. One of Juliana's clients, Martin, is upset by this policy and contacts the IRS, filing a formal complaint against Juliana. The IRS launches an investigation into Juliana's practices, and discovers that she has not provided a required copy of completed return to 105 of her clients. The penalty is $55 for each failure, multiplied by 105 clients, equals a preparer penalty of $5,775 against Juliana under IRC §6695(a).

IRC §6700–Promoting abusive tax shelters: This applies to people who organize or sell abusive tax shelters. The IRS will calculate the penalty differently, depending on the conduct:

- False statements about the tax benefits of the transaction: The penalty is 50% of the gross income the person made for the activity.
- Provides a gross valuation overstatement: The penalty is $1,000 or 100% (whichever is less) of the gross income the person made for the activity for each entity or arrangement (treated as a separate activity) and participation in each sale.

> **Example:** Simon is a CPA that starts marketing tax shelters to his clients, offering the tax shelter to eliminate or reduce personal income tax. Simon encourages the use of offshore trusts to reduce tax liability by overclaiming deductions and hiding income and assets offshore, to shelter them from taxation. The IRS eventually catches up with Simon and assesses him a penalty of promoting abusive tax shelters, calling the trusts a sham transaction. The IRS assesses a penalty of $1,000 for each sale of an abusive plan or arrangement. Simon sold the tax shelter to 250 of his clients, so his §6700 penalty would be $250,000 ($1,000 × 250).

IRC §6701–Penalties for aiding and abetting understatement of tax liability: The penalty is $1,000 ($10,000 for a corporate tax return) for aiding and abetting in an understatement of a tax liability. Any preparer subject to the penalty shall be penalized only once for documents relating to the same taxpayer for a single tax period or event.

IRC §6713 – (Civil penalty) Disclosure or use of information by preparers of returns: The penalty is $250 for each unauthorized disclosure or use of information furnished for, or in connection with, the preparation of a return. The maximum penalty is $10,000 a year. If a disclosure or use is made in *connection with a crime* relating to the misappropriation of another person's taxpayer identity, whether or not such crime involves any tax filing, the penalty increases to $1,000 for each use or disclosure, with a maximum of $50,000 per person per calendar year.

Criminal Statutory Provisions

IRC §7206 – Fraud and false statements: This penalty applies to people who commit fraud or make false statements on tax returns. This penalty also applies to fraudulent and false activities in connection with offers in compromise or a closing agreement. People assessed this penalty are charged with a felony crime and may be:

- Fined up to $100,000 ($500,000 in the case of a corporation)
- Imprisoned up to 3 years and required to pay for the costs of prosecution

IRC §7207 – Fraudulent tax returns, statements, or other documents: This penalty can apply to people who prepare fraudulent returns, statements or other documents. People assessed this penalty are charged with a misdemeanor crime and may be:

- Fined up to $10,000 ($50,000 in the case of a corporation)
- Imprisoned up to 1 year.

IRC §7216 – Disclosure or use of information by preparers of returns: This penalty applies to tax preparers who <u>knowingly or recklessly</u> disclose information given to them to prepare a tax return or use the information for any purpose other than to prepare a return. Tax preparers assessed this penalty are charged with a misdemeanor crime and may be:

- Fined up to $1,000
- Imprisoned up to 1 year, and required to pay for the costs of prosecution.

IRC §7407– Action to enjoin tax return preparers: A federal district court may enjoin a tax return preparer from engaging in certain proscribed conduct, or in extreme cases, from continuing to act as a tax return preparer altogether.

IRC §7408–Action to enjoin specified conduct related to tax shelters and reportable transactions: A federal district court may enjoin a person from engaging in certain proscribed conduct (including any action, or failure to take action, which is in violation of Circular 230).

If a penalty is assessed against a tax preparer and the preparer does not agree with the assessment, he or she may request a conference with the IRS officer or agent and explain why the penalty is not warranted. The preparer may also wait for the penalty to be assessed, pay the penalty within 30 days, and then file a claim for refund.

Return Preparer Penalties Quick Reference		
IRC	**Violation**	**Penalty**
§6695	§6695(a) Failure to furnish a copy of return/claim for refund to a taxpayer	$55 per failure
	§6695(b) Failure to sign a return/claim for refund	$55 per failure
	§6695(c) Failure to furnish a PTIN on a return	$55 per failure
	§6695(d) Failure to retain a copy or list for a return/claim for refund	$55 per failure
	§6695(e) Failure to file correct information returns	$55 per failure
	§6695(f) Endorse, cash, or deposit a taxpayer's refund check	$560 per failure/No maximum fine in 2023 (For 2022 tax returns)
	§6695(g) Failure to comply with EITC, CTC, ODC, AOTC, or HOH due diligence requirements	$560 per failure/No maximum fine in 2023 (For 2022 tax returns)
§6694	§6694(a) Understatement due to an unreasonable position	Greater of $1,000 per return or 50% of fees derived by the preparer
	§6694(b) Understatement due to negligent/willful disregard	Greater of $5,000 per return or 75% of fees derived by the preparer
§6700	A preparer who sells, organizes, or promotes abusive tax shelter (tax shelter promoter)	Lesser of $1,000 per activity, or 100% of gross income derived from the activity
§6701	Aiding/abetting understatement of tax liability	$1,000 per individual return, $10,000 per corporate return
§6713	Unauthorized disclosure of client information (civil)	$250 per disclosure (not per return)/ $10,000 maximum per year. If due to fraud, the penalty increases to $1,000 for each disclosure, with a maximum of $50,000 per person per year.
§7216	Unauthorized disclosure of client information (criminal)	$1,000 fine and/or up to one year in prison

(Test yourself and then check the correct answers at the end of this chapter.)

1. Adele is a sole proprietor who files a Schedule C. She meets with Carlos, her enrolled agent, and gives him a list of expenses she says she incurred for a home office, business mileage, travel, and business meals. She does not bring any receipts or other documentation to the meeting. What is Carlos required to do in order to prepare an accurate tax return for Adele?

A. Nothing further; Carlos can rely on the list of Adele's expenses without seeing any documentation.

B. Carlos must make appropriate inquiries of Adele about her list of expenses. However, he does not need to actually see any documentation if she tells him she did not retain any receipts or keep a mileage log.

C. Carlos must ask relevant questions of Adele to help determine if the expenses are allowable. He must also ask if she has receipts to support the expenses.

D. Carlos must review all of Adele's receipts and her mileage log prior to preparing her tax return.

2. Basil is a tax preparer. He does not want to include his PTIN on his client's returns. What penalty does Basil face for failing to include his PTIN on a client's return?

A. No penalty, but he may receive an official censure from the IRS.

B. $55 per failure to provide his PTIN.

C. $100 per failure to provide his PTIN.

D. $560 per failure to provide his PTIN.

3. What is the penalty for a taxpayer who has filed a return determined to be frivolous?

A. $600, plus any other penalty provided by law.

B. $1,000, plus any other penalty provided by law.

C. $5,000, plus any other penalty provided by law.

D. $10,000, plus any other penalty provided by law.

4. Norris was audited during the year, and a large deduction was disallowed on his return. He was assessed a penalty for substantial understatement. What percentage of the understatement of tax must a taxpayer pay if he is liable for this penalty?

A. 5%

B. 10%

C. 20%

D. 25%

5. Paulette is married to Ronald, and the couple usually files jointly. Paulette is self-employed, and she files a fraudulent Schedule C, greatly inflating her deductions and underreporting her income. The IRS later discovers that Paulette had been making large cash deposits in a hidden bank account, and none of that income was reported on her return. Ronald only earns wages and now he is terrified that the IRS will assess fraud penalties against him, too. All of the following statements regarding the fraud penalty are correct except:

A. If there is any underpayment of tax due to fraud, a penalty of 75% of the underpayment may be assessed against Paulette.
B. The fraud penalty on a joint return will automatically apply to both spouses.
C. IRS examiners who find strong evidence of fraud may refer the case to the IRS Criminal Investigation Division for possible criminal prosecution.
D. Negligence or simple ignorance of the law does not constitute fraud.

6. Suzie hires Gustav to prepare her income tax returns. Gustav has prepared returns for several years, but he is not a CPA, an attorney, or an enrolled agent. Although he knows that Suzie is single and childless, he prepares her tax return based on the head of household filing status with two qualifying children so that Suzie may qualify for the Earned Income Tax Credit, and thus a larger refund. Suzie reviews a copy of the tax return and signs it. Gustav also signs the return and submits it to the IRS for processing. If the IRS detects the fraudulent credit, which of the two, if either, will face potential penalties?

A. Gustav only.
B. Suzie only.
C. Both Gustav and Suzie.
D. Neither Gustav nor Suzie.

7. Which of the following statements is correct?

A. Tax avoidance and tax evasion are always illegal.
B. Taxpayers who commit fraud are subject to civil penalties only.
C. The IRS will assess a failure-to-file penalty or a failure-to-pay penalty, but never both.
D. A felony conviction against a taxpayer who deliberately failed to file taxes could mean a fine of up to $100,000 and a prison sentence of up to five years.

8. What is not considered a "badge of fraud" by the IRS?

A. Failing to deposit cash income into business accounts.
B. Taking clearly improper deductions.
C. Keeping two sets of books and records.
D. Claiming deductions for foreign travel.

9. At the end of April, Boris has not yet filed his individual tax return, and he did not file an extension. Boris estimates that he owes $2,000 in unpaid tax, but he doesn't have the money to pay this amount, so he doesn't file at all. Since he missed the filing deadline and did not file an extension, Boris will be subject to penalties for non-filing; which of the following penalties will accrue at a faster rate?

A. Failure-to-file penalty.
B. Failure-to-pay penalty.
C. Both penalties are equal.
D. Neither, as it is facts-and-circumstances dependent.

10. All of the following statements about the trust fund recovery penalty are correct except:

A. The penalty is equal to 100% of the trust fund taxes not properly paid.
B. The IRS primarily targets employees for this penalty.
C. The penalty involves payroll taxes withheld from the wages of employees.
D. The penalty can be assessed against anyone who is considered a responsible person and has failed to remit trust fund taxes to the U.S. government.

11. Colleen owns a business and has never filed a tax return. How long should she keep her records?

A. Three years if she owes additional tax.
B. Seven years if she files a claim for a loss from worthless securities.
C. For an unlimited period of time if she does not file a return.
D. Ten years.

12. Accuracy-related penalties in IRC §6662 are imposed for substantial understatement of income tax and also for:

A. Substantial misstatement of the value of assets.
B. Substantial overstatement of income tax.
C. Preparer fraud related to the Earned Income Tax Credit.
D. Negligence while representing a business entity.

13. If there is substantial unreported income (over 25%), the IRS may audit tax returns for up to _____ after the filing date.

A. Three years.
B. Four years.
C. Six years.
D. Indefinitely.

14. An enrolled agent (EA) can be sanctioned under Circular 230 in each of the following ways EXCEPT:

A. Monetary penalty.
B. Imprisonment.
C. Censure.
D. Disbarment.

15. Which of the following statements is <u>incorrect</u> regarding the statute of limitations on the assessment of additional tax?

A. If no other provisions apply, the statute of limitations is three years from the filing date or the unextended due date, whichever is later.
B. If more than 25% of gross income has been omitted from the tax return, the statute of limitations is six years after the return was filed.
C. If a fraudulent return is filed, the statute of limitations is seven years after the return was filed.
D. If a tax return is not filed at all, there is no statute of limitations on assessment.

16. What is the minimum penalty for failing to file a tax return more than 60 days late (assuming the taxpayer is not owed a refund)?

A. 100% of the unpaid tax.
B. A fee of $135 or 90% of the unpaid tax, whichever is greater.
C. The smaller of $450 or 100% of the unpaid tax.
D. A minimum of 25% of a taxpayer's unpaid tax.

17. Tommy is a tax preparer. He has a client without a bank account, so Tommy cashes the client's refund check for him. What penalty does Tommy face for cashing his client's tax refund check?

A. Nothing. This is acceptable as long as the client has given written permission to do so.
B. $55 for each violation.
C. $100 for each violation.
D. $560 for each violation.

Unit 7: Quiz Answers

1. The answer is C. Carlos must make reasonable inquiries if the information appears to be incorrect, inconsistent, or incomplete. Carlos can generally rely in good faith, without verification, on the information his client provides. However, he cannot ignore the implications of the information. Since Adele may not fully understand the tax laws and may incorrectly believe she can claim deductions for non-qualifying expenses, Carlos must ask probing and relevant questions to help determine if the expenses are allowable. He must also ask if Adele has receipts to support the expenses, and further instruct her to keep the receipts in case the IRS requests supporting documentation.

2. The answer is B. Basil may receive a penalty of $55 per failure (for 2022 tax year filings). IRC §6695 lists the penalties that may be assessed when it comes to the preparation of tax returns for other persons. The penalty is $55 (in 2023, for 2022 tax year filings) for each violation of the following:

- Failure to furnish a copy of a return or claim to a taxpayer.
- Failure to sign a return or claim for refund.
- Failure to furnish an identifying number (PTIN) on a return.
- Failure to retain a copy or list of a return or claim for refund.
- Failure to file correct information returns.

3. The answer is C. Any taxpayer who files a return found to be frivolous may be fined $5,000, in addition to any other penalties provided by law. This penalty may be doubled on a joint return.

4. The answer is C. The substantial understatement penalty is calculated as a flat 20% of the net understatement of tax. Norris may also face additional fraud-related penalties if he provided false information on his tax return.

5. The answer is B. The fraud penalty on a joint return will not automatically apply to a spouse unless some part of the underpayment is due to the fraud committed by that spouse. In other words, the fraud penalty would not automatically apply to Ronald, because the fraud of one spouse will not be automatically imputed to the other. If Ronald is innocent of any wrongdoing, he may qualify for innocent spouse relief.

6. The answer is C. Suzie is ultimately responsible for the accuracy of her own return. However, a tax return preparer, whether officially licensed or not, also signs a tax return attesting to its accuracy under penalties of perjury. Both Gustav and Suzie could face penalties and other legal action in relation to the fraudulently claimed Earned Income Credit.

7. The answer is D. This is the maximum penalty and prison sentence in a tax evasion case. The other statements are false. Tax avoidance is not illegal. Taxpayers who commit fraud are subject to criminal penalties as well as civil. The IRS may assess both failure-to-file and failure-to-pay penalties.

8. The answer is D. IRS auditors are trained to spot common types of deception and attempts to defraud on tax returns. These acts are known as badges of fraud and include deducting personal items as business expenses, the overstatement of deductions, and the understatement of income. Simply having deductions for foreign travel is not an indication of illegal behavior on the part of a taxpayer.

9. The answer is A. The penalty for filing late (the **failure-to-file** penalty) is more severe, and is usually 5% of the unpaid taxes for each month that a return is late. The penalty for not paying taxes by the due date is less severe; ½ of 1% (0.5%) (the failure-to-pay penalty). Boris should have filed on time, or filed an extension, because even if he could not pay the amount due, he is better off filing on time and paying as much as he can.

10. The answer is B. The trust fund recovery penalty is levied against employers, or other responsible persons, who have failed to pay the appropriate payroll taxes to the U.S. government.

11. The answer is C. A taxpayer must keep records as long as they are needed for the administration of any provision of the IRC. Taxpayers must keep records that support an item of income or deduction on a tax return until the statute of limitations for that return runs out. If a tax return is not filed, there is no time limit.

12. The answer is A. Accuracy-related penalties in IRC §6662 are imposed for substantial understatement of income tax and also for a substantial misstatement of the value of assets. IRC §6662 imposes penalties on taxpayers who misstate the value of assets in order to reap tax benefits. The penalty is 20% of the net understatement of tax for assets incorrectly valued at 150% or more than the correct amount of valuation or adjusted basis. The penalty increases to 40% of the net understatement of tax for assets incorrectly valued at 200% or more than the correct amount of valuation or adjusted basis.

13. The answer is C. In most cases, tax returns can be audited for up to three years after filing. However, the IRS may audit for up to six years if there is substantial unreported income (over 25%).

14. The answer is B. An enrolled agent can be sanctioned under Circular 230 in various ways, but imprisonment would be a consequence of criminal activity and would not fall under the jurisdiction of Circular 230. However, there are other Federal laws that could allow for the imprisonment of EAs (and other practitioners) under certain circumstances.

15. The answer is C. If a fraudulent tax return is filed, there is no statute of limitations. Under federal law, a tax return is fraudulent if the taxpayer files it knowing that the return either omits taxable income or claims one or more deductions that are not allowable.

16. The answer is C. For the 2022 tax year, the minimum penalty for filing a tax return more than 60 days late is the smaller of $450 or 100% of the unpaid tax.

17. The answer is D. It is illegal for tax return preparers to negotiate or cash a taxpayer's refund check. Tommy faces a fine of $560 for each IRC § 6695(f) violation in 2023 (for 2022 tax returns).

Unit 8: Practitioner Misconduct

More Reading:
Publication 947, Practice Before the IRS and Power of Attorney
Form 14157, Return Preparer Complaint

The IRS's Office of Professional Responsibility (OPR) is responsible for interpreting and applying the provisions of Circular 230 to ensure that tax professionals follow the law. OPR's oversight generally covers all individuals who interact with federal tax administration, whether in person, orally, in writing, or by the preparation and submission of documents. The following are subject to Circular 230 jurisdiction, and thus to OPR oversight:

- Attorneys and CPAs who interact with the IRS at any level.

- Enrolled agents (EAs), enrolled retirement plan agents (ERPAs), and enrolled actuaries.

- Qualified appraisers: persons providing appraisals used in connection with tax matters (such as valuing estate and gift assets).[58]

- AFSP certificate holders who represent taxpayers before the IRS examination division, IRS customer service, and Taxpayer Advocate Service in connection with returns they prepared and signed.

- Other licensed and unlicensed individuals who give written advice that has the potential for tax avoidance or evasion.

- Any person submitting a power of attorney in connection with limited representation or special authorization to practice before the IRS in a specific matter before the agency (for example, the executor of an estate, or the fiduciary of a trust).

The Office of Professional Responsibility has authority in matters related to practitioner standards and exclusive authority in matters involving discipline and sanctions. This authority includes:

- Receiving and processing referrals regarding allegations of misconduct under Circular 230 and initiating disciplinary proceedings against individuals or entities relating to allegations or findings of practitioner misconduct consistent with the applicable disciplinary rules under Circular 230.

- Making final determinations on appeals regarding practitioner eligibility or suitability decisions and recommending and imposing sanctions for violations under Circular 230.

- Making determinations on whether to appeal administrative law judge decisions and reviewing and determining petitions from practitioners seeking reinstatement to practice.

---

[58] A "qualified appraiser" is defined by the IRS as someone who has earned an appraisal designation from a recognized professional appraisal organization (such as the ASA, NACVA, IBA, or AICPA) or has met certain minimum education and experience requirements.

Four Categories of Practitioner Misconduct

There are **four** broad categories of practitioner misconduct, all of which may be reasons for the OPR to initiate disciplinary action against a tax professional:

- Misconduct while representing a taxpayer,
- Misconduct related to the practitioner's own tax return,
- Giving a false opinion knowingly, recklessly, or through gross incompetence,
- Misconduct not directly involving IRS representation (such as a conviction of certain criminal acts).

Example: Laverne is an enrolled agent. She has been preparing tax returns for compensation for over ten years, but has filed her own returns late multiple times. She completely stops filing her own returns and does not file for 2020, 2021 or 2022. The Office of Professional Responsibility sends multiple notices which Laverne ignores. OPR initiates disciplinary action against Laverne for misconduct related to her own returns.

Example: Milton is a CPA who prepares tax returns for compensation. In 2022, Milton is convicted of felony wire fraud in a multimillion-dollar real estate scheme. OPR initiates expedited disbarment proceedings against Milton after his conviction. Milton is disbarred from practice before the Internal Revenue Service.

Circular 230 outlines many instances in which the OPR might sanction a practitioner for incompetence or disreputable conduct. Types of disreputable conduct include, but are not limited to:

- Conviction of any criminal offense under federal tax laws, or conviction of any criminal offense involving dishonesty or breach of trust.
- Conviction of any felony under federal or state law in which the conduct renders the practitioner unfit to practice before the IRS.
- Giving false or misleading information or participating in any way in the giving of false or misleading information to the Department of the Treasury, including a practitioner's misrepresentation of their own credentials.
- Soliciting employment as prohibited under Circular 230 or making false or misleading representations with intent to deceive a client.
- Willfully failing to file a federal tax return, or willfully evading any assessment or payment of any federal tax.
- Willfully assisting a client in violating any federal tax law, or knowingly counseling a client to evade federal taxes.
- Misappropriating funds received from a client for purposes of payment of taxes.
- Attempting to influence any IRS officer by the use of threats, false accusations, duress, coercion, or bribery.

- Disbarment or suspension from practice as a CPA, actuary or attorney.[59]
- Knowingly aiding and abetting another person to practice before the IRS during a period of suspension, disbarment, or ineligibility of such other person.
- Contemptuous conduct in connection with practice before the IRS, including the use of abusive language, knowingly making false accusations or statements, or circulating or publishing malicious or libelous matter.
- Willfully disclosing or using private tax return information.
- Willfully failing to sign a tax return.
- Willfully failing to e-file a return.
- Willfully signing a tax return without a valid PTIN.
- Willfully representing a taxpayer before the IRS without appropriate authorization.

Example: Mirabella is an enrolled agent with her own tax preparation business. In 2022, she was convicted of forgery because she forged her father's signature on several checks and cashed them. Although this was a case unrelated to her tax preparation firm, Mirabella is guilty of disreputable conduct because she was convicted of a criminal offense involving dishonesty or breach of trust. The IRS can disbar her and strip her of her enrollment.

In addition, the most recent Circular 230 revision expands part of §10.51 that prohibits "giving a false opinion, knowingly, recklessly, or through gross incompetence." False opinions include those that reflect or result from:

- A knowing misstatement of fact or law.
- An assertion of a position known to be unwarranted under existing law.
- Counseling or assisting in conduct known to be illegal or fraudulent.
- Concealing matters required by law to be revealed.
- Consciously disregarding information indicating that material facts expressed in the opinion or offering material are false or misleading.

Note: This paragraph of §10.51 defines reckless conduct in light of giving a false opinion as a "highly unreasonable omission or misrepresentation involving an extreme departure from the standards of ordinary care that a practitioner should observe under the circumstances."

The IRS will consider a practitioner's pattern of conduct to assess whether it reflects gross incompetence, meaning "gross indifference, preparation which is grossly inadequate under the circumstances, and a consistent failure to perform obligations to the client."

Some other examples of practitioner misconduct include fee disputes and bad behavior such as physical threats against a client, former client, or any employee of the IRS.

---

[59] For example, an attorney or CPA who is disbarred and loses his license at the state level would also be disbarred by the OPR at the federal level and be unable to represent taxpayers before the IRS.

> **Example:** Anthony is a CPA who was caught charging unconscionable fees to one client, for withholding files from another client and for willfully failing to provide an accounting of deposited funds to a third client. In his initial disciplinary proceeding, Anthony made several false statements to authorities. As a result of all of these actions, the Office of Professional Responsibility (OPR) successfully initiated disbarment proceedings against Anthony, which were ultimately upheld against Anthony. He will not be able to practice before the IRS.

> **Example:** Annie is a tax preparer representing a business client before the IRS. She submits a Form 2848 for the entity to the CAF unit, but she misrepresents her credentials, listing herself as a CPA, when in fact she does not have a current CPA license. She is studying for the CPA exam but has not passed it yet. The IRS CAF Unit discovered the practitioner's misrepresentation of her credentials, and makes a referral to the OPR.

Referrals to the Office of Professional Responsibility (OPR)

Most disciplinary cases opened by the Office of Professional Responsibility (OPR) result from internal and external referrals. OPR relies heavily on referrals involving tax practitioner misconduct from several sources, including IRS employees, taxpayers, tax practitioners, law enforcement agencies, and U.S. state licensing authorities.

An IRS employee who believes a practitioner has violated any provision in Circular 230 is <u>required</u> to file a written report to the OPR. Referrals are also mandatory following the assessment of penalties for violations of IRC §6694(b) (a willful attempt to understate the liability for tax).

A referral *must* also be made when there are penalties or sanctions imposed that relate to the promotion of abusive tax shelters, or aiding and abetting the understatement of a tax liability.

Mandatory Referrals	Discretionary Referrals
§6700 - Promoting abusive tax shelters	§6662 - Accuracy related penalty
§6701 - Aiding and abetting understatement of a tax liability	§6694(a) - Understatement of liability due to an unreasonable position
§7407 - Injunction of a tax return preparer	§6695 - (a) Failure to furnish copy of return;
§7408 - Injunction for specified conduct relating to tax shelters and reportable transactions	§6695 - (b) Failure to sign return; 6695 - (d) Failure to keep a copy of tax return or list of taxpayers, §6702 - Frivolous tax returns or submissions[60]

---

[60] For more information on mandatory and discretionary referrals, see OPR: Frequently Asked Questions (FAQ's), https://www.irs.gov/tax-professionals/frequently-asked-questions.

Example: Ms. Rowena Smith is an IRS auditor who is examining a taxpayer's 2022 tax return. Ms. Smith discovers that the taxpayer has participated in an abusive tax shelter. When she asks the taxpayer about it, the taxpayer is bewildered and states that the tax shelter was suggested to him by his tax attorney, who also prepared the tax return currently under audit. Ms. Smith checks the preparer section of the taxpayer's return, and writes down the tax attorney's name, address, and PTIN. She is required to file a written report to the OPR.

OPR says other common reasons for referral include:

- Cashing, diverting, or splitting a taxpayer's refund by electronic or other means,
- Patterns of misconduct involving multiple years, multiple clients, or unprofessional conduct demonstrated to multiple IRS employees,
- Potential conflict of interest situations, such as the representation of both spouses (or ex-spouses) who have a joint tax liability.

A taxpayer may also file a complaint against a tax return preparer by using Form 14157, *Return Preparer Complaint,* and submitting it to the Return Preparer Office, which will undertake an initial investigation before referring a case to the OPR. The form allows identification of complaints within the following categories: theft of refund, e-file issues, preparer misconduct, PTIN issues, false documents, employment taxes, and other issues.

Form **14157** (June 2018)	Department of the Treasury - Internal Revenue Service **Return Preparer Complaint**	OMB Number 1545-2168

Use this form to file a complaint with the IRS against a tax return preparer or tax preparation business.

CAUTION: READ THE INSTRUCTIONS BEFORE COMPLETING THIS FORM. There may be other more appropriate forms specific to your complaint. (For example, if you believe you are a victim of identity theft, please complete Form 14039, Identity Theft Affidavit).

Section A - Return Preparer Information *(complete all known information)*

1. Preparer's professional status *(check all that apply)*

☐ Attorney   ☐ Certified Public Accountant   ☐ Other/Unknown

☐ Enrolled Agent   ☐ Payroll Service Provider

2. Preparer's name and address	3. Preparer's business name and address *(if different)*
4. Preparer's telephone number(s) *(include area code)*	5. Preparer's email address
6. Preparer's website	7. Preparer Electronic Filing Identification Number (EFIN)
8. Preparer Tax Identification Number (PTIN)	9. Employer Identification Number (EIN)

Form 14157-A, *Tax Return Preparer Fraud or Misconduct Affidavit,* is used to report possible tax preparer fraud, for example, if a preparer provided the taxpayer with a copy of a tax return which is different from what was filed with the IRS.

163

Anonymous complaints are allowed. However, if a taxpayer chooses to submit his or her name and other personal information when he files a complaint, the information will not be shared with the individual or business being reported.

Disciplinary Sanctions

The OPR may impose a wide range of sanctions upon practitioners and other preparers who are subject to Circular 230 jurisdiction:

1. **Reprimand:** A reprimand is the least severe sanction. It is a private letter from the director of the OPR, stating the practitioner has committed some kind of misconduct under Circular 230. Although the issuance of a reprimand is kept private, it stays on a practitioner's record.

2. **Censure:** Censure is a public reprimand, with the practitioner's name published in the Internal Revenue Bulletin. The facts of the case that triggered the censure are not published. Unlike disbarment or suspension, censure generally does not prevent a practitioner from representing taxpayers before the IRS. However, in certain situations, a censure may place conditions on a practitioner's future representations in order to promote high standards of conduct.

3. **Suspension from Practice before the IRS:** An individual who is suspended is not eligible to represent taxpayers before the IRS during the term of the suspension. Suspensions may be imposed for a period of one to 60 months (five years).

4. **Disbarment from Practice before the IRS:** An individual who is disbarred is not eligible to represent taxpayers before the IRS. Disbarment lasts a minimum of five years, and Circular 230 requires the practitioner to demonstrate that he has regained fitness to practice before the IRS before he may be reinstated. As a result of suspension or disbarment, the practitioner will have the matter that caused the disbarment or suspension published in the Internal Revenue Bulletin.

5. **Monetary Penalty:** A monetary penalty may be imposed on an individual or a firm, or both, and can be in addition to any censure, suspension, or disbarment. The amount of the penalty may be up to the gross income derived, or to be derived, from the conduct that triggered the penalty.

> **Example:** Maynard is a CPA whose personal income tax returns were audited by the IRS. The audit found he was improperly claiming personal expenses as business deductions, and he had not timely filed his own tax returns. Even though no misconduct was discovered that related to his clients, Maynard was suspended from practice by the OPR for a period of three years. The Internal Revenue Bulletin listed his name, length of time of the suspension, and personal tax compliance issues as the reasons for the disciplinary action.

The Official Complaint Process

The OPR's response to an official complaint about a tax preparer or other referral about possible misconduct will vary depending upon the seriousness of the allegation. The OPR will first investigate whether a violation has occurred, whether the violation is one that calls into question a practitioner's fitness to continue to practice, and if so, what an appropriate sanction might be.

When it has identified a violation following its preliminary investigation, the OPR will send a "pre-allegation notice" to the practitioner regarding the alleged conduct. The notice gives the practitioner an opportunity to provide evidence or documentation in the case. The OPR will then determine the appropriate level of discipline warranted for the violation and try to reach an agreement with the practitioner on a sanction. If an agreement cannot be reached, the OPR will draft a complaint and refer the case to the Office of Chief Counsel, General Legal Services (GLS). The practitioner will have one final opportunity to resolve the matter before a formal disciplinary hearing.

When a formal complaint is issued against a practitioner, the complaint must:
- Name the respondent.
- Provide a clear and concise description of the facts.
- Be signed by the director of the OPR.
- Describe the type of sanction.

If a suspension is sought, the duration must be specified. The complaint may be served to the practitioner in one of the following ways: certified mail; first-class mail if returned undelivered by certified mail; private delivery service; in person; or by leaving the complaint at the office of the practitioner. Electronic delivery, such as email, is not a valid means of serving a complaint.

The complaint must specify a date by which the practitioner is required to respond, which must be at least 30 days after it is served. Within ten days of serving the complaint, copies of the evidence against the practitioner must also be served.

When a practitioner responds to a complaint, he is expected to specifically admit or deny each allegation, or state that he does not have enough information to know whether it is true or false. He cannot deny a material allegation in the complaint when he knows it to be true. If the practitioner fails to respond to a complaint, it constitutes an admission of guilt, and sanctions may be imposed without a hearing.

After a practitioner responds to a complaint, a hearing will be scheduled for an administrative law judge to hear the evidence and decide whether the OPR has proven its case.

> **Note:** To prevail in a disciplinary action involving suspension or disbarment, the OPR must prove by "clear and convincing evidence" that the practitioner willfully violated one or more provisions of Circular 230. "Willful" is defined as a voluntary, intentional violation of a known legal duty. This is a higher standard than preponderance of the evidence (or "more likely than not").

During a hearing, the practitioner may appear in person or be represented by an attorney or another practitioner. The OPR may be represented by an attorney or by another IRS employee assigned to the case. Within 180 days of the conclusion of a hearing, the administrative law judge must enter a decision.

If there is no appeal, the decision by the administrative law judge becomes final. However, either party—the OPR or the practitioner—may appeal the judge's decision with the Treasury Appellate Authority within 30 days. The Treasury Appellate Authority will receive briefs and render what is known as the "Final Agency Decision."

For the OPR, this decision is final, but the practitioner may contest the Final Agency Decision in a U.S. district court. The judge will review the findings from the administrative law hearing, but will only set aside the decision if it is considered arbitrary or capricious, contrary to law, or an abuse of discretion.

A practitioner who has been disbarred may petition the OPR for reinstatement after five years. The OPR may reinstate the practitioner if it determines that his conduct is not likely to be in violation of regulations and if granting the reinstatement is not contrary to the public interest.

Under a provision in the latest revision to Circular 230, the OPR has the right to use expedited suspension procedures against a practitioner under certain circumstances. First, §10.82 allows for these procedures when an attorney or CPA has already had his license revoked for cause by any state licensing agency or board. Further, expedited procedures can be used when a practitioner has been convicted of a crime involving dishonesty or breach of trust, or when he has demonstrated a pattern of "willful disreputable conduct" by failing to comply with certain of his personal federal tax filing obligations.

§10.82 gives the OPR the ability to move more quickly in sanctioning practitioners. If a practitioner fails to respond to a §10.82 complaint or does not appear at a §10.82 conference, the OPR can suspend the practitioner immediately.

> **Example:** The OPR receives a referral from another practitioner regarding Gayle, an enrolled agent. After an investigation and preliminary discussions with Gayle, the OPR drafts a complaint citing violations of Circular 230. The case is referred to the Office of Chief Counsel, which sends the complaint by certified mail alleging that Gayle gave irresponsible advice to clients, forged client signatures, and falsified multiple documents. Thirty days later, Gayle offers a response in writing. The case goes before an administrative judge, who listens to evidence presented by the OPR and by Gayle's attorney. Within 180 days, the judge issues his ruling, which agrees with the OPR's recommendation that Gayle be disbarred. She chooses not to appeal and is banned from practice before the IRS.

Prohibited Actions during Suspension or Disbarment

During disbarment or suspension, a practitioner will not be allowed to practice in any capacity before the IRS (except to represent himself). A disbarred or suspended practitioner may not:

- Prepare or file documents or other correspondence with the IRS. The restriction applies regardless of whether the individual signs the documents and regardless of whether the individual personally files, or directs another person to file, documents with the IRS.

However, as a result of the Loving case, disbarred and suspended practitioners are eligible to prepare and file tax returns for compensation.[61]

- Render written advice with respect to any entity, transaction, plan, or arrangement having the potential for tax avoidance or evasion.
- Represent a client at conferences, hearings, and meetings.
- Execute waivers, consents, or closing agreements; receive a taxpayer's refund check; or sign a tax return on behalf of a taxpayer.
- File powers of attorney with the IRS.
- Accept assistance from another person (or request assistance) or assist another person (or offer assistance) if the assistance relates to a matter constituting practice before the IRS, or enlist another person for purposes of practicing before the IRS.
- State or imply that he or she is eligible to practice before the IRS.

However, a disbarred or suspended individual is still allowed to:

- Represent himself or herself in any matter.
- As mentioned previously, prepare tax returns for clients for compensation (due to the outcome of the *Loving* case[62]).
- Appear before the IRS as a trustee, receiver, guardian, administrator, executor, or other fiduciary if duly qualified/authorized under the law of the relevant jurisdiction.
- Appear as a witness for a taxpayer.
- Furnish information at the request of the IRS or any of its officers or employees.
- Receive IRS information pursuant to a valid tax information authorization. However, simply receiving this information does not entitle a disbarred or suspended preparer to practice before the IRS on behalf of any taxpayer.

Example: Bartlett is an attorney who was disbarred in 2022 for criminal wire fraud. Bartlett can no longer give tax advice or represent clients before the IRS. However, he is the legal guardian of his disabled adult daughter, Camilla. Bartlett is the fiduciary of Camilla's qualified disability trust. Despite the fact that he is a disbarred attorney, he may still represent his daughter (as her legal guardian) and the trust (as the trust's fiduciary) before the IRS.

Example: Adrianne is an enrolled agent who prepares tax returns and owns her own firm. In 2022, she hires another enrolled agent named Emery as an employee. Emery comes under investigation by the Office of Professional Responsibility during the year. Emery is later disbarred for financial fraud and loses his EA license. Adrianne must dismiss Emery as her employee. She cannot accept assistance from, or employ, a disbarred practitioner.

---

[61] The Office of Professional Responsibility released an official statement on this matter (OPR Statement 20052314). OPR determined that a suspension or disbarment from practice before the IRS may not include a restriction on return preparation for compensation, and that access to the PTIN required for such services may no longer be blocked based on discipline under Circular 230.

[62] In Loving v. IRS, a U.S. district court found that the IRS lacked the authority to issue tax preparer regulations.

(Test yourself and then check the correct answers at the end of this chapter.)

1. All of the following are considered examples of disreputable conduct for which an enrolled agent can be disbarred or suspended except:

A. Directly or indirectly attempting to influence the official action of any employee of the Internal Revenue Service by use of threats, or by bestowing any gift, favor or thing of value.
B. Misappropriation or failure to remit funds received from a client for the purpose of payment of taxes or other obligations due to the United States.
C. Knowingly aiding and abetting another person to practice before the Internal Revenue Service during a period of suspension or disbarment.
D. Nonwillful failure to timely pay personal income taxes.

2. How is a proceeding for a violation of the regulations in Circular 230 instituted against an enrolled practitioner once an official complaint has been made against the practitioner?

A. An aggrieved taxpayer files a petition with the United States Tax Court stating a claim against the enrolled practitioner.
B. The Commissioner of the IRS files a complaint against the enrolled practitioner with the United States Tax Court.
C. The Office of Professional Responsibility will draft a complaint and refer the case to the Office of Chief Counsel.
D. The Secretary of the Treasury files a complaint against the enrolled actuary in the United States District Court for the District of Columbia.

3. What is the shortest period of <u>suspension</u> that will be imposed upon a practitioner who has been found to violate a provision of Circular 230?

A. One month.
B. Six months.
C. One year.
D. Two years.

4. Alisha is an enrolled agent that was disbarred from practice by OPR. How long must Alisha wait in order to petition for reinstatement?

A. One year.
B. Five years.
C. Ten years.
D. Disbarment is permanent.

5. Which of the following types of disciplinary actions allow a practitioner to continue practicing before the IRS?

A. Disbarment
B. Suspension
C. Censure
D. All of the above

6. Bowie is an enrolled agent. The OPR receives a complaint about Bowie and launches an investigation. The OPR determines Bowie has violated provisions of Circular 230 by cashing his client's refund checks. Bowie wants to fight the determination. Which of the following **best describes** the due process procedures that Bowie will face?

A. After the formal OPR complaint is filed against Bowie; a disciplinary hearing is held with an administrative law judge presiding; either the OPR or the Bowie can appeal; a final decision is rendered by the Treasury Appellate Authority; at that point, Bowie must sue in court to contest the decision.
B. After the formal OPR complaint is filed against Bowie; a disciplinary hearing is held with an administrative law judge presiding; either the OPR or the Bowie can appeal; a final decision is rendered by the Treasury Appellate Authority; no further appeal is granted either side.
C. After the formal OPR complaint is filed against Bowie; a disciplinary hearing is held with an administrative law judge presiding; either the OPR or Bowie can appeal; a final decision is rendered by the judge; at that point, Bowie must sue the IRS to contest the decision.
D. After the formal OPR complaint is filed against Bowie; a decision is rendered by the Treasury Appellate Authority; no appeal can be made by either OPR or Bowie.

7. Under Treasury Department Circular 230, all of the following are considered to be incompetence and disreputable conduct EXCEPT:

A. Conviction of any criminal offense under the Federal tax laws.
B. Conviction of any criminal offense involving dishonesty or breach of trust.
C. Willfully disclosing tax return information with the consent of the taxpayer.
D. Willfully failing to sign a tax return prepared by the tax practitioner as required by Federal tax laws.

8. A suspended or disbarred practitioner may:

A. Appear before the IRS as a fiduciary.
B. File an IRS appeal request on a taxpayer's behalf.
C. Represent a client at IRS conferences, hearings, and meetings.
D. Execute a closing agreement for a client with a valid power of attorney.

9. Benedict is a lawyer who was disbarred from practice in 2022. Which of the following actions is he <u>not allowed</u> to do?

A. Represent his own child, whose tax return is under examination before the IRS.
B. Furnish information to the IRS at the request of a revenue officer.
C. Act as a representative for a client for a fee in an IRS audit.
D. Prepare his own federal tax return.

10. Renata Smith, an enrolled agent, advises her prospective clients that she is able to obtain approval of qualified retirement plans with unique vesting provisions because of her close relationship with the IRS territory manager of the Tax Exempt Government Entities operating unit in her locality. This type of solicitation constitutes:

A. Reasonable care
B. Disreputable conduct
C. Authorized disclosure
D. Conflict of interest

11. Under Circular 230, the OPR has the right to use <u>expedited</u> suspension procedures against a practitioner for "willful disreputable conduct" involving which of the following transgressions?

A. Violating due diligence procedures related to the Earned Income Tax Credit.
B. Failure to use a PTIN when filing clients' federal tax returns.
C. Failure to comply with his personal federal tax filing obligations.
D. Failure to abide by IRS standards related to advertising and fees.

12. Which of the following is not listed in Circular 230 as conduct that could cause a practitioner to be censured, suspended, or disbarred?

A. Abusive language in connection with practice before the IRS.
B. Willfully failing to sign a federal tax return.
C. Conviction of a felony charge.
D. Indictment on a criminal offense charge.

Unit 8: Quiz Answers

1. The answer is D. A failure to timely pay personal income taxes will not be considered disreputable conduct, as long as the failure to pay is not a willful attempt to evade tax. However, a willful failure to <u>timely file</u> a federal income tax return constitutes disreputable conduct as defined under 31 C.F.R. § 10.51(a)(6).

2. The answer is C. When OPR receives an official complaint about a practitioner, it will send a "pre-allegation notice" to the practitioner regarding the alleged conduct. The notice gives the practitioner an opportunity to provide evidence or documentation in the case. The OPR will then determine the appropriate level of discipline warranted for the violation and try to reach an agreement with the practitioner on a sanction. If an agreement cannot be reached, the OPR will draft a complaint and refer the case to the Office of Chief Counsel. The practitioner will then have one final opportunity to resolve the matter before a formal disciplinary hearing.

3. The answer is A. The OPR can <u>suspend</u> a practitioner who has violated the rules and regulations of Circular 230 for a period of one month and up to a maximum of 60 months (5 years). A suspension (unlike a disbarment) can be for a period shorter than 5 years.

4. The answer is B. Alisha may petition the OPR for reinstatement after a period of five years. Reinstatement will not be granted unless the Internal Revenue Service is satisfied that the petitioner is not likely to engage thereafter in conduct contrary to the regulations, and that granting such reinstatement would not be contrary to the public interest. In the case of a *suspension* (rather than a disbarment) a practitioner may petition for reinstatement immediately following the expiration of the suspension period, if shorter than 5 years (Title 31, CFR §10.81).

5. The answer is C. A practitioner who is censured by the OPR is still eligible to practice before the IRS. Censure is a public reprimand. Unlike disbarment or suspension, censure does not affect an individual's eligibility to represent taxpayers before the IRS, although the OPR may subject the individual's future representation of taxpayers to conditions designed to promote high standards of conduct.

6. The answer is A. After the formal complaint is filed against Bowie; a disciplinary hearing is held with an administrative law judge presiding; either the OPR or Bowie can appeal; a final decision is rendered by the Treasury Appellate Authority. At that point, if Bowie does not agree with the decision, he can sue in a U.S. district court. However, the district court judge will only reverse the decision if it is considered arbitrary or capricious, contrary to law, or an abuse of discretion.

7. The answer is C. Willfully disclosing tax return information <u>with the consent</u> of the taxpayer would not be considered disreputable conduct.

8. The answer is A. A disbarred practitioner may appear before the IRS as a trustee, receiver, guardian, administrator, executor, or other fiduciary, if duly qualified or authorized under the laws of the relevant jurisdiction.

9. The answer is C. Benedict cannot act as a representative for a client for a fee in an IRS audit. A practitioner who has been disbarred (or suspended) may not represent a client in front of the IRS, sign a tax return on behalf of a taxpayer, file powers of attorney with the IRS, or any other actions considered practice before the IRS. The other actions listed are allowed, even for a practitioner who has been disbarred or suspended.

10. The answer is B. This type of solicitation constitutes disreputable conduct, subjecting Renata to potential disbarment or suspension from IRS practice. A tax preparer cannot infer or imply any type of employer-employee or other close relationship with the IRS.

11. The answer is C. Under §10.82 of Circular 230, the OPR may move quicker to sanction practitioners by using expedited procedures in certain circumstances, including when a practitioner has been convicted of a crime involving dishonesty or breach of trust. The procedures are also allowed when a practitioner has demonstrated a pattern of "willful disreputable conduct" involving the following:

- Failing to file federal income tax returns in four of the five previous tax years.
- Failing to file a return required more frequently than annually (such as an employment tax return) during five of the seven previous tax periods.

12. The answer is D. Circular 230 §10.51 details a large number of violations related to incompetence or disreputable conduct for which a practitioner may face sanctions from the OPR. The statute specifically cites "conviction" of a criminal offense or felony charges, rather than merely an "indictment" on criminal offense or felony charges. Circular 230 also does not specify that a conviction of misdemeanor charges is a sanctionable offense. However, the statute warns that practitioners may be sanctioned for offenses that are not specifically listed.

Unit 9: Tax Payments and IRS Collections

> **More Reading:**
> **Publication 594, The Collection Process**
> **Publication 1035, Extending the Tax Assessment Period**
> **Publication 971, Innocent Spouse Relief**
> **Publication 556, Examination of Returns, Appeal Rights, and Claims for Refund**
> **Publication 1660, Collection Appeal Rights**

If a taxpayer owes a balance after filing their return, the IRS will send him a bill for the amount due, including any penalties and interest. This bill officially starts the collection process, which continues until the taxpayer's tax debt is paid, or until the IRS can no longer legally collect the tax; for example, when the statute for collection expires. The unpaid balance is subject to interest that compounds daily and a monthly late payment penalty up to the maximum allowed by law.

If a taxpayer *agrees* with the information on the bill but is unable to pay the full amount, the taxpayer is advised to pay as much as they can, and contact the IRS immediately to explain the situation. For taxpayers who cannot pay the tax they owe, payment options include: extensions of time to pay, installment agreements, and offers in compromise.

Approved Methods of Payment

The IRS offers numerous options for making payments. The following methods of payment are currently accepted by the IRS:

1. **Direct debit (note: this is not the same thing as "Direct Pay"):** A Direct Debit is a tax payment electronically withdrawn from a taxpayer's bank account through the tax software at the time of efiling; this option must be supported by the tax software.
2. **Credit card, debit card or digital wallet:** Individuals can pay online, by phone or with a mobile device through any of the authorized payment processors. The processor charges a fee. The IRS doesn't receive any fees for these payments.
3. **Personal check, cashier's check, or money order:** On all checks or money orders, the preparer should write the taxpayer's daytime phone number, EIN, TIN, or SSN, tax return type, and tax year to which the payment applies. The check or money order should be made payable to the "United States Treasury."
4. **Installment agreement:** A payment plan that allows a taxpayer to pay the taxes owed within an extended timeframe. An IRS Direct Debit Installment Agreement (DDIA) is when a taxpayer authorizes monthly payments to the IRS directly from their bank account.
5. **Electronic Federal Tax Payment System (EFTPS):** This is a free way for individual taxpayers and businesses to pay their taxes online. EFTPS allows taxpayers to schedule payments up to one year in advance. Corporations must deposit all income tax payments using EFTPS.

173

6. **Electronic funds withdrawal (EFW):** This option allows taxpayers to file and pay electronically from their bank account when using tax preparation software or a tax professional. This option is free and only available when e-filing a tax return.
7. **Federal Tax Application (same-day wire transfer):** If a taxpayer does not have a US bank account, (for example, a U.S. citizen that is living and working overseas) it is possible to make same-day wire transfers directly to the IRS. The foreign bank where the wire transfer originates must have a banking relationship with a US bank, although the US bank does not have to be an affiliate of the foreign bank.
8. **Direct Pay:** Direct Pay is free and allows taxpayers to securely pay their federal taxes directly from their checking or savings account without any fees or preregistration. Taxpayers can schedule payments up to 365 days in advance.
9. **Cash:** Cash payments can only be made through select, IRS-approved retail stores, and with dollar amount and frequency limitations.

Payments do not have to be sent at the same time an electronic return is transmitted. For example, the return may be transmitted in January, and the taxpayer may mail payment by check at a later date. As long as the payment is mailed by the due date of the return, it will be considered timely.

Tax Refunds

Taxpayers have several options related to their tax refunds. They may:

- Apply a refund to next year's estimated tax.
- Receive the refund as a direct deposit or as a paper check.
- Split the refund, with a portion applied to next year's estimated tax and the remainder received as direct deposit or a paper check, or split the refund between three different accounts.
- Use the refund (or part of it) to purchase U.S. Series I Savings Bonds. Taxpayers can purchase up to $5,000 (in $50 increments) in bonds for themselves or others.

Direct deposit is the fastest way to receive refunds. Refunds may be designated for direct deposit to qualified accounts in the taxpayer's name. Qualified accounts include savings, checking, share draft, or retirement accounts (for example, IRA or money market accounts).

Direct deposits cannot be made to regular credit card accounts, but can be made to prepaid debit cards. Qualified accounts must be in financial institutions within the United States. The number of refunds electronically deposited into a single account is limited to three.

A preparer is required to accept any direct deposit election to a qualified account at an eligible financial institution designated by the taxpayer. A preparer may not charge a separate fee for direct deposit.

A direct deposit election <u>cannot be rescinded</u> once a return is filed. In addition, changes cannot be made to the routing numbers of financial institutions or to the taxpayer's bank account number after the IRS has accepted the return. A preparer should verify account and routing numbers with the taxpayer each year.

Example: Karla filed her 2022 tax return on February 25, 2023. She e-filed and chose direct deposit for her refund. Three days later, her purse was stolen, and she had to close her bank account to prevent fraud. The direct deposit information cannot be changed on her return after it has been e-filed. The IRS will attempt to deposit her tax refund, but once the bank declines her deposit, her refund will default to a paper check.

Installment Agreements (Long-Term and Short-Term Payment Plans)

Installment agreements are long-term payment arrangements in which the IRS allows taxpayers to pay liabilities over time. Before applying for an installment agreement, the taxpayer (or business) must file all required tax returns.

Though interest and late-payment penalties continue to accrue on any unpaid taxes after the due date, the failure-to-pay penalty rate is cut in half while an installment agreement is in effect—from the usual penalty rate of 0.5% per month to a reduced rate of 0.25% per month.

A taxpayer who files electronically may apply for an installment agreement once the return is processed and the tax is assessed. Taxpayers must either submit Form 9465, *Installment Agreement Request,* or apply online if they qualify. The IRS charges a one-time user fee to set up an installment agreement, although this fee can be reduced or waived for low-income taxpayers with AGIs at or below 250% of the federal poverty level.

An installment agreement generally provides for full payment of the taxpayer's account before the expiration of the collection statute of limitations; however, there are exceptions if the taxpayer's financial circumstances warrant it. During the term of the installment agreement, penalties and interest continue to accrue. Future refunds are applied to the tax debt until it is paid in full. Equal monthly payments are specified in the agreement, but the taxpayer may choose to pay more than the required monthly amount.

Taxpayers may pay in a variety of ways, including by check, credit card, payroll deduction, or direct debit. Qualified taxpayers who owe $25,000 or less may have their Notice of Federal Tax Lien withdrawn after entering into a direct debit installment agreement. A taxpayer who owes $10,000 or less in tax cannot be turned down for an installment agreement, assuming that all of the following apply:

- The taxpayer (and spouse, if married) has timely filed all income tax returns and paid all tax due during the past five years;
- The IRS has determined the taxpayer cannot pay the tax owed in full when it is due;
- The taxpayer agrees to pay the full amount he owes within three years; and
- The taxpayer has not entered into an installment agreement with the IRS in the prior five years.

Applying for an Installment Agreement Online: Individuals must owe $50,000 or less in combined individual income tax, penalties, and interest, and have filed all required returns in order to apply for an installment agreement online. In the case of a business taxpayer with a payroll tax liability, the business must owe $25,000 or less in payroll taxes and must have filed all required returns.[63]

IRS Payment Plan Options	
Short Term Payment Plan	**Cost**
Short Term Payment Plan: This a free option for individuals and businesses that can pay their balance within 180 days (approximately 6 months). Payment options include: • Pay directly from a checking or savings account (Direct Pay) (Individuals only) • Pay electronically online or by phone using Electronic Federal Tax Payment System (EFTPS) (enrollment required) • Pay by check, money order or debit/credit card	• Apply online: $0 setup fee (only individuals can apply for a short-term payment plan online) • Apply by phone, mail, or in-person: $0 setup fee (up to 180 days) • Although there is no fee for this payment option, accrued penalties and interest will be assessed until the balance is paid in full
Long-Term Payment Plans	**Cost**
Option 1: Pay through Direct Debit (automatic monthly payments from a checking account). Also known as a Direct Debit Installment Agreement (DDIA). Direct Debit is required if the taxpayer's balance is more than $25,000.	• Apply online: $31 setup fee • Apply by phone, mail, or in-person: $107 setup fee • Low income: setup fee waived • Accrued penalties and interest will be assessed until the balance is paid in full
Option 2: Other payment options • Make monthly payment via Direct Pay (Individuals only) • Make monthly payment using Electronic Federal Tax Payment System (EFTPS) • Make monthly payment by check, money order or debit/credit card (additional fees apply when paying by credit card)	• Apply online: $130 setup fee • Apply by phone, mail, or in-person: $225 setup fee • Low income: $43 setup fee which may be reimbursed if certain conditions are met • Accrued penalties and interest will be assessed until the balance is paid in full

---

[63] For taxpayers with AGIs at or below 250% of the federal poverty level, the IRS will waive or reimburse user fees for an installment agreement.

> **Note:** Do not confuse a long-term installment agreement with a "short-term payment plan." Short-term payment plans do not require a fee, and typically the balances must be paid within 180 days. [64]

Direct Debit requirement: For individuals, balances over $25,000 must generally be paid by direct debit. For businesses, balances over $10,000 must be paid by direct debit.

Taxpayers that owe more than $100,000, may still qualify for an installment agreement, but *Form 433-A* or *Form 433-F, Collection Information Statement,* may have to be submitted along with the installment agreement request. As a result of the IRS Taxpayer Relief Initiative, as long as a taxpayer's case has *not been referred* to an IRS Revenue Officer, Forms 433-A or 433-F are not currently required for balances of $250,000 or less. The IRS generally will not take collection actions:

- When an installment agreement is being considered.
- While an installment agreement is in effect.
- For 30 days after an installment agreement request is rejected.
- During the period the IRS evaluates an appeal of a rejected or terminated agreement.

If a taxpayer fails to make a payment on an installment agreement, an automatic 30-day notice is generated. The IRS typically charges a fee for reinstating an installment agreement that has gone into default.

> **Example:** Glenda owes $36,000 in taxes and is not able to pay the balance due. She is under the $50,000 threshold, so she is eligible to apply for an installment agreement online. She applies online, and her installment agreement is approved by the IRS. Glenda has $500 deducted from her checking account every month via direct debit. Under the terms of the agreement, she must pay the entire amount within 72 months.

Extension of Time for Payment (Form 1127): A taxpayer who wants to extend the time they have to pay should file *Form 1127, Application for Extension of Time for Payment of Tax Due to Hardship,* by the due date of his return, or by the due date for the amount determined as a deficiency. The types of taxes covered by Form 1127 include income taxes, self-employment taxes, and gift taxes.

The term "undue hardship" does not mean a taxpayer will simply be inconvenienced by paying the tax. Rather, for the IRS to grant a Form 1127 request, a taxpayer must show he will sustain a substantial financial loss if he pays the tax on the date it is due. In the request for an extension, a taxpayer must:

- Enter the date he proposes to pay the tax,
- Provide a detailed explanation of the undue hardship that would result if he paid the tax on or before the due date, and

---

[64] Under the IRS *Taxpayer Relief Initiative,* short-term payment plans currently have up to 180 days to pay their taxes in full (increased from the prior 120-day period).

- Provide supporting documentation, including a statement of assets and liabilities and an itemized list of income and expenses for each of the three months prior to the due date of the tax.

Interest will continue to accrue on the amount due. The IRS generally will not grant an extension of more than six months to pay the tax shown on a return. An extension to pay an amount determined as a deficiency is generally limited to 18 months from the date payment is due, but an extension to pay a deficiency will not be granted at all if the deficiency is due to negligence, intentional disregard of rules and regulations, or fraud with intent to evade tax.

> **Example:** Reginald knew that he owed taxes on his return, but he had unexpected hospital expenses, which depleted his savings. To pay the $8,500 he owes in taxes, he would have to sell his car at a sacrifice price. Doing so would create an undue hardship because he would not have reliable transportation, which could cause him to lose his job. Prior to the tax deadline, Reginald files Form 1127, to request an extension of time to pay tax owed because of undue hardship. He provides a full explanation of his financial difficulties as well as the other required documentation. The IRS grants Reginald an extension of 6 months to pay the tax shown on his return.

The IRS Collection Process and the CSED

After a taxpayer files a return, if they have unpaid tax due, the IRS will send a bill, which officially starts the collection process.[65] The IRS has wide powers when it comes to collecting unpaid taxes. The first notice explains the balance due and demands payment in full. It will include the amount of the unpaid tax balance plus any penalties and interest calculated from the date the tax was due.

The collection process continues until the taxpayer's account is satisfied or until the IRS may no longer legally collect the tax, such as when the collection period has expired. The date that the IRS is no longer allowed to collect the tax is called the collection statute expiration date (CSED).

The CSED is normally ten years from the date of the assessment. The collection statute of limitations period can be **suspended** (also referred to as "tolled") which **extends the CSED.**

> **Note:** The collection period is suspended when the IRS is prohibited from collecting tax. During this suspension period, the collection period is extended whereby the IRS is legally authorized additional time to be added to the initial ten-years to collect. The IRS is not prohibited or stopped from collecting after the original 10-year period if the collection period is extended.

The CSED can be extended for a variety of reasons, including:

- While the IRS considers a request for an installment agreement or an offer in compromise,
- From the date a taxpayer requests a collection due process (CDP) hearing,
- While the taxpayer is residing outside the United States,

---

[65] Per Publication 594, the "collection process" is a series of actions that the IRS can take to collect the taxes you owe if you do not voluntarily pay them.

- A pending bankruptcy proceeding. The running of the collection period is extended for an additional 6 months upon the conclusion of the bankruptcy.

The amount of time the suspension is in effect will be added to the time remaining in the ten-year period. For example, if the ten-year period is suspended for six months, the time left in the period the IRS has to collect will increase by six months. If a taxpayer is delinquent filing their return, the date of assessment is the date the return is processed, and the taxpayer is legally liable for the tax.

> **Note:** Installment agreements do not suspend the collection statute. In other words, if a taxpayer is paying his or her tax debt under an installment agreement, the amount of time that the IRS has to legally collect the debt does not increase.

Bankruptcy

A filing in bankruptcy court immediately stops all assessment and collection of tax. This is called an automatic stay, and it remains in effect until the bankruptcy court lifts the stay or discharges liabilities, meaning they are eliminated or no longer legally enforceable. Income tax debt that may be discharged in bankruptcy must meet the following general conditions:

- The tax debt must be related to a return that was due at least three years before the taxpayer filed for bankruptcy.
- The tax return must have been filed at least two years ago.
- The tax assessment must be at least 240 days old.
- The taxpayer cannot be guilty of tax evasion, and the tax return cannot be fraudulent or frivolous.

> **Example:** On January 3, 2022, Damian has a car accident and broke both his legs. His medical insurance wasn't very good, and Damian ended up having insurmountable medical debts. Damian also had a tax debt from the prior year, which he was planning to pay, but after his accident he no longer had the funds to do so. The IRS had already sent Damian a bill, so his account was in collections when his accident occurred. On the advice of his attorney, he files for bankruptcy on June 1, 2022. The filing in bankruptcy court immediately stops all assessment and collection of tax, but the running of the collection period is also suspended during the time Damian's bankruptcy petition is pending with the courts, plus an additional 6 months upon the conclusion of his bankruptcy case.

Taxpayer's Ability to Pay

When there is a delinquent tax liability or when the taxpayer makes a request for an installment agreement or an offer in compromise, the IRS may use a variety of methods to assess the taxpayer's ability to pay. The IRS may consider the taxpayer's general financial health, including factors such as cash flow and assets, lawsuits against the taxpayer, garnishments, and whether the taxpayer has filed bankruptcy. Third-party research, such as property assessments, asset values, and state and local tax information, may also be used.

Collection Financial Standards: The IRS' Collection Financial Standards are used to evaluate a taxpayer's ability to pay a delinquent tax liability. These standards help determine allowable living expenses that are necessary to provide for a taxpayer's health and welfare and/or production of income while his tax debt is being repaid.

Allowances for housing, utilities, and transportation vary by location, while standard amounts are allowed nationwide for food, clothing, out-of-pocket health care expenses, and other items. In most cases, the taxpayer is allowed the amount actually spent, or the local standard, whichever is less.

For the items based on national standards, a taxpayer is allowed the total amounts applicable for the taxpayer's family size, without regard to the amounts actually spent. Generally, the number of persons for whom necessary living expenses are allowed is the same as the number of exemptions on the taxpayer's most recent income tax return.

The IRS uses these standards for taxpayers who do not qualify for streamlined installment agreements, which require little financial analysis or substantiation of expenses, or who cannot afford the streamlined payment amount. If a taxpayer believes he needs a higher amount for basic living expenses than the Collection Financial Standards allow, he must provide documentation to explain why.

Collection Information Statements: The information described above regarding allowable living expenses may be used to prepare a Collection Information Statement, using Form 433-A, Form 433-B, Form 433-F, Form 433-A (OIC), or Form 433-B (OIC). This statement also contains detailed financial information about the taxpayer's income, bank and retirement accounts, real estate and other assets, and outstanding debts. Further, it may include information concerning the taxpayer's obligations for court-ordered payments, such as child support and alimony, since the taxpayer will generally have little flexibility regarding these obligations.

"Currently Not Collectible" Status: The IRS can declare a taxpayer to be currently not collectible if the taxpayer's financial information shows no ability to pay his tax debts.

Before this status is declared, the IRS requires the taxpayer to submit a collection information statement in order to demonstrate that after paying necessary living expenses, he has no money left to make monthly payments to the IRS. Further, he must prove he has no assets that could be liquidated or sold to make a lump sum payment to the IRS.

Once a taxpayer is placed into "currently not collectible" status (also known as "Status 53"), the IRS must stop all collection activities, such as levies. Once a taxpayer is granted this status, the IRS may periodically review the taxpayer's financial information, or keep him in CNC status until his income increases.

While in "currently not collectible" status, penalties and interest continue to be added to the tax debt, and the collection statute of limitations continues to run.

IRS Enforcement to Collect Unpaid Taxes

Congress has given the IRS broad powers to compel taxpayers to produce information it requires to determine tax liability or to collect tax. The IRS is permitted to do the following:

- Examine any books, papers, records, or other data;
- Summon a taxpayer or any other person, requiring the person to appear, to produce books and records, and to give testimony under oath; and
- Take testimony under oath.

These powers are most commonly used in connection with collection proceedings, such as when a taxpayer refuses to provide information voluntarily, and in IRS audits, referred to as examinations (Even though the IRS uses the term "examination" rather than "audit" the terms mean essentially the same thing). IRS enforcement actions to collect unpaid taxes may include the following:

- **Levies:** Issuing a notice of levy on salary and other income, bank accounts, or property (legally seizing property to satisfy the tax debt);
- **Liens:** Filing a Notice of Federal Tax Lien;
- **Summons:** Issuing a summons to secure information to prepare unfiled tax returns or determine the taxpayer's ability to pay.
- **SFRs:** IRS employees will prepare a "*substitute for return*" (SFR) when a taxpayer refuses to file voluntarily, applying future federal tax refunds to any prior amount due, or offsetting a taxpayer's refund.

The **Automated Substitute for Return Program**, or ASFR Program,[66] identifies taxpayers who did not file a required tax return and attempts to bring these taxpayers into compliance. The IRS either secures an income tax return from these taxpayers or prepares a Substitute for Return for taxpayers with a proposed tax assessment based on information return data reported to the IRS combined with other internal data.

> **Example:** Ambrose has not filed tax returns for several years. The IRS has sent him notices repeatedly, which Ambrose ignored. The IRS prepares substitute for returns (SFRs) for all of Ambrose's unfiled years. The IRS does this so they can assess tax and begin collection activities. After the SFRs are filed, the IRS sends Ambrose a bill for each year, and collection activity can commence.

Under the Federal government's Treasury Offset Program ("TOP") there is generally no limit on the period during which an offset may be initiated or taken, meaning debts that are years, or even decades, old may be repaid by a refund offset.

Debts may include past-due federal income tax, other federal debts such as student loans, state income tax, child and spousal support payments, and state unemployment compensation debt. A state income tax refund may also be applied to a taxpayer's federal tax liability.

---

[66] These are called SFRs, or Substitutes for Returns. These "substitute returns" generally do not give credit for deductions and exemptions a taxpayer may be entitled to receive. Even if the IRS has already filed a substitute return, a taxpayer may still file his own return. The IRS will generally adjust the taxpayer's account to reflect the correct figures after they receive the filed returns from the taxpayer. Substitutes for returns are for core income tax returns only; they are not applicable to non-taxable Form 990 and similar returns.

> **Example:** Franklin has been expecting a $2,000 refund from his federal tax return. However, Franklin has past-due child support payments and a delinquent student loan totaling $3,800. The IRS notifies Franklin that the entire $2,000 he had been anticipating as a refund will be used to offset these debts.

Federal Tax Lien

A federal tax lien is a legal claim against a taxpayer's property, including property that the taxpayer acquires after the lien is filed. By filing a Notice of Federal Tax Lien, the IRS establishes its interest in the taxpayer's property as a creditor and as security for his tax debt, and publicly notifies the taxpayer's other creditors of its claim. A federal tax lien automatically arises after:

- The IRS assesses the taxpayer's liability,
- The IRS sends a notice and demand for payment, and
- The taxpayer neglects to pay the debt.

Once these requirements are met, a lien is created for the amount of the taxpayer's debt. The lien is a public document, to alert creditors that the government has a legal right to the taxpayer's property.

The lien attaches to all the taxpayer's property, such as a house or car, and to all the taxpayer's rights to property (such as accounts receivable, in the case of a business).

> **Example:** William owes the IRS $85,000 in back taxes from a prior year in which he won a big lottery prize. Although he filed his taxes on time, William does not want to pay the debt, and he ignores the IRS bills that come to his home. William's home is worth $250,000, and he has over $175,000 in equity in the home. The IRS files a Notice of Federal Tax Lien against William's assets. It is on public record, and the tax lien will give the government the authority to seize William's house if he fails to pay his delinquent debt. William is embarrassed by the public nature of the lien, and contacts the IRS to make payment arrangements. Within six months, he has paid his tax debt in full, which is the easiest and fastest way to eliminate a federal tax lien. The IRS releases William's lien within 30 days after he has paid his tax debt.

The general filing threshold for the amount taxpayers can owe before a Notice of Federal Tax Lien is issued has been increased from $5,000 to $10,000 in most cases. Once a lien is filed, the IRS generally cannot release it until the taxes are paid in full or until the government may no longer legally collect the tax.

Notice of Levy

An IRS seizure (or a levy) is the legal act of confiscating a taxpayer's property to satisfy a tax debt. The IRS may issue levies to attach a taxpayer's assets, such as wages, pension benefits, annuities, or Social Security benefits, that result in multiple payments over many years.

There are special rules regarding IRS seizures. The IRS generally must wait at least 30 days from the date of the notice of intent to levy before it can make a seizure. However, if the IRS has determined that the collection of tax is in jeopardy, it may immediately seize property without the normal waiting period. Typically, the IRS may not seize property in the following circumstances:

- When there is a pending installment agreement,
- While a taxpayer's appeal is pending,
- During the consideration of an offer in compromise,
- During a bankruptcy (unless the seizure is authorized by the bankruptcy court),
- If the taxpayer's liability is $5,000 or less in a seizure of real property,
- While innocent spouse claims are pending.

The IRS may not seize a main home without prior approval from the IRS Area Director; judicial approval is also required for the seizure of a primary residence. Further, the following items are <u>exempt</u> from IRS levy:

- Wearing apparel and school books.
- Fuel, provisions (food), furniture, personal effects in the taxpayer's household, arms for personal use, or livestock, up to an allowable amount.
- Books and tools necessary for the trade, business, or profession of the taxpayer, up to an allowable amount.
- Undelivered mail.
- Unemployment benefits.
- Workers' compensation, including amounts payable to dependents.
- Certain annuity or pension payments, but only if payable by the Army, Navy, Air Force, Coast Guard, or under the Railroad Retirement Act or Railroad Unemployment Insurance Act. Traditional and Roth IRAs are not exempt from levy.
- Judgments for the support of minor children (child support).
- Certain public assistance and welfare payments, and amounts payable for Supplemental Security Income for the aged, blind, and disabled under the Social Security Act. Regular Social Security payments are not exempt from levy.

If an IRS levy creates a severe economic hardship, it may be released at the discretion of the IRS. A levy release does not mean the taxpayer is exempt from paying the balance due.

> **Example:** Bradley owes $295,000 to the IRS because of a failed business venture. Bradley closed the business and starting working for a department store as a manager. The IRS issues a continuous levy under IRC §6331 to Bradley's employer and the department store withholds a portion of his paycheck every month for his outstanding tax debt, remitting the amount to the IRS each month for the next four years. In 2022, Bradley's teenage daughter, Mandy, becomes ill, and as a result, Bradley's living expenses increase significantly due to Mandy's large medical bills. The IRS levy is now causing a severe economic hardship to the taxpayer. Bradley contacts the IRS and asks the IRS to release the levy. The IRS determines that Bradley is experiencing severe economic hardship, and the IRS agrees to stop the wage garnishment temporarily.

IRS Summons

If a taxpayer or other witness refuses to comply with requests for IRS records or other information, the IRS has the power to issue a summons. An IRS examiner may issue an administrative summons to the taxpayer (or other third parties).

An administrative summons directs the person summoned to appear before the examiner and testify or produce information. IRC §7602 authorizes the IRS to issue summonses for the following purposes:

- To ascertain the correctness of any return,
- To prepare a return where none has been made,
- To determine the liability of a person for internal revenue tax,
- To determine the liability at law or in equity of a transferee or fiduciary of a person in respect of any internal revenue tax,
- To collect any internal revenue tax liability, or
- To inquire into any civil or criminal offense connected with the administration or enforcement of the internal revenue law.

The most common IRS summons is Form 2039. The form contains a blank area within which the IRS can describe the information or records being summoned. The IRS will use a summons to request documents and records from taxpayers and businesses, but usually only after other methods have been unsuccessful.[67] A summons cannot require a witness to prepare or create documents, including tax returns, which do not exist.

A summons cannot be issued solely to harass a taxpayer or to pressure the taxpayer into settling a dispute. The IRS must follow precise procedures in serving a summons upon a taxpayer or third party. The summons must be delivered in person to the taxpayer or left at his last known residence. Third-party record-keepers may also be served by certified or registered mail. When a summons is served in-person to a taxpayer or left at his home, the person serving the summons must sign a certificate of service.

This certificate must include the date and time the summons was served, the manner in which it was served (such as the address and whether it was left with a person), the server's title, and the server's signature. The certificate of service certifies that the taxpayer has been properly served. The server must also sign a certificate of notice when he serves a summons on a third-party record keeper.

An individual has the right to contest a summons based on various technical, procedural, or constitutional grounds. However, if a taxpayer or other witness fails to respond to a summons within the prescribed period, the IRS may seek judicial enforcement through a U.S. district court.

---

[67] During the audit process, the IRS will often issue an Information Document Request (IDR), asking the taxpayer for certain records. An IDR is issued on IRS Form 4564, and this is how the IRS requests information from a taxpayer or a business. If the taxpayer does not respond or comply to the Information Document Request, the IRS has the right to issue a summons.

Note: In recent years the IRS has given more scrutiny to cryptocurrency exchanges. The Department of Justice filed a court petition, asking the IRS to serve a "John Doe" summons on Coinbase, a popular cryptocurrency exchange. This "John Doe" summons directed Coinbase to produce records identifying U.S. taxpayers who have used its services. The summons was triggered after the IRS found instances of tax evasion involving Coinbase customers. Coinbase initially opposed the summons, arguing that it was too broad. The IRS subsequently narrowed the demand to a smaller number of heavy traders, and Coinbase eventually produced the requested records.

Taxpayer Collection Appeal Rights

A taxpayer may appeal an IRS collection action to the IRS Independent Office of Appeals. The Independent Office of Appeals is separate from and independent of the IRS Collection offices that initiate collection actions. The IRS ensures the independence of the Appeals office through a strict policy prohibiting ex parte communication with the IRS Collection office about the accuracy of the facts or the merits of each case.

Note: An "*ex parte communication*" is one that takes place between any IRS Appeals employee and employees of other IRS functions, without the taxpayer or his representative being given a chance to participate in the communication, whether it is written, on the phone, or in person.

The two main ways that taxpayers use to appeal an IRS collection action are collection due process and the collection appeals program. The first method is a **Collection Due Process** hearing, or a "CDP hearing." The second avenue is the **Collection Appeals Program**, or CAP. There are drawbacks and benefits to both of these appeals options.

Collection Due Process Hearings (CDP)

A taxpayer who wants to protest an IRS collection notice may complete Form 12153, *Request for a Collection Due Process or Equivalent Hearing,* and submit it to the address listed on the IRS notice. CDP procedures are available to taxpayers who have received any of the following notices:

- Final Notice of Intent to Levy and Notice of Your Right to a Hearing.
- Notice of Federal Tax Lien and Your Right to a Hearing.
- Notice of Jeopardy Levy and Right of Appeal.
- Notice of Levy on Your State Tax Refund – Notice of Your Right to a Hearing.
- Post Levy Collection Due Process (CDP) Notice.

A taxpayer has 30 days from the date of a collection notice to request a CDP hearing. Before the hearing, the taxpayer may attempt to work out a solution with the Collection office that sent the notice. If the issue cannot be resolved, the case will be forwarded to IRS Appeals for the taxpayer (or the taxpayer's representative) to schedule a conference with an Appeals officer. The conference may be by telephone, correspondence, or face-to-face for taxpayers who qualify.

Many taxpayers ignore IRS notices until they receive a final notice or a notice of intent to levy. Often, by the time this happens, it is too late to help the taxpayer solve these issues, and the IRS has already begun the collection process in earnest. A CDP hearing gives taxpayers a chance to issues that may be discussed during a collection due process hearing include:

- Whether or not the taxpayer paid all the tax owed,
- Whether the IRS assessed tax and sent the levy notice when the taxpayer was in bankruptcy,
- Whether the IRS made a procedural error in the assessment,
- Whether the time to collect the tax (the statute of limitations) has expired,
- Whether the taxpayer wishes to discuss collection options,
- Whether the taxpayer wishes to make a spousal defense (innocent spouse relief).

Example: Jennifer was married to Richard in 2019-2021, when Richard was the owner of a farming business that was very profitable for those years, but Richard reported only a small fraction of its taxable income for the business on the Schedule C. Jennifer was not involved in the business at all and no indication as to the profitability of the business. Jennifer and Richard filed jointly for all of those years. On March 31, 2022, Jennifer filed for divorce from Richard. The divorce became final on July 31, 2022. Several months later Jennifer receives a notice from the IRS, informing her of their intent to assert taxes and penalties against her and her ex-husband totaling $175,000 based on the unreported income of the business. Jennifer attempted to contact Richard about the notice, but he ignored her, and the deadline for Jennifer to challenge the proposed assessment has passed. The IRS eventually assessed income tax and penalties against both Jennifer and Richard. Following the assessment, Jennifer timely requested a collection due process (CDP) hearing because she wants to make a spousal defense claiming the business was her ex-husband's and not hers and that she was not aware of the high level of profitability of the business.

In a CDP hearing, a taxpayer may request specific action regarding a lien against his or her property or a collection alternative (installment agreement, offer in compromise, etc.). For example, a taxpayer may request a lien withdrawal on the grounds the IRS filed the Notice of Federal Tax Lien prematurely or did not follow established procedures. Alternatively, a taxpayer may request a lien discharge that removes a federal tax lien from a specific property, so it can be sold to satisfy the debt.

Example: Elwood owes $100,000 in delinquent taxes to the IRS. The IRS issues a notice of federal tax lien on Elwood's vacation condo in Florida. Elwood's attorney attends a CDP hearing and asks that the lien be discharged so Elwood may sell the condo and use the sales proceeds to pay the income tax he owes. The IRS Appeals officer agrees and releases the lien so that the property may be sold. Elwood uses the proceeds from the sale to pay his delinquent tax debt.

After a CDP hearing, the Appeals officer will issue a written determination letter. If the taxpayer disagrees with the determination, he can request judicial review by petitioning the U.S. Tax Court. The petition must be made within the time period specified in the Appeals' determination letter. The taxpayer cannot raise any issues with the Tax Court that he did not already raise during the appeals hearing.

If a taxpayer timely files a CDP hearing request, no collection action can be taken until a final determination is made following the hearing or a subsequent appeal to the Tax Court.

Collection Appeals Program (CAP)

The collection appeals program (CAP) is generally quicker than a CDP hearing and available for a broader range of collection actions. However, there is a significant drawback, and that is that the taxpayer cannot appeal an adverse decision made in a CAP heading. CAP is available in the following instances:

- Before or after the IRS levies or seizes a taxpayer's property.
- After the termination of an installment agreement.
- After the rejection of an installment agreement.

To appeal an installment agreement that has been rejected or that the IRS is proposing to be modified or terminated, the taxpayer should appeal by completing Form 9423, *Collection Appeal Request.* The form should be submitted within 30 days to the IRS office or revenue officer who took action regarding the installment agreement.

Example: Walter applied for an installment agreement in March 2022. Two months later, he was a victim of wire fraud, and his entire bank account was drained suddenly without his knowledge. It took Walter several months to correct the problem. In the meantime, he received notification that his installment agreement had been rescinded. Walter wants to appeal the cancellation of his installment agreement. He files Form 9423, *Collection Appeal Request.* He will explain his circumstances to an IRS employee and request reinstatement of his installment agreement.

Example: Danton was paying his tax debt under an installment agreement and missed a few payments, because he lost his job. The IRS sent a notice that the installment agreement was canceled, and he must now pay the full outstanding balance. Danton appealed the termination of the installment agreement by filing Form 9423 and requesting an appeal. In the meantime, he got a new job, and notified the IRS that he could begin making monthly payments again. Danton's appeal was granted, and his installment agreement was reinstated.

Form 9423, *Collection Appeal Request,* is also used in cases of liens, levies, and seizures. Generally, the taxpayer would first try to resolve the disagreement by telephone with an IRS employee, manager, or revenue officer. If the issue cannot be resolved, the taxpayer would submit a written request for Appeals consideration by completing Form 9423. The taxpayer must explain why he disagrees with the collection action and how he proposes to resolve his tax problem.

In an appeals hearing, a taxpayer may represent himself, or he may appoint a qualified representative (attorney, CPA, EA, spouse, or a family member). In the case of a business, the entity may be represented by a regular full-time employee, a general partner, or a bona fide officer. Once the IRS makes a determination under CAP, it is binding on both the taxpayer and the IRS. The determination is final and cannot be appealed to the U.S. Tax Court.

Abatement of Penalties and Interest

In certain cases, the IRS will waive or abate penalties and interest assessed against a taxpayer. A taxpayer may qualify for penalty relief in the following circumstances:

- **Disaster-related relief:** When the penalty is incurred due to a major disaster or emergency affecting a large number of taxpayers in a given geographical area. Relief is often provided in the form of extensions of time to file or pay.
- **Due to an IRS error:** When the penalty is due to an IRS computation or assessment error, or when the penalty is incurred as the result of erroneous written advice provided by an IRS employee.
- **Reliance on a tax advisor:** When the penalty is incurred as a result of the taxpayer relying on the advice of a tax advisor. This generally involves accuracy-related penalties and is limited to issues that are considered highly technical or complicated.

Penalty relief is most commonly granted if the taxpayer can demonstrate reasonable cause. This is when a taxpayer has established that, despite the "exercise of ordinary business care and prudence," he was assessed a penalty due to circumstances beyond his control.

The First Time (Penalty) Abate (FTA) waiver is an administrative waiver that the IRS may grant to relieve taxpayers from failure-to-file, failure-to-pay and failure-to-deposit penalties if certain criteria are met. An FTA waiver will only apply if none of the aforementioned penalties were assessed in the prior three years. The IRS will consider the FTA option only if the taxpayer has filed all returns and paid, (or arranged to pay), all tax currently due.

> **Example:** Kelly has always filed her tax returns on time and paid the amounts that she owes by the filing deadline. She self-prepares her own tax return using online software. She owes $900 in tax and fills out the information for the tax to be automatically withdrawn from her bank account when she submits her return. She attempts to submit the return, and believes that she has filed it, but she does not realize that her return was not submitted. She doesn't realize her mistake until June 15, well after the filing deadline has passed. She submits her return as soon as she realizes her mistake, but the IRS still assesses a $450 failure-to-file and an $8 failure-to-pay penalty, as well as $5 of interest on the amount due, because she did not file her return and pay the amount due by the deadline. She contacts the IRS customer service line and requests an FTA. Since Kelly has always had an excellent compliance history, the FTA is granted, and the failure to file and failure to pay penalties are waived. Kelly will still be required to pay the small amount of interest due.

Abatement of Interest: The IRS will not abate *interest* using the FTA procedure or for reasonable cause. Interest may be abated in the following instances:

- When it is excessive, barred by statute, or erroneously or illegally assessed,
- When it is assessed on an erroneous refund,
- When it was incurred on an account while the taxpayer was in a combat zone or in a federally declared disaster area.

Further, the IRS will waive interest that is the result of certain errors or delays caused by an IRS employee. The IRS will only abate the interest if there was an unreasonable error or delay in performing a managerial or ministerial act (defined below). The taxpayer cannot have caused any significant aspect of the error or delay. The interest can be abated only if it relates to taxes for which a notice of deficiency is required, which includes income taxes and estate and gift taxes.

> **Definition:** A "managerial" act is an administrative act that occurs during the processing of the taxpayer's case involving the temporary or permanent loss of records or the exercise of judgment or discretion relating to the management of personnel.

> **Example:** A revenue agent is examining Catrina's tax return. During the course of the examination, the agent is sent to an extended training course in another state. The agent's supervisor decides not to reassign the case, so the examination is unreasonably delayed until the agent returns. Interest caused by the delay can be abated since the decision to send the agent to the training class and the decision not to reassign the case are both managerial acts.

> **Definition:** A "ministerial" act is a procedural or mechanical act that does not involve the exercise of judgment or discretion, and that occurs during the processing of the taxpayer's case.

> **Example:** Bryant moves to another state before the IRS selects his tax return for examination. Notice of the examination was sent to his old address and then forwarded to his new address. When Bryant gets the letter, he responds with a request that the examination be transferred to the area office closest to his new address. The examination group manager approves his request. However, the original examination manager forgets about the transfer and fails to transfer the file for six months. The failed transfer is a ministerial act. The IRS can reduce the interest Bryant owes because of the unreasonable delay in transferring the case.

A taxpayer may request an abatement of penalties and/or interest on Form 843, *Claim for Refund and Request for Abatement.* The taxpayer should file the claim with the IRS service center where the examination was affected by the error or delay.

If a request for abatement of interest is denied, an appeal can be made to the IRS Independent Office of Appeals. When a portion of interest is abated, the IRS must recalculate the amount of remaining interest the taxpayer owes.

Seeking Relief from Joint Liability

Married taxpayers often file jointly because of benefits this filing status affords. In the case of a joint return, both taxpayers are liable for the tax and any interest or penalties, even if they later separate or divorce. "Joint and several liability" means that each taxpayer is legally responsible for the entire liability.

This is true even if only one spouse earned all the income, or if a divorce decree states that a former spouse is or is not responsible for any amounts due on previously filed joint returns. In some cases, however, a spouse who filed joint returns can receive relief from joint and several liability:

1. **Innocent Spouse Relief**: Provides relief from additional tax if a spouse or former spouse failed to report income or claimed improper deductions.
2. **Separation of Liability Relief:** Provides for the allocation of additional tax owed between the taxpayer and his spouse or former spouse because an item was not reported properly on a joint return. The tax allocated to the taxpayer is the amount for which he is responsible.
3. **Equitable Relief:** This type of relief may apply when a taxpayer does not qualify for innocent spouse relief or separation of liability relief for items not reported properly on a joint return and generally attributable to the taxpayer's spouse. A taxpayer may also qualify for equitable relief if the correct amount of tax is reported on his joint return but the tax remains unpaid.

Requesting Innocent Spouse Relief

The taxpayer must meet all of the following conditions in order to qualify for innocent spouse relief:

- The taxpayer filed a joint return that has an understatement of tax directly related to his spouse's erroneous items.
- The taxpayer establishes that, at the time he or she signed the joint return, the taxpayer did not know, and had no reason to know, that there was an understatement of tax.
- Taking into account all the facts and circumstances, it would be unfair for the IRS to hold the taxpayer liable for the understatement.
- A request for innocent spouse relief must generally be filed within two years after the IRS first takes collection action against the requesting spouse.

In order to apply for innocent spouse relief, a taxpayer must submit Form 8857, *Request for Innocent Spouse Relief*, and sign it under penalty of perjury. One form can cover multiple years.

A request for innocent spouse relief will be denied if the IRS proves that property was transferred between the taxpayer and the spouse or former spouse as part of a fraudulent scheme to defraud the IRS or another third party. If a taxpayer requests innocent spouse relief, the IRS cannot enforce collection action while the request is pending, but interest and penalties continue to accrue.

Example: Bettie and Christian are married and file jointly. At the time Bettie signed their joint return, she was unaware her husband had a gambling problem. The IRS examined their return and determined that Christian's unreported gambling winnings were $30,000. Christian kept the gambling proceeds for himself and hid the bank statements from his wife. Bettie was able to prove that she did not know about, and had no reason to know about, the additional $30,000 because Christian had concealed his gambling winnings. The understatement of tax due to the $30,000 qualifies for innocent spouse relief.

Requesting Separation of Liability Relief

To qualify for "separation of liability" relief, the taxpayer must have filed a joint return and be no longer married (including a taxpayer who is widowed), legally separated, or living apart for the 12 months prior to the filing of a claim. Living apart does not include a spouse who is only temporarily absent from the household, in which case the taxpayer would not qualify for separation of liability relief.

The spouse or former spouse who is applying for **separation of liability** relief must not have known about the understatement of tax at the time of signing the return. An exception is made for spousal abuse or domestic violence, if the taxpayer had been afraid that failing to sign the return could result in harm or retaliation.

A request for separation of liability relief must generally be filed within two years after the IRS first takes collection action against the requesting spouse.

> **Example:** Charlotte and Darwin have lived apart for several years and legally divorced on December 1, 2022. In the tax year before they separated, they filed a joint return showing Charlotte's wages of $35,000 and Darwin's self-employment income of $15,000. Their prior-year joint return was later selected for audit. During the audit, the IRS examiner found that Darwin failed to report $25,000 of self-employment income, which resulted in a $7,500 understatement of tax. Since she is now divorced from Darwin, Charlotte filed Form 8857 to request relief by separation of liability. However, the IRS was able to prove that Charlotte knew about the $25,000 of additional income because it was deposited into their joint bank account, and she had full ownership, access and use of the funds. She is not eligible for separation of liability relief, and the IRS denies her request.

Requesting Equitable Relief

A taxpayer who does not qualify for innocent spouse relief or separation of liability relief may qualify for equitable relief. The taxpayer must establish, based upon all the facts and circumstances, that it would be unfair to hold him liable for the understatement or underpayment of tax.

The IRS considers a taxpayer's current marital status, whether there is a legal obligation under a divorce decree to pay the tax, and whether he would suffer significant economic hardship if relief were not granted. The following factors weigh *in favor* of equitable relief:

- Abuse by the spouse or former spouse,

- Poor mental or physical health on the date the taxpayer signed the return or requested relief.

> **Note:** Unlike innocent spouse relief or separation of liability, if you qualify for equitable relief, you can get relief from an understatement of tax or an underpayment of tax. (An underpayment of tax is an amount properly shown on the return, but not paid.)

> **Example:** Shanice and Wyatt were married in 2019 and filed a joint return that showed they owed $12,000 in unpaid income tax. Shanice had $7,000 of her own money, and she took out a loan to pay the remaining $5,000. Shanice gave Wyatt the money to pay their full $12,000 tax liability. Without telling Shanice, Wyatt gambled away the entire $12,000 rather than paying their tax liability. The couple divorced on January 15, 2022, and the IRS later selects their joint return for audit. Shanice did not know at the time she signed the return that the tax would not be paid. These facts indicate to the IRS that it may be unfair to hold Shanice liable for the underpayment. Shanice's request for equitable relief is granted.

Congress has expanded the amount of time to request equitable relief in the Taxpayer First Act. A taxpayer seeking relief from a balance due has up to ten years to file a request, the same period the IRS has to collect the tax. If the taxpayer is making a claim for a refund, he must file his request within the statute of limitations for refunds.

More time may be allowed for taxpayers who are physically or mentally unable to manage their financial affairs or who live in federally-declared disaster areas.

Injured Spouse Claims

Innocent spouse relief should not be confused with an injured spouse claim. A taxpayer may qualify as an injured spouse if he filed a joint return and his share of the refund was applied against past due amounts owed by his spouse.

An injured spouse may be entitled to recoup only his share of a tax refund. When a joint return is filed, and the refund is used to pay one spouse's past-due federal tax, state income tax, child support, spousal support, or federal nontax debt (such as a delinquent student loan), the other spouse may be considered an injured spouse. The injured spouse can request his share of the refund using *Form 8379, Injured Spouse Allocation.*

> **Example:** Andrea and Cesar marry and file jointly in 2022. Unknown to Andrea, Cesar has unpaid child support as well as delinquent student loan debt. Their entire refund is retained to pay Cesar's outstanding debts. Andrea may qualify for injured spouse treatment and recoup her share of the tax refund. Andrea can file Form 8379 to recoup her share of the refund. The IRS will keep Cesar's share of the refund to pay his delinquent debts.

Offer in Compromise Program

An offer in compromise (OIC) is an agreement between a taxpayer and the IRS that settles the taxpayer's tax liabilities for less than the full amount owed. Submitting an offer application does not guarantee that the IRS will accept the offer.[68] It begins a process of evaluation and verification by the IRS.

Generally, the IRS will accept an offer if it represents the most the agency can expect to collect within the remaining collection statute of limitations. Absent special circumstances, an offer will not be accepted if the IRS believes that the liability can be paid in full as a lump sum or through a payment agreement. The IRS will consider each taxpayer's unique set of facts and

---

[68] The acceptance rate of OIC offers from the Internal Revenue Service averaged around 32% in the previous year.

circumstances in determining whether to grant an OIC, including his ability to pay, income, expenses, and asset equity.

To apply for an OIC on the grounds of "doubt as to collectibility" or "exceptional circumstances," a taxpayer must submit an application fee and initial nonrefundable payment along with Form 656, *Offer in Compromise*. Fees may be waived for low-income taxpayers. There is no fee required to apply for an OIC on the grounds of "doubt as to liability," and Form 656-L is used instead.

The taxpayer may appeal a rejected offer in compromise within 30 days. An offer in compromise can be applied to all taxes, including interest and penalties. A taxpayer may submit an OIC on three grounds: (1) doubt as to collectibility, (2) doubt as to liability and (3) effective tax administration.

Doubt as to Collectibility

Doubt exists that the taxpayer could ever pay the full amount of tax liability owed within the remainder of the statutory period for collection. This is the most commonly submitted OIC, and it is utilized when a taxpayer does not have enough in assets and income to pay the full amount.

> **Example:** Constance owes $80,000 for unpaid tax liabilities and agrees that the tax she owes is correct. Constance is terminally ill and cannot work. She does not own a home, and does not have the assets or the ability to pay the liability now, or through monthly installment payments. Constance may qualify for an OIC under "doubt of collectability."

Doubt as to Liability

Doubt as to liability exists where there is a genuine dispute as to the existence or amount of the correct tax debt under the law. A legitimate doubt must exist that the assessed tax liability is correct. The taxpayer must provide a written statement explaining why the tax debt or portion of the tax debt is incorrect. In addition, the taxpayer should provide supporting documentation or evidence that supports the inaccuracy of the disputed debt.

> **Note:** To request an OIC under "doubt as to liability," the taxpayer will need to complete a *Form 656-L, Offer in Compromise (Doubt as to Liability).* This is a different form than is used for other types of offers, and *no fee* is required when this form is submitted.

> **Example:** Darla was the vice-president of a corporation from 2006 to 2021. After her departure from the company, the business started having financial difficulties. In 2022, the corporation accrued unpaid payroll taxes, and Darla was later assessed a trust fund recovery penalty. However, Darla had resigned from the board of directors prior to any of these delinquent payroll taxes accruing. Since there is legitimate doubt that the assessed tax liability is correct, she may apply for an OIC under doubt as to liability.

Exceptional Circumstances (Effective Tax Administration)

This type of OIC is rare. This type of OIC can be based on the client's financial hardship or on public policy or equitable considerations. In this case, there is potential to collect the full amount of the tax owed, but an exceptional circumstance exists. A taxpayer must demonstrate that the collection of the tax would create a serious economic hardship or would be unfair.

> **Example:** Valerie and Walter Smith have sufficient assets to satisfy their tax liability. However, they provide full-time care to their dependent child, who has a serious chronic illness. The unpaid taxes were a result of the Smiths providing necessary medical care for their sick child. They will need to continue to use their assets to provide for basic living expenses and ongoing care for the child. There is no doubt that the tax is correct, but to pay the tax would endanger the life of their child and would create a serious hardship.

Unit 9: Study Questions

(Test yourself and then check the correct answers at the end of this chapter.)

1. Aziza owes $20,000 of unpaid federal tax liabilities. She agrees she owes the tax, but she has a serious medical problem, and her monthly income does not meet her necessary living expenses. She does not own any real estate and does not have the ability to fully pay the liability now or through monthly installment payments. What type of offer in compromise may she qualify for?

A. Doubt as to liability.
B. Doubt as to collectibility.
C. Effective tax administration.
D. Collection advocate procedure.

2. Douglas owed $5,500 in back taxes, and he wants to set up an installment agreement, because he cannot pay the full amount currently. The installment agreement will allow Douglas to do all of the following except:

A. Pay his tax debt in equal monthly payments over a period of time.
B. Eliminate interest accruals while the agreement is active.
C. Pay his tax debt by check, payroll deduction, or direct debit.
D. Avoid IRS collection actions, including levies.

3. Cohen is married to Emma, and they live together and file joint returns. In which scenario would Cohen qualify as an <u>injured spouse</u>?

A. Cohen files a joint return, and his share of the refund is applied against Emma's past-due student loans.
B. Cohen files a joint return with Emma, and one of them fails to report income.
C. Cohen files a separate return and has the refund offset by his own past-due student loan obligations.
D. Cohen files for bankruptcy protection.

4. Belinda and Neil file jointly. They report $15,000 of income, but Belinda knows that Neil is not reporting $3,000 of dividends. The income is not hers, and she has no access to it since it is in Neil's separate bank account. She signs the joint return. The return is later chosen for examination, and penalties are assessed. Does Belinda qualify for innocent spouse relief?

A. Yes, because she can file for divorce later.
B. Yes, because she had no control over the income.
C. No, but she is eligible for injured spouse relief.
D. No, because she knew about the understated income.

5. When can the IRS issue a summons?

A. When a taxpayer refuses to comply with IRS requests for records or other information.
B. When a taxpayer immediately complies with IRS requests for records or other information.
C. When a taxpayer requests an enrolled practitioner to represent them at a hearing.
D. When a taxpayer chooses not to file a return.

6. If the IRS rejects an offer in compromise, a taxpayer may appeal within:

A. 30 days.
B. 60 days.
C. 90 days.
D. 120 days.

7. If the IRS has filed a notice of seizure, how long must it wait before <u>actually seizing</u> a taxpayer's nonexempt property?

A. Immediately, with the exception of a taxpayer's home, which requires judicial approval.
B. Seven days.
C. 30 days.
D. 60 days.

8. A levy allows the IRS to:

A. Publicly notify a taxpayer's creditors of a claim against his property.
B. Confiscate and sell a taxpayer's property to satisfy a tax debt.
C. Collect tax beyond the statute of limitations.
D. Sell property on behalf of the taxpayer.

9. Payton's only income comes from wages. He has a high-paying job as a medical doctor, but did not properly estimate his withholding for several years. As a result, he currently owes $255,000 to the IRS. He would like to set up an installment agreement. Which of the following statements regarding his payment options is <u>correct</u>?

A. Payton may qualify for an installment agreement for this amount of unpaid tax.
B. Payton is not eligible for an installment agreement because he owes more than $100,000.
C. Payton may qualify for an installment agreement, but an offer in compromise must first be completed.
D. Payton must enroll in EFTPS and have automatic withdrawals in order to have his installment agreement approved.

10. Farida is an enrolled agent. She prepared a tax return for her client, Josue. Josue has a balance due of $25,900, but he cannot pay the entire amount upon filing and would like to set up an installment agreement. Which of the following is required before an installment agreement will be approved?

A. Since Josue owes more than $25,000, the taxpayer must submit a paper application.
B. Josue must authorize the installment agreement by contacting the IRS directly.
C. Josue must be in filing compliance.
D. Josue must be a U.S. Citizen.

11. "Separation of liability" relief does not apply to taxpayers who are:

A. Divorced.
B. Legally separated.
C. Widowed.
D. Single (never married).

12. The IRS generally does not pursue collection enforcement action against a taxpayer who has been placed in "currently not collectible" status for a minimum of:

A. Six months
B. One year
C. Two years
D. Five years

13. Sheila and Dale were married in 2022. They are owed a refund on their joint return, but the refund is offset against Dale's past-due child support. Does Sheila have any recourse to recover her portion of the refund?

A. Since they filed jointly, Sheila's portion of the refund cannot be recovered.
B. Sheila may be eligible for injured spouse relief.
C. Sheila may be eligible for innocent spouse relief.
D. Sheila may be eligible for equitable relief.

14. All of the following property is exempt from an IRS levy except:

A. Undelivered mail.
B. Child support payments.
C. Social Security payments.
D. Unemployment benefits.

15. The statute of limitations on collection activity can be suspended in certain instances. The ten-year collection period may be suspended in each of the following instances except:

A. While the IRS considers a request for an installment agreement.
B. While a collection due process (CDP) hearing is pending.
C. While the taxpayer is in prison.
D. While the taxpayer lives outside the United States.

16. Rosalyn is receiving a federal tax refund this year. Which of the following methods is not available for her to receive her refund?

A. She may apply the refund to next year's estimated tax.
B. She may receive the refund as a direct deposit to her retirement account.
C. She may use her refund to purchase U.S. Series I Savings Bonds.
D. She may direct deposit her refund to her credit card account.

17. Which of the following amounts is the IRS least likely to challenge when evaluating a taxpayer's offer in compromise?

A. Rent.
B. Prescription drugs.
C. Child support.
D. Food.

18. Ignacio files his tax return on time, but does not pay the $750 balance due. How would the IRS begin the collection process against Ignacio?

A. With an email to Ignacio shortly after he files his tax return.
B. With a certified letter, immediately after Ignacio's tax return is processed and flagged.
C. With a written examination notice when Ignacio is notified of the possibility of an audit.
D. With a notice and demand for payment mailed to Ignacio.

19. All of the following statements regarding IRS installment agreements are correct except:

A. During the course of the installment agreement, penalties and interest continue to accrue.
B. A taxpayer who owes $10,000 or less in taxes will be automatically approved for an installment agreement if certain requirements are met.
C. An installment agreement allows a taxpayer to pay a set amount toward a tax liability on a monthly basis.
D. An IRS levy may be served during an installment agreement.

20. The IRS may legally seize property in which of the following circumstances?

A. If the collection of tax is in jeopardy.
B. During the consideration of an offer in compromise.
C. If the taxpayer's liability is $5,000 or less in a seizure of real property (real estate).
D. While an innocent spouse claim is pending.

21. Penalties and interest continue to accrue on a taxpayer's unpaid tax liability in which of the following instances?

A. When an installment agreement is in place.
B. When a taxpayer has been declared currently not collectible.
C. When a taxpayer requests innocent spouse relief.
D. All of the above.

22. Jason cannot pay his tax liability because of a serious health issue. How much extra time will the IRS grant for Jason to pay his tax liability under the undue hardship extension?

A. Three months.
B. Six months.
C. One year.
D. 18 months.

Unit 9: Quiz Answers

1. The answer is B. Aziza may apply for an offer in compromise under doubt as to collectibility. Doubt exists that she could ever pay the full amount of tax liability owed within the remainder of the statutory period for collection.

2. The answer is B. An installment agreement will allow Douglas to pay his tax liability over a period of time if he cannot pay the amount when it is due. During the time an installment agreement is in place, penalties and interest continue to accrue.

3. The answer is A. If Cohen files a joint return with his wife, and his share of the refund is applied against Emma's past-due student loans, then he would qualify as an "injured spouse." A taxpayer may qualify as an injured spouse if he filed a joint return and his share of the refund was applied against past due amounts owed by a spouse. The injured spouse may be entitled to recoup only his share of a tax refund.

4. The answer is D. Belinda is not eligible for innocent spouse relief because she knew about the understated income. She signed the return knowing that the income was not included, so the IRS will not grant her relief.

5. The answer is A. The IRS can use its summons authority when a taxpayer or other witness refuses to comply with IRS requests for records or other information. Answer "B" is incorrect, because a summons would not be used in a situation where the taxpayer immediately complied with a records request. Answer "C" is incorrect, because a taxpayer can always seek representation from an enrolled practitioner to represent them in any tax matter before the IRS. Answer "D" is incorrect, because an IRS summons cannot force or compel a taxpayer to file a return.

6. The answer is A. The IRS requires a taxpayer whose offer in compromise has been rejected to file an appeal within 30 days.

7. The answer is C. After the IRS has filed a notice of intent to seize, it must wait 30 days before actually seizing a taxpayer's nonexempt property. It legally cannot seize items such as clothing, food, fuel, furniture, and personal effects up to a specified, inflation-adjusted amount. Undelivered mail, books, and tools of the trade needed for the taxpayer's business are also exempt, up to a certain amount. Further, the IRS cannot seize unemployment benefits, worker's compensation, child support payments, and certain disability and public assistance payments. However, most Social Security benefits and retirement fund proceeds may be seized to fulfill a taxpayer's debt obligation. Before a taxpayer's home is seized, there generally must be judicial approval.

8. The answer is B. A levy allows the IRS to confiscate and sell property to satisfy a tax debt. An IRS levy refers to the *actual seizing* of property authorized by an earlier tax lien. Answer "A" refers to a lien, which gives the IRS a legal claim to a taxpayer's property as security for a tax debt.

9. The answer is A. Even though he owes more than $50,000, Payton may still qualify for an installment agreement, but he will be required to fill out Form 433-F, *Collection Information Statement,* as well as 433-A, *Collection Information Statement for Wage Earners and Self-Employed Individuals.*

10. The answer is C. In order to set up an installment agreement, Josue must be in filing compliance (all tax returns must be filed). Josue must also remain tax compliant for the entire term of the installment agreement.

11. The answer is D. To qualify for separation of liability relief, the taxpayer must have filed a joint return, meaning the taxpayer must have been married at one time. Separation of liability applies to taxpayers who are no longer married (including a taxpayer who is widowed), legally separated, or living apart for the 12 months prior to the filing of a claim.

12. The answer is B. If the IRS has determined a taxpayer's status is currently not collectible, it is generally prohibited from pursuing all collection activities for at least one year, or until the taxpayer's income has increased.

13. The answer is B. Sheila may be eligible for injured spouse relief. She can file Form 8379, *Injured Spouse Allocation,* and request injured spouse relief. If married taxpayers file a joint return and the refund is offset, the injured spouse can file Form 8379 to request the portion of the refund attributed to him or her.

14. The answer is C. Regular Social Security payments are not exempt from IRS levy. Certain types of income are exempt from IRS levy, such as unemployment compensation, court-ordered child support payments, and welfare.

15. The answer is C. The ten-year collection period is not suspended when a taxpayer is in prison. The ten-year collection period may be suspended in the following cases:

- While the IRS considers a request for an installment agreement or an OIC.
- From the date a taxpayer requests a collection due process (CDP) hearing.
- For tax periods included in a bankruptcy.
- While the taxpayer is residing outside the United States.

16. The answer is D. Rosalyn may not designate a credit card account for direct deposit of their federal tax refund. However, the IRS will deposit refunds onto a prepaid debit card.

17. The answer is C. The IRS Collection Financial Standards are used to evaluate a taxpayer's ability to pay a delinquent tax liability. These standards help determine allowable living expenses that are necessary to provide for a taxpayer's (and his family's) health and welfare and/or production of income while his tax debt is being repaid. Allowances for housing, utilities, and transportation vary by location, while standard amounts are allowed nationwide for food, clothing, out-of-pocket health care expenses, and other items. Consideration is also given to the taxpayer's income, bank and retirement accounts, real estate and other assets, and outstanding debts. Further, the taxpayer may have obligations for court-ordered payments, such as child support and alimony. Since the taxpayer will have little flexibility regarding these obligations, the IRS would be unlikely to challenge amounts that are supported by evidence the taxpayer provides.

18. The answer is D. Since Ignacio did not pay in full when filing his tax return, he will receive a bill in the mail from an IRS service center. The first notice will explain the balance due and demand payment in full. It will include the amount of the tax plus any penalties and interest added to Ignacio's unpaid balance from the date the tax was due. The IRS will never email a taxpayer about an unpaid liability.

19. The answer is D. No levies may be served during installment agreements. During the course of an installment agreement, penalties and interest continue to accrue. A taxpayer who owes less than $10,000 in taxes will automatically be approved for an installment agreement under most circumstances.

20. The answer is A. The IRS may seize or levy property if the collection of tax is in jeopardy, and may do so without the normal waiting period if a jeopardy assessment has been made. Typically, the IRS may <u>not</u> seize property in the following circumstances:

- When there is a pending installment agreement.
- While a taxpayer's appeal is pending.
- During the consideration of an offer in compromise.
- During a bankruptcy (unless the seizure is authorized by the bankruptcy court).
- If the taxpayer's liability is $5,000 or less, in a seizure of real property.
- While innocent spouse claims are pending.

21. The answer is D. The IRS will continue to assess penalties and interest on a taxpayer's unpaid tax liability in most circumstances, including during the period when an installment agreement is in place, when a taxpayer has been declared "currently not collectible," and when a taxpayer requests innocent spouse relief.

22. The answer is B. The IRS generally will not grant an extension of more than six months to pay the tax due on a return. A taxpayer may file Form 1127, Application for Extension of Time for Payment of Tax Due to Hardship, to explain why he cannot pay the tax. He must provide a detailed explanation of the undue hardship that would result if he paid the tax when it is due and provide adequate documentation of his financial situation.

Unit 10: The IRS Examination Process

More Reading:
Publication 556, Examination of Returns, Appeal Rights, and Claims for Refund
Publication 1, Your Rights as a Taxpayer
Publication 3498, the Examination Process
Publication 3598, The Audit Reconsideration Process
Publication 3605, Fast Track Mediation: A Process for Prompt Resolution of Tax Issues

Overview of the IRS Audit Process

An IRS examination is also commonly called an "IRS audit." The IRS accepts most tax returns as they are filed, but selects a small percentage for examination. The IRS generally audits around 1% of the total number of individual tax returns filed. However, the IRS audit rate dropped below 1% in the last few years due to the COVID-19 pandemic.

Higher-income earners are audited more frequently than those who earned less. Returns claiming refundable credits, such as the EITC, are also audited at a higher rate than normal returns.

An IRS examination is a review of the accounts and financial information supporting the items reported on a tax return. An examination evaluates whether information on the return is being reported correctly and according to the tax laws, and verifies that the amount of tax reported is accurate. Due to disclosure requirements, the IRS will always notify a taxpayer about an examination by mail, (never by email). Filing an amended return does not affect the selection process for original returns. Amended returns go through a separate screening process and may also be selected for audit.

Selecting a return for examination does not necessarily suggest that the taxpayer has made an error or has been dishonest. However, a taxpayer's responsibility to provide support for entries, deductions, and statements made on a tax return is known as the burden of proof. The taxpayer must be able to substantiate expenses in order to deduct them. Taxpayers can usually meet their burden of proof by having the receipts for the expenses. After an examination, if any changes to a taxpayer's return are proposed, the taxpayer can either agree or disagree with the changes. If the taxpayer disagrees with the examiner's adjustments, the taxpayer can appeal the IRS's determination. This is done through the appeals process. We will cover the examination process in this chapter.

Types of Audits

There are three types of IRS examinations:

1. **Correspondence audit,** which is conducted entirely by mail,
2. **Office audit,** which takes place at a nearby IRS field office, and
3. **Field examinations,** which typically take place at the taxpayer's home or place of business.

The IRS conducts most examinations entirely by mail.[69] In these correspondence audits, a taxpayer will receive a letter asking for additional information about certain items shown on the return, such as proof of income, expenses, and itemized deductions.

Correspondence audits typically occur when there is a minor issue that the IRS needs to clarify. For example, the IRS may have detected a math error, or there may be a discrepancy between the tax return and the 1099 statements sent by brokers, banks, or mutual funds. Other times, the IRS simply requests evidence that a particular transaction has transpired as reported on the tax return.

Similar in purpose to that of formal examinations, CP-2000 notices are typically issued to a taxpayer when information on the IRS computer systems on a taxpayer differs from that on a return filed by the taxpayer.

Example: The IRS selects Evelyn's return for examination. Evelyn had claimed her older half-brother as a qualifying child based on his permanent disability, and she had also claimed head of household (HOH) status. The IRS asks for proof of disability and residency, and Evelyn provides copies of doctors' records and additional evidence that her brother lives with her full-time. The IRS accepts Evelyn's documents and closes the case as a no-change audit. Evelyn does not have to meet with the IRS auditor, as the entire audit is conducted by mail.

Example: Rocio receives a CP-2000 notice saying that she has unreported wages. Rocio carefully reads the notice and realizes that the missing Form W-2 has her name and Social Security number, but she has never worked for the company. In fact, the company is in a completely different state than where she currently resides. Someone has stolen Rocio's Social Security number. Rocio is a victim of employment-related identity theft. Her SSN is being used by another person without her permission for employment purposes. Rocio responds to the notice and also files Form 14039, Identity Theft Affidavit, reporting the identity theft. A few weeks later, the IRS sends her a letter that it has accepted her return as filed. Rocio should also consider obtaining an Identity Protection PIN (IP PIN) to protect her account against tax-related identity theft.

In an "office audit," the IRS interviews the taxpayer and inspects the taxpayer's records at an IRS office. The issue under examination is typically not a complex one. Office audits generally involve issues with Schedule A, Schedule C (small business), or rental activity on Schedule E. Office audits usually cover a few specific issues or an uncomplicated tax matter. Taxpayers can choose to represent themselves, or have an enrolled practitioner represent them.

The least common type of audit is a field audit. Field audits are the most detailed and thorough of IRS examinations. Field audits are conducted only by IRS Revenue Agents, who are highly trained and have many years of experience. Field audits may take place at:

- The taxpayer's home or place of business.
- An IRS office.
- The office of the taxpayer's authorized representative.

---

[69] The majority of IRS audits, 78.4 percent, were conducted via correspondence. The remaining 21.6 percent were conducted in the field, according to the official IRS Data Book. https://www.irs.gov/pub/irs-pdf/p55b.pdf.

If a taxpayer is selected for a field audit, the taxpayer's return will most often be examined in the area where he lives and where the books and records are located. But if the return can be examined more conveniently in another area, the taxpayer can request the audit to be transferred to that area.

> **Example:** Natalia runs a marketing business, and she frequently travels in order to meet with clients. She lives in Los Angeles; however, her CPA lives in Chicago, her old hometown. Natalia's prior-year tax return is selected for examination, and she chooses to have her CPA represent her. Her CPA requests that the examination be transferred to Chicago, where Natalia's records are located. The IRS grants the transfer, so Natalia's CPA can represent her in Chicago.

How Returns are Selected for Examination

The IRS examines a percentage of all federal tax returns to determine if income, expenses, and credits are being reported accurately. The IRS selects returns for examination using various methods, which include random sampling, computerized screening, and comparison of information received by the IRS such as Forms W-2 and 1099 (this is also called "third-party" information).

When tax returns are filed, they are compared against the norms for similar returns. The IRS selects returns for examination using a variety of methods, including:

- **Potentially Abusive/Tax Avoidance Transactions:** Some returns are selected based on information obtained by the IRS through efforts to identify promoters of and participants in abusive tax avoidance transactions.

- **Computer Scoring/DIF Score:** Returns may be chosen on the basis of computer scoring. A computer program called the Discriminant Inventory Function System (DIF) assigns a numeric score to each individual and certain corporate tax returns after they have been processed.[70]

- **Information Matching:** Some returns are examined because third-party reports, such as Forms W-2 or 1099, do not match the applicable amounts reported on the tax return.

- **Related Examinations:** Returns may be selected for audit when they involve transactions with or issues related to other taxpayers, such as business partners or investors, whose returns were selected for examination.

- **Third-Party Information:** Returns may be selected as a result of information received from other third-party sources or individuals. Sources may include state and local law enforcement agencies, public records, and individuals. The information is evaluated for reliability and accuracy before it is used as the basis of an examination (or a possible criminal investigation).

---

[70] IRS computers automatically check tax returns and assign a Discriminant Inventory Function System (DIF) score based on the probability that the return contains errors, excessive tax deductions, or other issues. This does not necessarily mean that the return was prepared incorrectly. However, the screening is intended to identify aberrations and questionable items. If a taxpayer's return is assigned a high score under the DIF system, the return has a high probability of being chosen for audit. The IRS does not release information about how it calculates a taxpayer's DIF score.

A taxpayer's odds of being audited increase if his income is over $200,000, he is self-employed, or his itemized deductions were much higher than other taxpayers with similar incomes.

Other issues that may draw IRS attention include taking large charitable deductions; claiming the home office deduction; claiming rental losses; deducting business meals, travel; claiming 100% business use of a vehicle; deducting losses for a hobby activity; running a cash business; failing to report a foreign bank account; and engaging in currency transactions.

> **Example:** Harvey is an EA with a client, Jamila, who received an audit notice this year. Jamila's prior-year tax return was selected because she had a large number of tax credits and very little taxable income. However, her tax return was prepared correctly. Jamila had adopted four special-needs children and was able to take the Earned Income Credit and a large Adoption Credit. Harvey provided proof of the adoptions to the examining officer, which resulted in a positive outcome for Jamila: a "no-change" audit.

> **Example:** Alfred embezzled money from his former employer and was arrested for felony embezzlement. The case was made public, and the police shared its information with the IRS. The IRS then contacted Alfred and proposed adjustments to his tax returns, assessing additional tax, interest, and penalties for fraud for failing to report the embezzled funds as income. This is an example of third-party information that can trigger an IRS criminal investigation.

Taxpayer Examination Rights and Obligations

The IRS chooses to conduct some audits face-to-face, which are known as field audits. After notification of the planned audit, the taxpayer or the taxpayer's representative must make an appointment to meet with the IRS examiner. Before or during an initial interview, the IRS examiner must explain the examination and collection process and the taxpayer's rights. These rights include:

- A right to professional and courteous treatment by IRS employees.

- A right to privacy and confidentiality about tax matters.

- A right to know why the IRS is asking for information, how the IRS will use it, and what will happen if the requested information is not provided.

- A right to representation, either by oneself or an authorized representative.

- A right to appeal disagreements, both within the IRS and before the courts.

During an examination, the IRS has the right to confirm every item on a taxpayer's return. Form 4564, *Information Document Request (IDR),* is used to request information from the taxpayer. The taxpayer must make available any documents the IRS requests, including providing access to bookkeeping files such as QuickBooks.

If a taxpayer fails to produce requested documents, an examiner must determine whether to issue a summons to secure the documents.

The Taxpayer's Representative

Taxpayers may always represent himself during an examination. Alternatively, the taxpayer may use a qualified representative before the IRS. The taxpayer does not have to attend the audit if the representative has the proper power of attorney authorization and is an enrolled practitioner under Circular 230, or meets one of the other qualified representative criteria (such as certain family members of the taxpayer).

Example: Kimberly is an EA. A taxpayer named Lloyd hires her to represent him before the IRS during the examination of his tax return, which he self-prepared. Lloyd does not want to attend the audit. He signs Form 2848 indicating that Kimberly is now his authorized representative for all his tax affairs. Kimberly attends the examination on Lloyd's behalf.

Example: Mitchell is a 23-year-old accounting student who is not an enrolled practitioner, but is currently studying for the CPA exam, so he has some tax knowledge. The IRS mails an audit notice to Mitchell's older sister, Aimee. Aimee does not want to speak to the IRS, so she designates Mitchell as her authorized representative by signing and submitting Form 2848 to the IRS. Mitchell may practice before the IRS in this limited circumstance because of the familial relationship with the taxpayer. Mitchell has full representation rights before the IRS with regards to his sister's tax issue.

Example: Alexander is a full-time bookkeeper who also volunteers for his favorite animal rescue organization, Tri-County Greyhound Rescue, a 501(c)(3) organization. Alexander prepares the organization's annual returns and does the monthly bookkeeping. He is not an enrolled practitioner, but he is listed as the organization's treasurer (many exempt organizations have officers who are volunteers and not paid for their services). Tri-County Greyhound Rescue receives an examination notice from the IRS during the year. Alexander files a Form 2848 for the organization, listing himself as the entity's treasurer. As an officer of the organization, Alexander has full representation rights before the IRS, and can represent the Tri-County Greyhound Rescue during the examination.

When a jointly-filed (MFJ) tax return is selected for examination, either spouse may meet with the IRS, or the qualified representative may meet with the IRS without either spouse present. Without an administrative summons, the IRS cannot compel a taxpayer to accompany an authorized representative to an examination interview.

Example: Lucia and Javier are married and have always filed jointly. During the year, Lucia and Javier receive an audit notice. Lucia tries to encourage Javier to hire a representative, but Javier refuses to respond to the notice or participate in the audit process. Since it is a joint return, both spouses are jointly and severally liable for all the items shown on the return. Lucia contacts Mohammed, a licensed CPA, and hires him to represent her during the audit process. Mohammed obtains a signed Form 2848 from Lucia, and speaks with the IRS on his client's behalf. Mohammed does not represent Javier; he only represents Lucia. Lucia can have Mohammed represent her during the IRS audit process and she does not need to be present. Mohammed will do his best to represent Lucia during the audit process.

Just as a taxpayer is required to do, a representative is required to produce documents the IRS requests if he has them. If the representative does not have the requested documents, he must disclose what he knows about them.

A representative cannot knowingly mislead the government, and he cannot allow his client to do so by presenting fraudulent documents or putting forth a frivolous argument. If a representative fails to submit taxpayer records promptly, fails to keep scheduled appointments, or fails to return phone calls or written correspondence, the examiner has the right to initiate procedures to bypass the representative and deal directly with the taxpayer.

Audit Location and Procedures

IRS examiners are instructed to work out times, dates, and locations that are convenient for the taxpayer. However, the IRS retains the right to make the final determination of when, where, and how the examination will take place.

Regardless of where an examination takes place, an examiner has the right to visit the taxpayer's place of business or home to establish facts (such as information about inventory or verification of assets) that can only be accomplished by a direct visit.

The examination interview may be recorded by the taxpayer or his representative, or by the IRS, but whoever initiates the recording must notify the other party in writing ten days in advance. The taxpayer may request a copy of the IRS' recording. If a taxpayer becomes uncomfortable during the audit and wishes to consult with a qualified representative, the IRS must suspend the interview and reschedule it.

Example: Brandon is a self-employed mechanic who owns an auto body shop. The IRS is auditing his return (the amounts reported on his Schedule C). A licensed CPA prepared his return, but Brandon doesn't want to pay the CPA to represent him during the audit. Brandon decides to represent himself during the examination of his business in order to save money. Brandon meets with the IRS auditor at his shop. The auditor begins asking complicated questions, and Brandon becomes uncomfortable right away. He regrets not hiring someone to represent him. Brandon tells the IRS auditor that he wants to discontinue the audit, because he wants to hire someone to represent him. The auditor must immediately suspend the audit and allow Brandon time to seek representation.

Notice of IRS Contact of Third Parties

The IRS may contact third parties during the examination process. "Third parties" may include neighbors, banks, employers, or employees. An IRS auditor must notify the taxpayer that they intend to contact third parties.

Note: A third-party contact (TPC) is made when the taxpayer is unable or unwilling to provide the necessary information or when the examiner needs to verify information provided. An IRS examiner will generally request the information on a Form 4564, Information Document Request, before making a third-party contact.

The Taxpayer First Act of 2019 (TFA) revised IRC §7602(c)(1) to require the IRS to provide advance notice of the intent to contact third parties, specify in the notice the time period (i.e., not to exceed one year) in which contact will be made, and send the notice 45 days before the first contact with a third party.

- When the auditor notifies the taxpayer, he or she must actually intend to contact the third parties

- The auditor must notify the taxpayer at least forty-five (45) days before contacting a third party, and

- The auditor must tell the taxpayer the time period in which he or she intends to make the contact, and the period must not exceed more than a year.

The IRS Chief Counsel has stated that contacts with other governmental agencies are *not* subject to TFA's advance notice requirements.[71]

> **Example:** Feliciano is a business owner, but he uses his business to launder money from illicit activities. The IRS selects Feliciano's tax return for audit. The auditor sees several clues and immediately suspects unreported income related to possible criminal activity. The IRS auditor later discovers that Feliciano is also being investigated by the FBI and the Department of Justice for drug trafficking. Because this is a pending criminal investigation, the IRS is not required to give Feliciano notice before contacting the FBI or the Department of Justice about Feliciano's tax matters.

Revenue Agent Report (RAR)

When the fieldwork portion of an examination is completed, the revenue agent must prepare a detailed written report on his findings, known as a revenue agent report (RAR). A RAR is supposed to clearly state the amount of adjustments to a taxpayer's return and demonstrate how the tax liability was computed. Taxpayers have the right to disagree with a RAR and may choose to contest the agent's findings.

If the taxpayer agrees with the IRS's proposed changes in the report, the taxpayer may immediately sign an agreement. The taxpayer is responsible for paying interest and penalties on any additional tax.

If the taxpayer pays the additional tax owed when he or she signs the agreement, the interest and penalties are calculated from the due date of the tax return to the date of the payment.

If the taxpayer does not pay the additional amounts when he signs the agreement, he will receive a bill, including interest and penalties. If the taxpayer pays the entire balance within ten business days of the billing date, he will not have to pay any more interest or penalties. This period is extended to 21 calendar days if the amount due is less than $100,000.

---

[71] IRS Office of Chief Counsel Memorandum 202013015, The Application of I.R.C. §7602(c) to Government Contacts in the Context of DOJ Settlements with a Taxpayer.

Audit Determinations

An audit can be closed in one of three ways:

1. **No Change:** An audit in which the taxpayer has substantiated all of the items being reviewed, resulting in no changes.

2. **Agreed:** An audit in which the IRS proposes changes and the taxpayer understands and agrees with the changes.

3. **Unagreed (or "Disagreed"):** An audit in which the IRS proposes changes and the taxpayer understands, but disagrees with the changes. A conference with an IRS manager may be requested for further review of the issues. In addition, the taxpayer may request fast track mediation or an appeal. A taxpayer does not have to file a written protest to request fast-track mediation. The taxpayer may also choose to go to court and contest the IRS determination.

The IRS will not typically reopen a closed examination case to make an unfavorable adjustment and assess additional tax unless:

- There was fraud or misrepresentation,

- There was a substantial error based on an established IRS position existing at the time of the examination, or

- Failure to reopen the case would be a serious administrative omission.

Audit Reconsideration

In certain cases, the IRS will reevaluate the results of a prior audit if additional tax was assessed and remains unpaid or a tax credit was reversed. A taxpayer may request reconsideration if he disagrees with an earlier audit assessment, but he must provide new information, with documentation, that was not considered during the original examination. The IRS may accept a taxpayer's reconsideration request if:

- Information that is submitted has not been considered previously.

- The taxpayer filed a return after the IRS completed a substitute return for him.

- The taxpayer believes the IRS made a computational or processing error in assessing his tax.

- The tax liability remains unpaid, or credits are denied.

In filing a request for reconsideration, the taxpayer must attach a copy of his examination report (Form 4549), if available, along with copies of any new documentation that supports his position. The IRS will not accept an audit reconsideration request if:

- The taxpayer previously agreed to pay the amount of tax owed by signing a closing agreement or compromise agreement.

- The amount of tax owed is the result of final partnership item adjustments related to a TEFRA partnership examination.

- The U.S. Tax Court, or another court, has issued a final determination on the tax liability.

The IRS is under no obligation to approve a request to reopen an audit. However, the taxpayer retains the right to appeal an IRS assessment.

> **Example:** Cedrick is a sole proprietor who files on Schedule C. After an IRS examination, he was assessed $1,900 of additional taxes because he had lost the file with his receipts and other documentation supporting his business deductions. Cedrick disagrees with the findings of the examination, and a couple of weeks later, he finds the missing file, which includes his original receipts. Cedrick requests an audit reconsideration due to the new documentation.

> **Example:** In 2022, Gracie received a Notice Number CP504. The notice says – "Urgent! The IRS intends to levy Certain Assets." Gracie had moved in the prior year and also hadn't filed a tax return, so the IRS did not have an updated address for her. She did not respond to any prior notices because she did not receive them. The tax has already been assessed, but Gracie doesn't believe that she owes the amount listed on the notice. Gracie may request an audit reconsideration.

Repeat Examinations

The IRS tries to avoid repeat examinations of the same items, but sometimes this happens. If a taxpayer's return was audited for the same items in the previous two years and no change was proposed to tax liability, the taxpayer may request the IRS discontinue the examination (IRM 4.10.2.8.5). However, approval of the request is subject to the discretion of the IRS.

> **Example:** Eleanor donates a large percentage of her salary to her church. The IRS has selected Eleanor's return for examination for the last two years based on her large donations. In both instances, Eleanor was able to substantiate all her donations, and no change was made to her tax liability. Her tax return is selected again for the same reason in 2022. Eleanor contacts the IRS to request that the examination be discontinued, and the examining officer agrees to do so.

> **Example:** Terrance's tax return has been selected for examination three years in a row. In 2020 and 2021, his tax return was selected to verify compliance with the EITC requirements. There was no change to his tax liability in either year. In 2022, Terrance's tax return is selected for audit again. This time, the IRS is questioning an education credit that he claimed on the return. Terrance cannot request that the examination be discontinued because it was selected for a different reason than in the previous two examinations.

Unit 10: Study Questions

(Test yourself and then check the correct answers at the end of this chapter.)

1. When do the IRS rules regarding notice of third parties <u>not apply</u>?

A. To any pending criminal investigation.
B. When providing notice would jeopardize the collection of any tax liability.
C. When providing notice may result in reprisal against any person.
D. All of the above.

2. Aria's prior-year return was selected for audit in 2022. Regarding the audit process, which of the following statements is correct?

A. Aria must appear before the IRS in person.
B. Aria may choose to be represented by a federally-authorized practitioner and is not required to appear unless she chooses to do so.
C. Aria must communicate directly with the IRS, even if she hires a lawyer, EA, or CPA.
D. If Aria feels that she is not being treated fairly during an IRS audit, she cannot appeal to the auditor's manager.

3. Which of the following is a reason that the IRS would reopen a closed audit case?

A. There was fraud or misrepresentation from the taxpayer during the audit process.
B. The taxpayer is deceased, and the IRS sees an opportunity to assess more tax against the estate.
C. The taxpayer has a successful business and makes over $1 million.
D. The taxpayer filed a request for fast-track mediation.

4. Which of the following is not a term the IRS uses to classify an audit determination?

A. No change.
B. Agreed.
C. Acknowledged.
D. Unagreed.

5. For a jointly-filed tax return that has been selected for examination, which of the following statements is correct?

A. Both spouses must be present during an examination because both are liable for the tax.
B. Only one spouse must be present.
C. Each spouse must have his or her own representative.
D. Neither spouse may use a representative.

6. Rahim's tax return was chosen by the IRS for examination. He moved recently to another state, but the IRS notice says that his examination will be scheduled in the city where he used to live. Which of the following statements is correct?

A. Rahim can request that his tax return examination be moved to another IRS service center since he has moved to another area.
B. Rahim must schedule the examination in his former city of residence, but he can have a practitioner represent him there.
C. Rahim must meet with the examiner at least once, in person, to move the examination to another location.
D. None of the above.

7. Joshua received a notice from the IRS saying a prior year's tax return had been examined, creating a tax assessment of $2,875. Joshua disagrees with the amount of tax assessed. He could request an audit reconsideration in all of the following situations EXCEPT:

A. The full amount owed has already been paid.
B. There is new documentation for the examination that could help the taxpayer's case.
C. Joshua neither appeared for the examination nor sent information to the IRS.
D. Joshua moved and never received the examination notice.

8. What is a revenue agent report (RAR)?

A. An agreement a taxpayer makes with the IRS after an examination.
B. A report detailing the in-person interview of a taxpayer or his representative.
C. A concluding report by a revenue agent that states the amount of adjustments to a taxpayer's return.
D. A preliminary report by a revenue agent that is made when a taxpayer's return is first flagged for audit.

9. Hazel trades a large number of stocks every year, although she is still just a casual investor. Hazel's 2020 and 2021 tax returns were audited for investment expenses. Both examinations resulted in no change to the return as filed. Hazel was notified that her 2022 return was selected again for examination for investment expenses. What should Hazel do?

A. Since Hazel has two prior no change audits, she should notify the Internal Revenue Service to see if the examination should be discontinued.
B. Hazel should contact the Office of Professional Responsibility and report the repeat examinations.
C. Hazel should notify the Treasury Inspector General to see if the repeat examinations should be considered abusive.
D. Hazel should file a whistleblower claim due to the repeat examinations.

10. Gibson is being audited for a prior year, and he wishes to record the audit using an audio device. What must he do in order to record the audit?

A. Make a request the same day as the examination.
B. Notify the examiner ten days in advance, in writing.
C. Notify the examiner one week in advance, in writing.
D. Nothing. Examinations are automatically recorded by the IRS to ensure compliance.

11. Shane's tax return was chosen for examination, but he does not want to communicate with the IRS directly. Who may represent Shane in an examination, assuming the proper power of attorney authorization is in place?

A. Shane's sister, Belinda, who is an accounting student, but does not have any type of licensing.
B. Eve, the unenrolled preparer who prepared the return under audit. Eve has an AFSP certificate.
C. Gary, a tax attorney who is Shane's college buddy.
D. All of the above may represent Shane before the IRS examination division.

Unit 10: Quiz Answers

1. The answer is D. During the examination process, the IRS must give the taxpayer reasonable notice before contacting other persons about his individual tax matters. This provision does not apply:

- To any pending criminal investigation.
- When providing notice would jeopardize collection of any tax liability.
- When providing notice may result in reprisal against any person.

2. The answer is B. Aria is not required to be present during an IRS examination if she has provided written authorization, such as Form 2848, to a qualified representative per Circular 230. Aria may choose to be represented by a federally-authorized practitioner and is not required to appear unless she chooses to do so.

3. The answer is A. Only in rare circumstances will the IRS reopen a closed examination case and assess additional tax. In general, the IRS will not reopen a closed examination case to make an unfavorable adjustment unless:

- There was fraud or misrepresentation,
- There was a substantial error based on an established IRS position existing at the time of the examination, or
- Failure to reopen the case would be a serious administrative omission.

4. The answer is C. There are three types of audit determinations. In other words, an IRS audit can be closed in one of three ways:

- **No change:** An audit in which the taxpayer has substantiated all of the items being reviewed, resulting in no changes.
- **Agreed:** An audit in which the IRS proposes changes and the taxpayer understands and agrees with the changes.
- **Unagreed (or "Disagreed"):** An audit in which the IRS proposes changes and the taxpayer understands but disagrees with the changes. A conference with an IRS manager may be requested for further review of the issues. In addition, the taxpayer may request fast-track mediation or an appeal. The taxpayer may also choose to go to court and contest the IRS determination.

5. The answer is B. For taxpayers who file jointly, only one spouse is required to meet with the IRS. Alternatively, the taxpayers can use a qualified representative to represent them before the IRS. They could be present along with the representative, or they could choose not to be at the meeting.

6. The answer is A. Rahim can request that his tax return examination be moved to another IRS service center since he has moved to another area. If a taxpayer has moved or if his books and records are located in another area, he can request that the location of his audit be changed to another IRS service center. IRS examiners are instructed to work out times, dates, and locations that are convenient for the taxpayer. However, the IRS retains the right to decide when, where, and how the examination will take place.

7. The answer is A. Joshua could request audit reconsideration in all of the following situations except if the full amount owed has already been paid (based on a prior exam question).

8. The answer is C. An IRS examiner files a revenue agent report (RAR) after he has completed the fieldwork part of an examination. The report should clearly state the amount of adjustments to be made to a taxpayer's return and demonstrate how the tax liability was computed. A taxpayer may agree with the RAR and pay any additional tax owed, or he may contest the agent's findings. He may appeal to the IRS or fight the tax in court.

9. The answer is A. Since Hazel has two prior no change audits, she should notify the Internal Revenue Service to see if the examination should be discontinued.

10. The answer is B. Gibson must notify the examiner ten days in advance, in writing. If a taxpayer, his representative, or the IRS examiner wishes for an audit to be recorded, he must notify the other parties in writing ten days in advance. If the IRS records the interview, the taxpayer may request a copy.

11. The answer is D. All of the people listed could potentially represent Shane before the IRS during an examination. Shane's sister can represent him because she is a close family member, and Eve can represent him because she prepared the return, and she has an AFSP certificate. Attorneys, CPAs, and Enrolled Agents have unlimited rights of representation before all offices of the IRS, so Gary would be able to represent Shane, as well. A Form 2848 (power of attorney) would be required.

Unit 11: IRS Appeals and the U.S. Tax Court

> **More Reading:**
> **Publication 5, Your Appeal Rights & How to Prepare a Protest If You Don't Agree**
> **Publication 556, Examination of Returns, Appeal Rights, and Claims for Refund**
> **Publication 4227, Overview of the Appeals Process**
> **Publication 4167, Appeals: Introduction to Alternative Dispute Resolution**

Because taxpayers often disagree with the IRS on tax matters, the IRS has a formal appeals process. The IRS Independent Office of Appeals ("IRS Appeals") is independent of any other IRS office and serves as an informal administrative forum for any taxpayer who wishes to dispute an IRS determination.

IRS Appeals provides taxpayers an alternative to going to court to fight disagreements about the application of tax law. The role of appeals is to resolve disputes on a fair and impartial basis that does not favor either the government or the taxpayer. Appeals officers are directed to give serious consideration to settlement offers by taxpayers or their representatives.[72]

> **Note:** In general, only attorneys, certified public accountants or enrolled agents are allowed to represent a taxpayer before IRS Appeals. An unenrolled preparer may be a witness at the conference, but not a representative. Exceptions also apply under the rules for limited practice (for example, a parent may represent their own child).

IRS Appeals System Overview

The mission of the IRS Appeals is to resolve tax controversies without litigation. The IRS Appeals Office is a separate division and independent of IRS examinations and collections. A taxpayer has three choices when protesting an IRS determination:

1. Appeal within the IRS appeals system.
2. Take the case directly to the U.S. Tax Court.
3. Bypass both IRS Appeals and the Tax Court and take the case to the U.S. Court of Federal Claims or to a U.S. District Court.

The contested tax does not have to be paid first if a taxpayer opts for either IRS Appeals or the Tax Court, but if the taxpayer goes directly to the Court of Federal Claims or a U.S. District Court, the contested tax must be paid first, and then the taxpayer must sue the IRS for a refund.

An IRS appeal does not normally abate penalties and interest on the tax due. These continue to accumulate until one of two events occurs:

- The balance of the debt is paid, or
- The taxpayer wins his appeal, and he is granted a no-change audit.

---

[72] Treas. Reg. §601.106(d)(2): "Appeals will ordinarily give serious consideration to an offer to settle a tax controversy on a basis which fairly reflects the relative merits of the opposing views in the light of the hazards which would exist if the case were litigated. However, no settlement will be made based upon the nuisance value of the case to either party."

Reasons for an appeal must be supported by tax law. An appeal cannot be based solely on moral, religious, political, constitutional, conscientious, or similar grounds.

Appealing After an Examination

The 30-Day Letter: Within a few weeks after a taxpayer's closing conference with an IRS examiner, the taxpayer will receive a 30-day letter. This letter includes:

- A notice explaining the taxpayer's right to appeal the proposed changes within 30 days,
- A copy of the revenue agent report explaining the examiner's proposed changes,
- An agreement or waiver form,
- A copy of *Publication 5, Your Appeal Rights,*
- The taxpayer has 30 days from the date of notice to accept or appeal the proposed changes.

If the taxpayer chooses to appeal an examiner's decision through the IRS system, he can contact a local Appeals Office, which is separate and independent of the IRS office that conducted the examination. Conferences with Appeals Office personnel may be conducted in person, through correspondence, or by telephone with the taxpayer or his authorized representative. Only practitioners are allowed to represent taxpayers before an IRS appeals hearing. The taxpayer does not need to attend if his representative has power of attorney authorization via a signed Form 2848 or any other properly written POA authorization.

> **Note:** An unenrolled tax return preparer may be a witness for a taxpayer at an appeals conference, but may not serve as an authorized representative for the taxpayer.

Filing a Formal Protest: A formal written protest is required in all cases to request an Appeals conference, unless the taxpayer qualifies for the small case request procedure. Amounts in dispute of not more than $25,000 qualify for the "small case" procedure, which allows for the initiation of an appeal through IRS Form 12203, *Request for Appeals Review,* which must be signed by the taxpayer. The protest statement must go into greater detail than the small case request. It must include the facts supporting the taxpayer's position and the law or authority that the taxpayer is relying upon in making his case. The protest must be signed by the taxpayer under penalties of perjury. If an Enrolled Agent or other practitioner prepares and signs the protest for a taxpayer, he must substitute a declaration that states whether he knows personally that the facts in the protest and accompanying documents are true and correct.

> **Example:** Ozzy is an EA who represents Tracy, a sole proprietor who runs a small restaurant. The IRS audited Tracy's business return and found discrepancies on her Schedule C. Tracy receives a 30-day letter stating that she owes an additional $32,000 in tax. Tracy disagrees with the amount, so Ozzy files a formal protest within 30 days with the IRS Appeals office. In the protest, Ozzy details why the proposed assessment is incorrect and the legal basis for his argument. He also submits the required practitioner declaration and a copy of Form 2848. Ozzy then schedules a conference with an Appeals Officer. When they meet, they discuss the matter and reach a settlement agreeable to each party. Since the IRS has a signed Form 2848 authorizing Ozzy to be Tracy's representative, she was not required to attend the appeals hearing.

The 90-Day Letter (Notice of Deficiency)

If a taxpayer does not respond to a 30-day letter, or if he cannot reach an agreement with an Appeals Officer, the IRS will send the taxpayer a Notice of Deficiency, which is also known as the 90-day letter. A Notice of Deficiency is required by law and is used to advise the taxpayer of his appeal rights to the U.S. Tax Court.

> **Note:** A Notice of Deficiency is a formal legal notice, sent by certified or registered mail. This letter is the <u>final notification</u> a taxpayer will receive before the IRS makes its final assessment of tax due.

A Notice of Deficiency must be issued before a deficiency is assessed and the taxpayer can go to the Tax Court. The taxpayer has 90 days (150 days if addressed to a taxpayer outside the United States) from the date of this notice to file a petition with the Tax Court.

> **Example:** Max was sent several IRS notices about an audit for a prior-year return, but he ignored them all. On March 30, 2022, he receives a Notice of Deficiency (a 90-day letter) and finally decides to respond. He has only 90 days from the date of the letter to file a petition with the Tax Court, otherwise the IRS will make a final assessment and begin collection action. Max responds to the letter on May 1, 2022, challenging the tax that the IRS has proposed by filing a Tax Court petition in the U.S. Tax Court. His file will be sent to the IRS appeals office first, giving him a prior opportunity to resolve his case before going to an actual hearing in the Tax Court.

> **Example:** Svetlana is a U.S. citizen that lives and works in Russia. She files U.S. tax returns as required by law. Her prior year return comes under audit, and she receives a 90-day letter, which is mailed to her residence in Russia. Since she has a foreign address, she has 150 days to respond to the letter, rather than the normal 90 days.

If the taxpayer does not file the petition in time, the tax will be assessed, and the taxpayer may not take his case to Tax Court. If the taxpayer does file a petition in time and the case is docketed before the Tax Court, his file will go to an IRS Appeals office to see if it can be resolved before going to court if the taxpayer did not have a prior opportunity in appeals in this controversy. More than 90% of all tax cases are resolved without a trial.

U.S. Tax Court

The U.S. Tax Court is a federal court separate from the IRS, and the only court where taxpayers may choose to contest their tax deficiencies <u>without having to pay</u> the disputed amount first. For most taxpayers, the U.S. Tax Court is the optimal court in which to challenge an adverse IRS decision, as payment is not a requirement for jurisdiction and the judges possess specialized tax expertise.

Under current law, however, taxpayers generally may litigate in Tax Court only if the IRS determines they owe more tax and it issues a notice of deficiency. When taxpayers are solely seeking a refund because they believe they overpaid their tax, they are barred from the Tax Court and must litigate in either the U.S. District Court or the U.S. Court of Federal Claims.

If a taxpayer does not receive a notice of deficiency and seeks judicial review of an adverse IRS determination, the taxpayer must pay the tax, penalty, or interest and file suit in a U.S. District Court or the U.S. Court of Federal Claims. This situation generally arises when the taxpayer is claiming a refund of tax, penalty or interest that has been paid. Taxpayers solely seeking refunds cannot litigate their cases in the Tax Court.

Example: Bernice files her income tax return on time. Her return reflects a tax liability of $15,000. Bernice had $12,000 of withholding taken from her wages, and she pays an additional $3,000 using direct debit when she e-files her return. Six months after filing her original return, she discovers a significant error that would result in a refund, and Bernice files an amended return, Form 1040-X, showing a tax liability of $11,000 and claiming a refund of $4,000. The IRS denies her claim. Under current law, Bernice could not go to Tax Court because there is no deficiency (i.e., no tax is due). To litigate her refund claim, she would have to file a refund suit in the U.S. District Court or the U.S. Court of Federal Claims to pursue her $4,000 refund claim. Bernice is at a disadvantage, because this type of suit would involve greater court fees, and potentially additional discovery burdens.

The U.S. Tax Court issues both **regular** and **memorandum** decisions. A **regular decision** is when the Tax Court rules on an issue for the first time. A **memorandum decision** is when the Tax Court has previously ruled on identical or similar issues. The Tax Court has jurisdiction over the following tax disputes:

- Notices of deficiency for income and estate and gift tax,
- Review of the failure to abate interest,
- Notices of transferee liability,
- Adjustment of partnership items,
- Administrative costs,
- Worker classification (employee versus independent contractor),
- Review of certain collection actions,
- Relief from joint and several liability on a joint return,
- Certification of seriously delinquent tax debt (passport cases)
- Whistleblower awards.

Any individual taxpayer may represent himself before the U.S. Tax Court. A taxpayer may choose to represent himself; this is referred to as "pro se" or "self-represented" which is a legal term meaning "for oneself" or "on one's own behalf." A taxpayer may also choose to be represented by a person admitted to practice before the Tax Court.

Note: Enrolled agents and CPAs must be "admitted to practice" before the U.S. Tax Court by first passing a separate exam specific to this purpose. "Practice before the IRS" does not include practice before the U.S. Tax Court. Licensed attorneys are the only practitioners who are not required to pass the U.S. Tax Court exam before practicing before the court.

> **Note:** The U.S. Tax Court has generally held that taxpayers who rely on software to justify errors on self-prepared returns are liable for the IRC §6662 accuracy-related penalty.[73]

> **Example:** Clyde has always prepared his own tax returns using tax preparation software. In 2022, one of his prior-year returns comes under examination. Clyde underreported a significant amount of income because he thought the income was not taxable. After his return goes under examination, He is assessed income tax on the amount that should have been reported and a substantial accuracy-related penalty. Clyde concedes that he should have reported the income, but he contests the accuracy-related penalty because he believes that the software steered him in the wrong direction. He files a petition with the U.S. Tax Court, requesting an abatement of the penalty due to reasonable cause. The Tax Court rejects his argument, and the accuracy-related penalty is upheld. That is because taxpayers cannot justify errors on self-prepared returns using reliance on software as an excuse.

U.S. Tax Court Small Tax Case Procedure

Small tax case procedures (also known as S-case procedures) in the Tax Court are one avenue to resolve disputes between taxpayers and the IRS. Small tax cases are handled under simpler, less formal procedures than regular cases. Often, decisions are handed down quicker than in other courts.

However, the Tax Court's decision in a small tax case cannot be appealed by the taxpayer. The decision is final, as the IRS is not allowed to appeal, either, if it loses the case. In contrast, either the taxpayer or the IRS can appeal a decision in a regular, non-S case to a U.S. Court of Appeals.

The taxpayer, the IRS, and the Tax Court must all agree to proceed with the small case procedure. Generally, the Tax Court will agree with the taxpayer's small case request if the taxpayer otherwise qualifies. Dollar limits for the Tax Court Small Case Division vary:

- **For a Notice of Deficiency:** $50,000 is the maximum amount, including penalties and interest, for any year before the court.

- **For a Notice of Determination:** $50,000 is the maximum amount for all the years combined.

- **For a Notice of Deficiency related to a request for relief from joint and several liability:** $50,000 is the maximum amount of spousal relief for all the years combined.

- **For an IRS Notice of Determination of Worker Classification:** The amount in the dispute cannot exceed $50,000 for any calendar quarter.

A decision entered in a small tax case is not treated as precedent for any other case and is not typically published. Since the taxpayer cannot appeal a decision under the Small Tax Case procedures, he or she must consider whether using the small case procedure is worth the risk of not being able to contest an adverse decision in a higher court.

---

[73] IRC §6662; 6664(c); Treas. Reg. §1.6664-4(b)(1); and *Anyika v. Commissioner*, T.C. Memo. 2011-69.

Note: Do not confuse the Tax Court's *"Small Tax Case Procedure"* with the IRS' *"Small Case Request."* They are **not** the same thing. One procedure is with the U.S. Tax Court, the other procedure is within the IRS Appeals system. Within the IRS appeals system, a taxpayer may also file a "Small Case Request" if the total amount of tax, penalties, and interest for each tax period involved are if the total amount for any single tax period is $25,000 or less. To make a Small Case Request, the taxpayer may use *Form 12203, Request for Appeals Review,* or prepare a brief written statement requesting an appeals conference. The taxpayer must also specify why he does not agree with the proposed tax assessment.[74]

Delay Tactics are Prohibited

If a taxpayer unreasonably fails to pursue the internal IRS appeals system, if the taxpayer files a case with the U.S. Tax Court primarily to cause a delay, or if the taxpayer's position is frivolous, the Tax Court may impose a penalty of up to $25,000.

Frivolous positions include those that contend that:

- The income tax is not valid,

- Payment of tax is voluntary,

- A person or a type of income is not subject to tax, or

- Espouse other arguments that the courts have previously rejected as baseless.

The Tax Court may also impose sanctions of up to $25,000 on those who misuse their right to a court review of IRS collection procedures merely to stall their tax payments.

This rule is targeted at taxpayers who do not have a legitimate complaint and are instead using the Tax Court simply to delay collection action in their case.[75]

Example: Jamillah worked as an employee of a California University. When she filed her tax return, she attached a statement that her wages were not subject to Federal income tax because she was not engaging in the "exercise of Federal privileges." Jamillah claimed that since she was not a federal officer, employee or elected official, she was not "exercising a Federal privilege" when performing services for the University and should therefore not be taxed. The court found her argument to be patently frivolous. The IRS' attorney urged the court to impose a section 6673 (frivolous return) penalty of $25,000 against Jamillah, but the taxpayer told the judge presiding over the case that she was currently unemployed and that a penalty would cause her financial hardship. Taking her at her word, the court assessed a tax deficiency of $5,326 and a modest penalty of $250. The judge warned Jamillah that she would risk a much more severe penalty if she advances frivolous positions in any future appearance before the Tax Court (based on Muhammad v. Comm'r, TC Memo 2021-77).

---

[74] Employee retirement plans (Form 5500), exempt organizations, S corporations, and partnerships are not eligible for small case requests.
[75] The IRS makes public the names and cases of taxpayers who have been assessed these §6673 penalties by the Tax Court. The cases are published on the IRS website as well as in the Tax Court Historical Opinion area.

Other Types of Court Appeals

The vast majority of taxpayers who use the court system to appeal their federal tax disputes do so in the Tax Court. However, a minority of taxpayers choose to challenge the IRS in a U.S. District Court or Court of Federal Claims. In this case, a taxpayer must pay the contested tax deficiency first before filing the case in these courts. If either party loses at the trial court level, the court's decision may be appealed to a higher court.

> **Example:** During the course of an audit, the IRS disallows a large deduction on Cassie's return. Cassie disagrees with the assessment, and the IRS eventually issues a notice of deficiency in the amount of $45,000. Cassie knows the deduction she has taken on her return is contrary to the IRS position, but there is a recent court case where another taxpayer took a similar deduction and prevailed against the IRS. Cassie does not wish to contest the tax through the IRS Appeals Office or the Tax Court. Instead, she feels that she would have better luck if she went straight to a U.S. District Court. She must first pay the contested liability in full and then sue the IRS for a refund.

> **Note:** Although Enrolled Agents and CPAs have unlimited rights of representation before all levels and officers of the IRS, they cannot represent taxpayers in disputes with the IRS before U.S. District Courts, bankruptcy courts, courts of appeal, or the U.S. Supreme Court. That authority is reserved only for licensed attorneys.

Taxpayer Rights to Bring Civil Action

Taxpayers generally have the right to take their cases to court. The government cannot ask a taxpayer to waive his or her right to sue the United States or a government employee for any action taken in connection with the tax laws. Taxpayers have the right to file a refund suit in a United States District Court or the United States Court of Federal Claims.

The burden of proof: In most cases, the burden of proof lies with the taxpayer; however, the burden of proof can shift to the IRS[76] during court proceedings, if the taxpayer meets the following requirements:

- Adhered to IRS substantiation requirements.

- Maintained adequate records.

- Cooperated with reasonable requests for information from the IRS.

- Introduced credible evidence relating to the issue.

This burden of proof "shift" applies to both individual taxpayers as well as business entities However, in the case of a trust, corporation, or partnership, it only applies if the entity had a net worth of $7 million or less and not more than 500 employees at the time of contested tax liability. This only applies only in court proceedings on civil tax matters, not criminal cases.

---

[76] In the case of an individual taxpayer, the IRS shall have the burden of proof in any court proceeding with respect to any item of income which was reconstructed by the IRS solely through the use of statistical information from unrelated taxpayers (IRC § 7491(b)).

Example: Dustin owns a laundromat business as a sole proprietor. His laundromat accepts coins in all the machines, making it a cash-intensive business. Dustin's prior-year tax return goes under audit. Dustin's accounting records appear to be correct and complete, and his bank statements match the amounts that are listed on his return. The IRS examiner believes that Dustin is concealing cash, but does not have any proof. The IRS examiner issues an audit report, assessing additional tax for "phantom income," based on statistical data taken from other taxpayers, which Dustin vehemently disagrees with. He waits for the 90-day-letter (the Notice of Deficiency) and immediately files a petition with the U.S. Tax court. In this case, the IRS will have the burden of proof with respect to any item of income on the return that it has reconstructed.

Recovering Litigation Costs

A taxpayer may be able to recover the expenses incurred to defend a position while contesting tax assessed by the IRS. Under IRC §7430, the IRS is compelled to pay "reasonable litigation and administrative" costs incurred by a taxpayer in most administrative proceedings before the IRS and in court proceedings before most U.S. federal courts. To recover court costs, the following general requirements must be met:

- The costs must be incurred in an administrative or court proceeding brought by or against the United States.
- The taxpayer must be the prevailing party.
- The taxpayer must have exhausted all administrative remedies within the IRS.
- The costs must be reasonable. They must have been incurred as a result of assessment, collection, or refund of tax, interest, or penalty imposed pursuant to the Internal Revenue Code.
- The taxpayer must not have unreasonably delayed any IRS proceeding.

Example: Aurora is a registered nurse. During an examination, she disagreed with an IRS assessment that disallowed educational expenses she had claimed while pursuing an MBA degree for health professionals. After receiving a notice of deficiency, she took her case to the Tax Court and won. Aurora may be able to recover attorney fees and other court costs she incurred in her fight with the IRS.

The taxpayer will not be treated as the prevailing party if the IRS establishes that its position was substantially justified. In order to request the recovery of litigation costs from the IRS, the taxpayer must meet certain net worth requirements:

- For individuals, net worth cannot exceed $2 million as of the filing date of the petition for review. Spouses filing a joint return are treated as separate individuals.
- For estates, net worth cannot exceed $2 million as of the date of the decedent's death.
- For exempt organizations and certain cooperatives, the entity cannot have more than 500 employees as of the filing date of the petition for review.

For all other taxpayers, net worth cannot exceed $7 million, and the entity must not have more than 500 employees as of the filing date of the petition for review.

Unit 11: Study Questions

(Test yourself and then check the correct answers at the end of this chapter.)

1. A Statutory Notice of Deficiency is also known as a "90-day letter" because:

A. The taxpayer generally has 90 days from the date of the letter to file a petition with the U.S. District Court.
B. The taxpayer generally has 90 days from the date of the letter to file a petition with the United States Tax Court.
C. The IRS generally has 90 days from the date of the letter to issue a notice of intent to levy.
D. The IRS generally only has 90 days from the date of the letter to collect the amount due.

2. At the conclusion of an audit, Daniel was unhappy with the outcome, and he wants to appeal the examiner's decision to a local IRS Appeals Office. Which statement regarding appeal procedures is <u>not correct</u>?

A. If the total amount under dispute is not more than $25,000, a formal written protest is not required, but instead an appeal is initiated through IRS Form 12203.
B. Daniel may represent himself at his appeals conference.
C. A written protest does not require a signature.
D. All partnership and S Corporation cases require formal written protests.

3. Armando's tax return was selected for audit, and he went through the examination. He was represented by Ginny, an unenrolled preparer with an AFSP certificate. Ginny prepared the return under audit. Armando wishes to appeal the examination, and prefers that Ginny represent him before IRS Appeals. What are his options?

A. Armando may ask Ginny to represent him before IRS Appeals, because she prepared the return and she has an AFSP certificate.
B. Armando may be represented by Ginny, as long as he is present during the IRS Appeals process. He doesn't have to speak, though.
C. Ginny cannot represent him before IRS Appeals. Armando may represent himself or hire an enrolled practitioner (CPA, attorney, or EA) to represent him at the Appeals level.
D. Armando may ask an IRS employee to represent him at IRS Appeals.

4. If a taxpayer wishes to challenge the IRS in a District Court, the taxpayer must:

A. First attempt to resolve the contested tax with the IRS Appeals office.
B. Pay the contested liability first and then sue the IRS for a refund.
C. Pay a retainer to the IRS for a refund.
D. Go first to the U.S. Tax Court before appealing to a U.S. District Court.

5. Which of the following best states the purpose of the IRS Independent Office of Appeals?

A. To help the taxpayer and the government settle their tax dispute and reach an equitable settlement.
B. To advocate for the taxpayer in connection with the taxpayer's disagreement with the collection or examination divisions of the IRS.
C. To advocate for the government and convince the taxpayer to pay his fair share before he pursues his case through the court system.
D. To look at the facts and circumstances of each case, and then take a side in the tax dispute.

6. Danielle owes a substantial sum to the IRS. She files a petition with the U.S. Tax Court. Her case is later determined to be frivolous, wholly without merit, and merely to cause delay. As a repercussion to Danielle's action, the Tax Court may impose a penalty of:

A. Up to $10,000.
B. Up to $25,000.
C. Up to $50,000.
D. Up to $25,000 and one year in prison.

7. Kevin and Javier are general partners in a body shop business. They decided to elect out of the Centralized Partnership Audit Regime. Both had their individual returns examined, in separate examinations, and based on how each of them treated flow-through items from the partnership, the IRS assessed additional tax on both Kevin and Javier. However, both of them disagreed with the IRS. Kevin decided to take his case to the IRS Appeals office. After the conference, he and the IRS still disagreed. Javier decided to bypass the Appeals office altogether and go directly to court. Which of the following statements is correct?

A. Neither may petition the U.S. Tax Court.
B. Both Kevin and Javier can take their cases to the following courts: U.S. Tax Court, U.S. Court of Federal Claims, or the U.S. District Court.
C. Only Kevin may petition the Tax Court, because he went through the IRS appeals process first.
D. Both can take their cases to the Tax Court, but not to other U.S. courts.

8. Alyssa disagrees with the IRS examiner regarding her income tax case. Her appeal rights are explained to her, and she decides to contest the tax by pursuing the case in the U.S. Tax Court. Which of the following statements is correct?

A. Alyssa must receive a Notice of Deficiency before she can petition the U.S. Tax Court.
B. Alyssa must wait for the IRS examiner to permanently close her audit case.
C. Alyssa must request a collection due process hearing before she can go to the U.S. Tax Court.
D. Alyssa cannot go to the U.S. Tax Court unless she agrees with the auditor's findings.

9. At the beginning of each examination, the IRS auditor must explain:

A. A taxpayer's appeal rights.
B. A taxpayer's right to a fair trial.
C. A taxpayer's right to remain silent.
D. A taxpayer's right to confidentiality.

10. The Tax Court has generally held that taxpayers who rely on software to justify errors on self-prepared returns are:

A. Not liable for the §6662 accuracy-related penalty.
B. Liable for the §6662 accuracy-related penalty.
C. Liable for 20% of the §6662 accuracy-related penalty.
D. Liable for 40% of the §6662 accuracy-related penalty.

11. Which of the following statements is *correct* regarding a taxpayer's right to appeal a tax assessment?

A. A taxpayer must first pay the contested tax before he can appeal in the U.S. Tax Court.
B. A taxpayer has the right to appeal a tax assessment on the basis of political grounds.
C. The taxpayer can bypass the IRS Independent Office of Appeals by appealing to his state representative.
D. A taxpayer must first pay the contested tax before he can appeal in a U.S. District Court.

12. Geraldine is an EA. Which of the following tasks can she perform on behalf of a client?

A. Prepare and file a suit for refund in U.S. District Court.
B. Prepare and sign a U.S. Tax Court petition to contest a notice of deficiency.
C. Prepare and sign a protest to challenge examination results in the IRS Appeals Office.
D. Prepare and file a bankruptcy petition in United States Bankruptcy Court due to unpaid tax balances.

13. If a taxpayer and the IRS fail to settle a <u>non-docketed</u> examination controversy in the IRS Appeals Office, the next event to occur is:

A. Issuance of a notice of deficiency.
B. Issuance of notice and demand for payment.
C. Return of the case to the Revenue Agent for further review.
D. Referral of the case to the Taxpayer Advocate.

14. An Enrolled Agent may NOT represent a taxpayer in a dispute before:

A. An IRS revenue agent.
B. An IRS revenue officer.
C. A U.S. District Court judge.
D. The IRS Independent Office of Appeals.

15. Which of the following statements is correct about an IRS appeal?

A. An appeal does not abate the interest on a tax liability. Interest continues to accrue.
B. A taxpayer must pay the disputed tax before filing an appeal with the IRS.
C. The IRS is prohibited from filing a federal tax lien if the taxpayer is outside the U.S.
D. Taxpayers who disagree with the IRS changes may not appeal to the U.S. Tax Court.

1. The answer is B. A Statutory Notice of Deficiency is also known as a 90- day letter because the taxpayer generally has 90 days from the date of the letter to file a petition with the United States Tax Court.

2. The answer is C. A formal written protest is required in all cases above $25,000 in dispute to request an IRS Appeals conference, and each protest must be signed by the taxpayer under penalties of perjury. For amounts in dispute of $25,000 or less, the appeal is initiated through Form 12203 instead of a more formal written protest. Form 12203 also requires the signature of the taxpayer.

3. The answer is C. Armando can appear before IRS Appeals by himself, or hire a qualified representative to appear on his behalf. Ginny cannot represent him before IRS appeals, because she only has an AFSP certificate. Only enrolled practitioners (attorneys, CPAs, and EAs) are allowed to represent taxpayers before an appeals hearing (unless a special exception applies, for example, an executor representing an estate or a parent representing their own child).

4. The answer is B. In order to appeal in District Court, the taxpayer must first pay the contested liability and then sue the IRS for a refund. If either party loses at the trial court level, the court's decision may be appealed to a higher court.

5. The answer is A. The Office of Appeals helps taxpayers resolve their tax disputes with the IRS without going to Tax Court. The IRS Appeals Office is an independent organization within the IRS. After the applicable IRS compliance division has made its decision, Appeals reviews a case and works to settle disagreements on the basis that is both fair and impartial to both the government and the taxpayer.

6. The answer is B. Danielle may be liable for a $25,000 penalty. If a taxpayer unreasonably fails to pursue the internal IRS appeals system, if the case is filed primarily to cause a delay, or if the taxpayer's position is frivolous, the Tax Court may impose a penalty of up to $25,000.

7. The answer is B. Both Kevin and Javier can take their cases to court. A taxpayer is not required to use the IRS appeals process. If a taxpayer and the IRS still disagree after an appeals conference or a taxpayer decides to bypass the IRS appeals system altogether, the case may be taken to the U.S. Tax Court, the U.S. Court of Federal Claims, or a U.S. District Court. Although Kevin and Javier are not required to take their claim to the U.S. Tax Court, it is the only court that will allow Kevin and Javier to contest their liability *before* paying the amount in dispute. In any other court, they would be required to pay the tax first, and then sue the IRS for a refund.

8. The answer is A. A Notice of Deficiency (90-day letter) must be issued before a taxpayer can petition the U.S. Tax Court. A taxpayer has 90 days from the date of the notice to respond and file a petition with the court (or 150 days if addressed to a taxpayer outside the United States).

9. The answer is A. At the beginning of each examination, the IRS auditor must explain a taxpayer's appeal rights.

10. The answer is B. The Tax Court has generally held that taxpayers who rely on software to justify errors on self-prepared returns are still liable for the §6662 accuracy-related penalty.

11. The answer is D. A taxpayer has the right to appeal a tax assessment through the IRS Appeals office, the U.S. Tax Court, or a U.S. District Court or the Court of Federal Claims. The contested tax does not have to be paid first if the taxpayer petitions the U.S. Tax Court. However, if the taxpayer opts to have his appeal heard in a district or Federal Claims court, the taxpayer must first pay the contested tax and sue the IRS for a refund.

12. The answer is C. An Enrolled Agent may prepare and sign a protest to challenge examination results in the IRS Appeals Office.

13. The answer is A. If a taxpayer and the IRS fail to settle a non-docketed examination controversy in the IRS Appeals Office, the next event to occur is the issuance of a notice of deficiency. Once the notice of deficiency is issued, the taxpayer has 90 days (150 days if addressed to a taxpayer outside the United States) from the date of this notice to file a petition with the U.S. Tax Court.

14. The answer is C. An Enrolled Agent may represent taxpayers at all levels of the IRS, but does not have the same practice rights in the U.S. court system.

15. The answer is A. An IRS appeal does not abate the interest, which continues to accrue until the balance of the debt is paid, or until the taxpayer wins his appeal and he is granted a no-change audit. A no-change audit means the IRS has accepted the tax return as it was filed.

Unit 12: The IRS E-File Program

More Reading:
Publication 3112, IRS e-file Application and Participation
Publication 1345, Handbook for Authorized IRS e-file Providers
Publication 4557, Safeguarding Taxpayer Data: A Guide for Your Business
Publication 5426, Taxpayer First Act Report to Congress

The IRS e-file program allows taxpayers to transmit their returns electronically. Approximately 92 percent of individual taxpayers e-filed during processing year (PY) 2022.[77] whereas business income tax returns had an e-file rate of 70%. Employment tax returns (Form 940, 941, 944, etc.) had an e-file rate of only 58%.

According to the IRS, the processing of e-file returns is not only quicker, but is also more accurate than the processing of paper returns. However, as with a paper return, the taxpayer is responsible for ensuring an e-filed return contains accurate information and is filed on time.

The IRS enacted an e-file mandate for tax preparers because e-filed returns cost less for the government to process, contain fewer errors, and result in faster refunds. Paid preparers who prepare more than ten individual and/or trust returns a year are required to e-file these returns.[78]

This preparer e-file mandate only covers returns for individuals, trusts, and estates (Form 1040 and Form 1041). The e-file mandate does not apply to tax preparers who are not paid. This includes volunteer preparers, including returns prepared under the Volunteer Income Tax Assistance (VITA) program.

For the purposes of the e-file mandate, members of firms must count their returns *in aggregate.* If the number of applicable income tax returns is 11 or more, then all members of the firm generally must e-file the returns they prepare and file. This is true even if an individual preparer expects to prepare and file fewer than 11 returns.

If a single preparer files 11 or more returns for the calendar year, all preparers of a firm must e-file the returns they prepare and file. This is true even if, on an individual basis, a member prepares and files fewer than the threshold. Some preparers are exempt from the e-file mandate.

The IRS e-file does not accept foreign preparers without social security numbers into their e-file program, so those preparers are exempt.

---

[77] Taxpayer Advocate Service's 2022 Annual Report to Congress (ARC), Publication 2104
[78] The e-file mandate only applies to paid preparers. Individual taxpayers are not bound by this mandate. A taxpayer may choose to file on paper, if he or she chooses to do so. The mandate does not apply to tax returns that are not prepared for compensation, such as a tax return that an enrolled agent files for a family member at no charge. Financial institutions and fiduciaries that file Forms 1041 as a trustee or fiduciary are not required to e-file and are not subject to the mandate. The e-file mandate also does not apply to payroll tax returns. Note that there are some states, like New York, that have a stricter e-file mandate that requires taxpayers as well as preparers to e-file.

> **Example:** Whitney is a licensed CPA who is a Canadian citizen. She lives and works in Canada, and is a specialist in cross-border accounting for Canadians who own U.S. businesses and have U.S. investments. Whitney specializes in the preparation of U.S. tax returns for nonresident aliens. She is not a U.S. citizen or U.S. resident, and does not have a Social Security number. She is therefore ineligible for an EFIN. She cannot e-file returns, so she is exempt from the e-file mandate. She is required to have a PTIN, and she must report her preparer information and sign the preparer section of her client's returns.

> **Example:** Ashley is an enrolled agent who works as a full-time employee for Appleby Accountancy, Inc. a small CPA firm that offers accounting and tax services to individuals and businesses in her city. Ashley also has a side business preparing tax returns from her home. Ashley specializes in fiduciary and estate tax issues and does not prepare very many individual tax returns. For the coming tax year, Ashley expects to prepare and file around ten Form 1041 returns (for estates and trusts) while working for the CPA firm. She also expects to prepare and file seven Form 1040 tax returns as a self-employed preparer. Since she expects to file 11 or more forms between her regular job and her side-business, Ashley is required to e-file all of the returns she prepares.

Fiduciaries that file returns <u>in their fiduciary capacity</u> are not considered "tax preparers" and are also not subject to the e-file mandate, even if they are compensated for their fiduciary duties. This would include situations where the fiduciary is paid for their services.[79]

> **Example:** Samantha is not a professional preparer. She is the executor of the Estate of Brian Smith, her deceased cousin. In her capacity as executor (a fiduciary), Samantha completes a 1041 return for the estate and signs the return as the fiduciary. Even if she receives fees as an executor for completing the return, this return will not be subject to the e-file requirement, because Samantha is preparing the return as a fiduciary. She will not sign the return as a paid preparer. Instead, she signs the return as a fiduciary of the estate.

In some cases, preparers may qualify for a waiver of the e-file requirement. A tax preparer may request an exemption from the e-file program due to financial hardship situations (including being in a Presidentially declared disaster area) by submitting Form 8944, *Preparer e-file Hardship Waiver Request,* to request a waiver.

Waivers are reviewed and approved in cases where the preparer demonstrates that complying would be an undue hardship. Hardship exemptions are rare and considered only on a case-by-case basis. The IRS will deny the waiver if the request is made because the preparer does not have appropriate software or simply prefers not to e-file.

A tax preparer that is a member of a recognized religious group that is conscientiously opposed to filing electronically is not required to apply for a waiver using Form 8944.

---

[79] Fiduciaries, as contemplated by IRC §7701(a)(36)(B)(iii), that file returns **in their fiduciary capacity** are not considered tax return preparers and are therefore not covered by the e-file requirement.

Preparers who claim a religious exemption to e-filing must attach Form 8948, *Preparer Explanation for Not Filing Electronically*, to their clients' paper returns and check the appropriate box.

> **Example:** Abraham is an accountant that belongs to a conservative Mennonite community. His faith encourages strict limits on computer use, limiting it to recordkeeping only, and forbids Internet altogether. Abraham will prepare tax returns on a computer, but he is conscientiously opposed to using the internet for any tasks, including filing electronically. He does not have to request a waiver to the e-file mandate, because he automatically qualifies for a religious exemption. When he prepares a return for a client, he should attach Form 8948, marking box 3: "The preparer is a member of a recognized religious group that is conscientiously opposed to filing electronically." The tax return can be mailed in by the client.

Entity E-file Mandates

Certain corporations, partnerships, and tax-exempt organizations are required to file their returns electronically. For the 2022 tax year, corporations with $10 million or more in assets are required to e-file Form 1120 and Form 1120S.

Also for the 2022 tax year, any entities that file more than 250 information returns (including Forms W-2, 1099, and Schedule K-1), during a calendar year are also required to e-file. This requirement applies regardless of whether the entity uses a paid preparer or not.

> **Example:** Placerville Construction, Inc. is a calendar-year S corporation with 13 shareholders, 110 employees, 160 independent contractors, and assets of $25 million. The company files a total of 270 information returns (including Forms W-2, Schedule K-1s, Forms 1099-NEC, and 1099-MISC). Since Placerville Construction has more than $10 million in assets it is required to file its Form 1120-S electronically. Even if it had 250 or fewer information returns for the year, it would still be required to e-file its Form 1120-S electronically because it had more than $10 million in assets at the end of the year.

For partnerships, those with <u>more than</u> 100 partners must file their income tax returns electronically. Partnerships with 100 <u>or fewer</u> partners (Schedules K-1) may voluntarily file their returns electronically, but are not required to do so in 2022. A partnership has more than 100 partners if, over the course of the taxable year, the partnership had over 100 partners on any particular day in the year, regardless of whether a partner was a partner for the entire year.

> **Note:** On February 23, 2023, The Department of the Treasury and the Internal Revenue Service published final regulations amending the rules for filing information returns and other documents electronically. These regulations will impose a much lower threshold than the current 250-return threshold, but these regulations will not take effect until **2024.**

These e-file requirements currently apply to Forms 1120 or 1120-S (for corporations) and Form 1065 (for partnerships). However, extension requests and payroll tax returns are not required to be e-filed in 2022, and are not subject to the e-file mandate (Forms 7004 and Form 940/941/944).

> **Example:** Pasadena Brokerage, LLP, is a limited liability partnership with 115 partners, most of whom are merely investors and do not work in the business. The partnership has 10 employees and two general partners that work at the main office. Pasadena Brokerage is required to e-file its 2022 partnership return (Form 1065), because it has over 100 partners. Pasadena Brokerage requests an extension of time to file its return by filing Form 7004. The extension can be mailed in on paper because extension requests are not subject to the e-file mandate. The partnership is also allowed to file its payroll tax forms by mail (Form 940 and Form 941) because payroll returns are also not subject to the e-file mandate.

Applying to the IRS E-file Program

Preparers need an EFIN (Electronic Filing Identification Number) to file tax returns electronically. To obtain an EFIN, a tax preparer must apply to become an authorized IRS e-file provider. There is no fee to apply for an EFIN, but the process can take up to 45 days.

The first step is to create an IRS e-Services account by providing required personal information including a Social Security number, an address where confirmation of the account will be mailed, and the preparer's adjusted gross income from the current or prior tax year. If the preparer is accepted into the file program, the IRS will issue the preparer an EFIN.

Providers must protect their EFINs and passwords from unauthorized use and never share them. This includes accepting payment for the use of an EFIN (i.e., renting, leasing, or purchasing an EFIN is prohibited.) In addition, if an e-file provider or software provider resells software, the provider cannot include the EFIN.

A preparer who wants to e-file for clients must be approved as an electronic return originator (ERO). The application must also identify a firm's principals and at least one responsible official. Each person on an e-file provider application must:

- Be a United States citizen or a legal U.S. alien lawfully admitted for permanent residence, (i.e., green card holder)
- Be at least 18 years of age as of the date of application, and
- Meet applicable state and local licensing and/or bonding requirements for the preparation of tax returns.

If the responsible official is certified or licensed (such as an attorney, CPA, or Enrolled Agent), the person must enter their current professional status information. All other individuals must be fingerprinted as part of the application process.[80]

After September 25, 2022, the IRS implemented a new electronic fingerprinting process for EFIN applications. Each new Principal and Responsible Official listed on a new e-file application, or added to an existing application, who is not an enrolled agent, CPA, or attorney is required to schedule an appointment with Fieldprint®, the IRS authorized vendor. Fieldprint® will perform livescan fingerprinting, so fingerprint cards are no longer needed.

---

[80] If the Principal or Responsible Official is an attorney, CPA or enrolled agent, they do not have to submit fingerprints. All other individuals need to provide fingerprints to the IRS.

Example: Michelle is a professional bookkeeper. She mainly does bookkeeping for small businesses, but has never prepared tax returns for clients. She has always prepared her own returns and the tax returns for her family, but she has never charged them. This year, Michelle decides to start preparing tax returns for compensation. She needs to request an EFIN. Michelle first creates an IRS e-services account. Michelle is not an attorney, CPA, or enrolled agent, so she is required to provide fingerprints to the IRS. and makes an appointment to be fingerprinted using livescan procedures through the IRS' official provider. She must also go through a suitability check. About two months later, Michelle gets her acceptance letter from the IRS with her Electronic Filing Identification Number (EFIN).

Example: Sadie is a tax preparer that has worked for an accounting firm for several years. She has an AFSP certificate and a PTIN, but has never had her own EFIN because she has never had her own clients. In 2022, she sits for the EA exam and passes all three parts. She submits Form 23 to the IRS and receives her EA license number and Treasury Card about eight weeks later. Sadie decides that she wants to pursue her own clients working from home part-time. She applies for an EFIN. Since she is already an enrolled agent, she will not have to be fingerprinted as part of the application process. A week after she submits her application, the IRS issues Sadie an EFIN. Now she has a PTIN, as well as an EFIN. She does some research on available software options, and on December 26, 2022, she purchases an affordable professional software suite. Now she can e-file returns from her home office during the 2023 filing season, using her own EFIN and PTIN. She can also continue working for her employer, if she wishes.

After the EFIN application is submitted, the IRS will conduct a suitability check on each person listed on the application as either a principal or responsible official. Suitability checks may include the following:

- A criminal background check.
- A credit history check.
- A tax-compliance check to ensure that the applicant's personal returns are filed and paid.
- A check for prior noncompliance with IRS e-file requirements.

The IRS requires firms with multiple physical locations to obtain separate EFINs for each different location.

Note: An EFIN is *not transferable*; if you sell your businesses, the new owner must obtain their own EFIN. An EFIN identifies a tax practice location—in other words, there must be an EFIN application for each office location. If you expand your business to multiple locations, an application is required for each location where e-file transmissions will occur.

A preparer's e-file application must be current and must list all the form types (1120, 1065, 990, etc.) that he will transmit to the IRS. If the preparer does not list a certain form on the e-file application, and later attempts to transmit that form, the IRS will reject the return.

Example: Rosemarie is an EA. When she first applied to be an e-file provider, she only prepared individual returns. In 2022, she prepares her first partnership return. However, Rosemarie forgets to update her e-file application. When she submits the partnership return, it is rejected. Rosemarie will have to update her e-file application in order to submit partnership returns electronically.

All preparers in a firm based in the same physical location can be covered by the same EFIN. For example, a tax preparation business with ten employee-preparers in one location would all file using the same EFIN. Each preparer would then use their own PTIN on the returns that he or she individually prepares.

Note: An "IRS e-file provider" is an umbrella term for anyone authorized to participate in e-file. This does not only include tax professionals. The program also includes software developers and transmitters.

Electronic Return Originators

An ERO is an authorized IRS e-file provider who originates the electronic submission of tax returns to the IRS. Although EROs typically engage in tax return preparation, (most do), tax preparation is a distinct and separate activity from the electronic submission of tax returns to the IRS. An ERO may submit a taxpayer's return **only** after the taxpayer has authorized the e-file transmission. The return must be either:

- Prepared by the ERO; or
- Collected from a taxpayer who has self-prepared his own return and is asking the ERO to e-file it on the taxpayer's behalf.

An ERO is required to:

- Timely submit returns.
- Submit any required supporting paper documents to the IRS.
- Provide a copy of the return to taxpayers.
- Retain records of each return filed, and make those records available to the IRS.
- Work with the taxpayer to correct a rejected return.
- Enter the preparer's identifying information (name, address, and PTIN).
- Be diligent in recognizing fraud and abuse, reporting it to the IRS and preventing it when possible.
- Cooperate with IRS investigations by making documents available to the IRS upon request.

An ERO who originates returns that he has not prepared, but only collected, becomes an income tax return preparer when he makes substantive changes to the tax return. A "non-substantive change" is a correction limited to a transposition error, misplaced entry, spelling error, or arithmetic correction. The IRS considers all other changes substantive. As such, the ERO may be required to sign the return as the preparer.

Example: Carolina is a tax preparer as well as an ERO. Sergey, a new client, brings a tax return that he self-prepared on paper with a ballpoint pen. He wants Carolina to e-file the return. She notices gross errors on the tax return and talks with Sergey about the mistakes. Sergey agrees to correct the return, and Carolina makes the necessary adjustments on the return for a small fee. Carolina is now required to sign the return as the preparer.

Authorized Transmitters

After an ERO submits a tax return, it is sent to an authorized transmitter (an "authorized transmitter" is *usually* a software company, like Lacerte, ProSeries, TaxSlayer, Drake, etc.). The transmitter submits the return to the IRS.

Example: Bruce is an enrolled agent who uses UltraTax-Pro software to prepare returns. Once he has completed a tax return, he gives a printed copy of the return to the client. Bruce also gives each client a Form 8879, which is an e-file signature authorization. After the client signs the Form 8879, Bruce then transmits the return to UltraTax-Pro, which is an authorized transmitter. UltraTax-Pro then transmits the return to the IRS. Most tax practitioners use this method; all the major tax preparation software companies have e-file transmission options.

Once a tax return is received at the IRS, it is automatically checked for errors. If the return contains an e-file error and cannot be processed, the IRS sends it back to the originating transmitter.

After an e-file rejection, the preparer typically will attempt to correct the return and re-submit it via their professional tax software (the transmitter). The transmitter will then *retransmit* the return to the IRS. If the corrected return is accepted, the IRS sends an acknowledgment to the transmitter stating the return is accepted for processing. This is called an electronic postmark, and it is the taxpayer's proof of filing and assurance that the IRS has the return.

Authorized e-file providers must retain a record of each electronic postmark until the end of the calendar year and provide the record to the IRS upon request. Most tax software packages automatically retain a record of the return transmission report and electronic postmark.

Electronic Signature Requirements

Electronically filed returns have signature requirements, just as paper tax returns do. There are *two methods* of signing individual income tax returns with an electronic signature available for use by taxpayers.[81] Both methods allow taxpayers to use a Personal Identification Number (PIN) to sign the return and the Declaration of Taxpayer.

- **Self-Select PIN Method:** The Self-Select PIN method requires taxpayers to provide their prior-year Adjusted Gross Income (AGI) amount or prior year PIN for use by the IRS to authenticate the taxpayer's signature. This method may be completely paperless if the taxpayers enter their own PINs directly into the electronic return record using keystrokes after reviewing the completed return. Taxpayers may also authorize EROs to

---

[81] Publication 1345, *Handbook for Authorized IRS e-file Providers of Individual Income Tax Returns.*

enter PINs on their behalf, in which case the taxpayers must review and sign a completed signature authorization form after reviewing the return.

- **Practitioner PIN Method:** This method is the most commonly used method, and does not require the taxpayer to provide their prior-year AGI amount or prior-year PIN. Instead, taxpayers must sign a completed signature authorization form (Form 8879, *IRS e-file Signature Authorization.*)

Form 8879 includes a taxpayer's consent to electronic filing; a declaration that the e-filed return is true, correct, and complete; and an indication of which method of signature authorization is used on the e-filed return. The preparer must retain this form for at least three years from the return due date or the IRS received date, whichever is later. Unless the IRS requests to see the form, it is not submitted with the return.

Sometimes, a tax return will require certain attachments. Form 8453, *U.S. Individual Income Tax Transmittal for an IRS e-file Return*, is used to send any required paper forms or supporting documentation that may be needed with an e-filed return.

Form 8453 must be mailed to the IRS within three business days after receiving an acknowledgment that the IRS has accepted the electronically-filed return. If the ERO is signing the tax return as a representative, Form 2848, *Power of Attorney and Declaration of Representative*, must be attached to Form 8453.

Example: Dexter is an enrolled agent and ERO. He has power of attorney for a client, Desiree, who has been living and working overseas in Spain for over 9 months. Dexter uses his practitioner PIN and signs Desiree's tax return on her behalf. He e-files the return and then mails Form 8453 to the IRS the next day. Dexter attaches Form 2848, showing he is Desiree's authorized representative, and has met the specific requirements to sign his client's tax return.

Practitioners who accept electronic signatures must take additional security steps to verify the identity of the taxpayer. For in-person transactions, the preparer must inspect a valid government-issued picture ID, compare the picture to the applicant, and record the name, Social Security number, address, and date of birth. A credit check or other identity verification is optional. For remote transactions, the preparer must verify that the name, Social Security number, address, date of birth, and other personal information on record are consistent with the information provided through record checks with applicable agencies or institutions, or through credit bureaus or similar databases. The IRS has clarified that an electronic signature via remote transaction does not include **handwritten signatures** of Forms 8879 sent to the ERO by hand delivery, U.S. mail, private delivery service, fax, email, or an Internet website.

Example: Charles is an enrolled agent. He has a new client named Kiana who comes to his office to consult with him about her tax return. Charles verifies Kiana's identity by inspecting her driver's license. Another long-term client, Vinnie, lives in a different state. Charles uses an online service that provides identity verification services to confirm Vinnie's identity. After confirming the identity of each client, Charles can prepare their returns and allow each to sign Form 8879 with electronic signatures.

Note: Although no specific technology for e-signatures is required, the IRS gives the following examples of acceptable electronic signature methods: a handwritten signature input onto an electronic signature pad; a handwritten signature, mark, or command input on a display screen by means of a stylus device; a digitized image of a handwritten signature that is attached to an electronic record; a typed name (e.g., typed at the end of an electronic record or typed into a signature block on a website form by a signer); a digital signature; or a mark captured as a scalable graphic.

E-File Rejections

If the IRS rejects an e-filed return and the preparer cannot rectify the reason for the rejection, the preparer must inform the taxpayer of the rejection within 24 hours.

The preparer must provide the taxpayer with the IRS reject codes accompanied by an explanation. If the taxpayer chooses not to have the electronic return corrected and retransmitted to the IRS, or if the IRS cannot accept the return for processing, the taxpayer must file a paper return.

The due dates for filing paper income tax returns also apply to electronic returns, however, if an e-filed return is rejected, the taxpayer does have some time to rectify the problem. This is officially called the "perfection period." During the *perfection period,* the preparer can either correct the return and re-transmit it electronically or, they can paper-file the return.

Perfection Periods: Sometimes, a taxpayer cannot correct the e-filed return to resubmit it electronically, and is therefore forced to file a paper return. This happens most commonly in the case of identity theft. In order to timely file after an e-file rejection, the taxpayer must either correct the return and attempt to resubmit it electronically, or file the return on paper, by the *later* of:

- The due date of the tax return, or

- **For business returns:** Ten calendar days after the date the IRS gives notification that it rejected the e-filed return. This is called the *"ten-day transmission perfection period."*[82] It is additional time the IRS gives a preparer and taxpayer to correct errors in the electronic filing and resubmit a tax return without a late filing penalty.

- **For individual returns:** Five calendar days after the date the IRS gives notification that it rejected the e-filed return. This is called the *"five-day transmission perfection period."*[83] It is additional time the IRS gives a preparer and taxpayer to correct errors in the electronic filing and resubmit a tax return without a late filing penalty.

The "perfection period" varies based on the type of return. This is an official period of time during which a preparer can correct a previously rejected e-filing.

---

[82] See IRS Publication 4163, *Modernized e-File (MeF) Information for Authorized IRS e-file Providers for Business Returns,* for the detailed procedure for perfecting previously-rejected business returns.
[83] See IRS Publication 1345, *Handbook for Authorized IRS e-file Providers of Individual Income Tax Returns,* for the detailed procedure.

The perfection period for Form 1040 returns and Form 4868 (individual extensions) is usually **five** days, ending on April 20. The perfection period for Forms 1120, 1120-S, 1065, 1041 and 990 is **ten** days, and the deadline will depend on the entity type and whether or not the entity is on a calendar year or a fiscal year.

Rejected individual e-filed returns can be corrected and retransmitted without new signatures or authorizations if the changes do not differ from the amount on the original electronic return by more than $50 to "total income" or "AGI," or more than $14 to "total tax," "federal income tax withheld," "refund," or "amount you owe."

Example: Harvey is an EA who e-files a 2022 tax return for his client, Joelle, right on April 18, 2023, which is the filing deadline for 2022 returns. Six hours later, Harvey receives an IRS notice that Joelle's return was rejected. Harvey notifies Joelle of the rejection within 24 hours. Someone else has used Joelle's SSN on another tax return, so the issue cannot be corrected through another e-filed return. Joelle is likely the victim of ID theft and will be forced to file a paper return. Harvey gives a copy of the return to Joelle on April 19, 2023, and she mails it that day, using certified mail as an additional precaution. Joelle's tax return will be considered filed timely, because the paper return was filed within 5 days of the rejection and the original e-filing of the return was attempted in a timely manner. If Joelle had owed tax, however, she would have needed to send payment by the due date in order to avoid a late payment penalty.

If a taxpayer is forced to file on paper after an e-file rejection, the following information must be included:

- An explanation of why the paper return is being filed after the due date
- A copy of the rejection notification
- A brief history of actions taken to correct the electronic return
- The taxpayer should write in red at the top of the first page of the paper return:

"REJECTED ELECTRONIC RETURN-(DATE)"

The date should be the date of the first e-file rejection. The paper return must be signed by the taxpayer. The PIN that was used on the rejected e-filing may not be used as the signature on the paper return.

If an e-file submission is rejected, a return can be corrected within the ten-day transmission period and not be subject to a late filing penalty, but this is not the case for a late payment penalty. If a return is rejected on the due date, an electronic payment should not be transmitted with the return, because a tax payment must still be submitted or postmarked by the due date. Paper-filed returns must be mailed to the IRS, and must have original, ink signatures (a "wet signature").

Safeguarding IRS e-File

Authorized IRS e-file providers are responsible for helping recognize and prevent fraud and abuse in IRS e-file. The IRS has mandated six security, privacy, and business standards to which providers must adhere, including the reporting of security incidents.

Providers who e-file individual income tax returns must report incidents to the IRS as soon as possible, but no later than the next business day. Any unauthorized disclosure, misuse, modification, or destruction of taxpayer information is considered a reportable security incident.

Paper Returns

A taxpayer may choose to file their return on paper, even one that has been prepared by a tax preparer. The taxpayer must mail the return himself. A preparer is required to attach Form *8948, Preparer Explanation for Not Filing Electronically,* to a client's paper return.

Some returns are impossible to e-file for various reasons and are therefore exempt from the e-file requirement. The following tax returns cannot be processed using IRS e-file:

- Estate tax returns (Form 706)
- Older amended individual tax returns (with the exception of 2019-2022 returns),[84]
- Individual tax returns with fiscal year tax periods (very rare),
- Returns containing forms or schedules that cannot be processed by IRS e-file,
- Tax returns with taxpayer identification numbers within the range of 900-00-0000 through 999-99-9999 (with the exception of certain ITIN and ATIN returns),
- Returns with rare or unusual processing conditions (for example, many nonresident and dual-status alien returns cannot be e-filed).

Example: Samuel Smith died on June 30, 2022. When Samuel died, he owned over $39 million in assets, so an estate tax return must be filed for his estate. The executor of Samuel Smith's estate is Angela, Samuel's adult daughter and his only heir. Angela hires an enrolled agent, Donna, to file the estate tax return (Form 706). Estate tax returns cannot be e-filed. Therefore, Donna is required to paper-file the estate tax return. This tax return is not subject to the e-file mandate. Donna has no choice but to submit the return on paper.

Example: Gregory files as head of household and claims his two daughters as dependents. He attempts to e-file his 2022 return on March 2, 2023. His e-filed return is rejected because one of his dependent's SSN has already been used on another return. Gregory is widowed and there is no one else who can legally claim his daughters. He is forced to file his return on paper. He should also complete and file *Form 14039, Identity Theft Affidavit,* and submit it with his paper tax return.

The IRS also may grant administrative exemptions when technology issues prevent specified preparers from filing returns electronically.

Form W-2 Requirements for E-Filing

An e-file provider is prohibited from submitting electronic returns prior to the receipt of all Forms W-2, W-2G, and 1099-R from the taxpayer. A provider also cannot advertise that he can file a tax return using only pay stubs or earning statements.

---

[84] At the time of this book's printing, only tax year 2019 through 2022 Forms 1040 and 1040-SR returns can be amended electronically, and only if the original tax return was also filed electronically. Taxpayers who cannot file their 1040-X electronically must file a paper Form 1040-X. Please see IR-2020-107 and IR-2020-182 for additional information.

If the taxpayer cannot provide a correct Form W-2, W-2G, or 1099-R, the return may be filed after *Form 4852, Substitute for Form W-2, Wage and Tax Statement*, or *Form 1099-R, Distributions from Pensions, Annuities, Retirement or Profit-Sharing Plans, IRAs, Insurance Contracts, etc.*, is completed. This is the only time information from pay stubs or earnings statements is permitted.[85]

The taxpayer must first make an attempt to obtain all the necessary forms from the employer. Form 4852 should only be used as a last resort.

Example: Kristen is a tax preparer. She advertises in her local newspaper that she will prepare a taxpayer's return "early" by using just their final earnings statement or their final pay stub, so taxpayers can get their refund as quickly as possible. This is prohibited, and Kristen can be expelled from the IRS e-file program for doing this.

Example: Nikolai is an enrolled agent. His client, Rosalie, did not get a Form W-2 from her last employer. Rosalie tells Nikolai that her employer went out of business last year, and did not issue a Form W-2 to any of the employees. The owner of the business later filed for bankruptcy. Nikolai believes it is unlikely that Rosalie will ever get a Form W-2 from her former employer, so he uses Rosalie's final pay stub and Form 4852 to create a "substitute W-2" so she can file her tax return as accurately as possible, based on the information they have.

E-File Advertising Standards

Once accepted to participate in IRS e-file, a tax preparation firm may represent itself as an "Authorized IRS e-file Provider." Practitioners may not use the regular IRS logo (the eagle symbol) or IRS insignia in their advertising, or imply any type of relationship with the IRS. They may use the IRS e-file logo, but cannot combine the e-file logo with the IRS eagle symbol, the word "federal," or with other words or symbols that might suggest a special relationship with the IRS.

---

[85] A leave and earning statement (LES) is a document given on a monthly basis to members of the U.S. military that documents their pay and leave status.

A practitioner must not use improper or misleading advertising in relation to IRS e-file, including promising a time frame for refunds.

Advertising materials must not carry the official IRS logo, or any other Treasury seals, but may use the IRS e-file logo. Use of any type of logo or insignia that copies the IRS "eagle" logo is strictly prohibited. If an e-file provider uses radio, television, Internet, signage, or other methods of advertising, the practitioner must keep a copy and provide it to the IRS upon request if any fee information is included in the advertising.

Copies of any advertising specifically containing fee information or a fee schedule must be retained for a period of at least 36 months from the date of the last transmission or use.

E-file Revocations and Sanctions

The IRS may revoke e-file privileges if a firm or individual is either:

- Prohibited or disbarred from filing returns by court order, or
- Prohibited from filing returns by any federal or state legal action that forbids participation in e-file.

The IRS may also sanction any e-file provider who fails to comply with e-file regulations. Before sanctioning a provider, the IRS may issue a warning letter that describes specific corrective action the provider must take.

The IRS categorizes the seriousness of infractions as Level One (the least serious), Level Two, and Level Three (the most serious). Sanctions may be a written reprimand, suspension, or expulsion from participation from IRS e-file. Suspended providers are generally not eligible to participate in e-filing for one to two years, depending on the seriousness of the infraction. If a principal or responsible official is suspended or expelled from participation in the IRS e-file program, every entity listed on the firm's e-file application may also be expelled.

Providers who are denied participation in IRS e-file usually have the right to an administrative review. In order to appeal, a provider must mail a written response within 30 days addressing the IRS's reason for denial or revocation and include supporting documentation. During this administrative review process, the denial of participation remains in effect.

In certain circumstances, the IRS can immediately suspend or expel an authorized IRS e-file provider without prior notice.

> **Example:** Frankie was a CPA who was convicted of felony embezzlement because he was stealing from his clients and illegally forging checks from their bank accounts. After his conviction, Frankie was immediately stripped of his CPA license by his state accountancy board. The IRS revoked his e-file privileges without prior notice.

(Test yourself and then check the correct answers at the end of this chapter.)

1. Lucas meets with a brand new client, Patty. Lucas has never worked with Patty before and does not know her personally. Under the IRS' verification requirements, what must Lucas do to authenticate Patty's identity if he is using electronic signatures, even if he is meeting with Patty in person?

A. Lucas is required to inspect Patty's client's Social Security card.
B. Perform a credit check or take other identity verification measures through a third party.
C. Inspect Patty's government-issued picture ID, compare the picture to the applicant, and record the name, Social Security number, address, and date of birth.
D. No verification is required if a client meets the preparer in person.

2. John recently opened a new tax practice and is advertising for his business. Which of the following presentations will violate the IRS' e-file advertising standards?

A. John offers to e-file a client's tax return for a flat fee.
B. John offers to prepare a client's tax return using only a pay stub.
C. John offers to e-file a client's tax return for no additional charge.
D. John offers to e-file a client's tax return as quickly as possible.

3. The IRS may sanction providers who fail to comply with e-file regulations. It uses a specific system of categorizing how serious infractions are. Which is the most serious?

A. Level One
B. Level Two
C. Level Three
D. Level Four

4. Elizabeth e-filed a return for her new client, Bobby. The IRS rejected the e-filed tax return and the reason for the rejection cannot be rectified with the information that Bobby already provided to Elizabeth. What is her responsibility at that point?

A. Elizabeth is not legally required to notify the taxpayer.
B. Elizabeth must attempt to notify the taxpayer within 24 hours and provide the taxpayer with the rejection code accompanied by an explanation.
C. Elizabeth is required to notify the taxpayer in writing within 72 hours.
D. Elizabeth is required to file the tax return on paper within 36 hours.

5. The IRS may excuse a preparer from the mandate to e-file in which of the following instances?

A. An administrative exemption due to technology issues.
B. An individual case of hardship documented by the preparer.
C. Lack of access to tax preparation software.
D. A preparer who does not like using a computer and prefers to fill out tax forms by hand.

6. What is the first step of the process for an individual to become an authorized e-file provider?

A. Apply for a PTIN.
B. Be fingerprinted and undergo a background check by the IRS.
C. Become a federally-authorized practitioner.
D. Create an authorized e-Services account online.

7. Electronic filing identification numbers (EFINs) are issued:

A. On a firm basis.
B. On a preparer basis.
C. On a client basis.
D. Only to foreign firms.

8. Sylvia is an enrolled agent who e-files an individual return for her client, Emiliano. However, Emiliano's e-filed return is rejected by the IRS. They cannot resolve the rejection issue, and the return must be filed on paper. In order to timely file Emiliano's tax return, what is the deadline for filing a paper return?

A. The due date of the return, or up to 14 days after the date the IRS rejects the e-filed return.
B. The due date of the return, or up to 5 days after the date the IRS rejects the e-filed return.
C. Forty-eight hours after the date the IRS rejects the e-filed return.
D. Ten days after the first e-file rejection.

9. Which of the following tax preparers would be subject to the mandate that requires preparers to e-file their clients' returns?

A. Oslo, a bookkeeper who prepares a tax return for himself and his family (free of charge).
B. Amy, a Certified Payroll Professional who prepares 200 payroll tax returns for various businesses.
C. Scott, who files sixteen individual tax returns and fifty payroll tax returns for compensation.
D. Brandon, a professional fiduciary, who files 25 estate and trust tax returns and signs them in his role as a fiduciary of those estates and trusts.

10. Which logo may an enrolled practitioner use in their advertising?

A. The official IRS logo.
B. The IRS e-file logo.
C. The official seal of the U.S. Treasury.
D. The IRS eagle symbol.

1. The answer is C. For in-person transactions, where an electronic signature is used, Lucas must inspect a valid government-issued picture ID, compare the picture to the applicant, and record the name, Social Security number, address, and date of birth. For remote transactions, the preparer must verify that the name, Social Security number, address, date of birth, and other personal information on record are consistent with the information provided through record checks with applicable agencies or institutions, or through credit bureaus or similar databases.

2. The answer is B. John cannot offer to prepare a client's tax return using only a pay stub. Authorized IRS e-file Providers are prohibited from submitting electronic returns to the IRS prior to the receipt of all Forms W-2, W-2G, and 1099-R from the taxpayer.[86]

3. The answer is C. Under the IRS system of rating e-file infractions, Level One is the least serious, Level Two is moderately serious, and **Level Three** is the most serious. There is no Level Four infraction.

4. The answer is B. Elizabeth must attempt to notify her client, Bobby, within 24 hours and provide him with the rejection code accompanied by an explanation. After receiving a rejection, a tax professional is not required to file a tax return on paper (that choice would be up to the client). The preparer and the client should attempt to correct the e-file. However, if the return continues to be rejected, the taxpayer may be forced to file on paper.

5. The answer is B. An individual case of hardship documented by the preparer may be grounds for a waiver. E-file waivers due to hardship will also be granted, but only on a rare case-by-case basis and typically only for a single year. The preparer must submit *Form 8944, Preparer e-file Hardship Waiver Request,* to request a waiver. An individual preparer's dislike of using a computer or the fact that he does not have appropriate software are not considered legitimate reasons to grant a hardship waiver. The IRS will grant e-file waivers in cases when technology makes it impossible to file electronically. Waivers are reviewed and approved in cases where the preparer demonstrates that complying would be an undue hardship.

6. The answer is D. To become an authorized e-file provider, an individual must first register with the IRS by creating an IRS e-Services account online. The individual will need to provide personal information, including a Social Security number and an address where confirmation of the account will be mailed.

---

[86] If the taxpayer is unable to provide a correct Form W-2, the return may be electronically filed after Form 4852, Substitute for Form W-2, is completed in accordance with the use of that form. This should only be done as a last resort, after other avenues at obtaining these required documents have failed. This is the only time information from pay stubs or earnings statements is permitted.

7. The answer is A. Electronic filing identification numbers (EFINs) are issued on a firm basis. A single EFIN can cover all tax return preparers in a firm with the same physical location. Providers need an EFIN to file tax returns electronically.

8. The answer is B. In order to timely file his tax return, Emiliano must file a paper return by the later of:
- The due date of the return, or
- Five calendar days after the date the IRS gives notification that it rejected the e-filed return.

This is called the *five-day transmission perfection period*. This is not an extension of time to file; rather, this is an additional time that the IRS gives a preparer and taxpayer to correct and resubmit a tax return without a late filing penalty. Most businesses are granted a ten-day perfection period.

9. The answer is C. Scott would be subject to the mandate, because he filed more than 11 individual tax returns, (although payroll tax returns are not subject to an e-file mandate). Any paid preparer who files 11 or more individual or trust returns in aggregate in a calendar year is required to e-file. There are limited exceptions, such as for returns that cannot be e-filed (returns that require paper attachments, certain nonresident returns, amended returns, etc.). Answers "A" is incorrect because the e-file mandate does not apply to tax returns that are not prepared for compensation. Answer "B" is incorrect because the e-file mandate does not apply to payroll tax returns. Answer "D" is incorrect because although the e-file mandate does apply to trust returns (Form 1041) it does not apply to fiduciaries, that file returns in their fiduciary capacity. These people are not considered tax return preparers and are therefore not covered by the e-file requirement.

10. The answer is B. A practitioner may use the IRS e-file logo. A tax preparer may not use the IRS logo or insignia, or imply a relationship with the IRS. A practitioner may not combine the e-file logo with the IRS eagle symbol, the word "federal," or with other words or symbols that suggest a special relationship between the IRS and the practitioner. Advertising materials must not carry the IRS or other U.S. Treasury Department seals.

Unit 13: Identity Theft and Safeguarding Taxpayer Data

> **More Reading:**
> Publication 4557, Safeguarding Taxpayer Data
> Publication 5293, Data Security Resource Guide for Tax Professionals
> Publication 5199, Tax Preparer Guide to Identity Theft
> Publication 4524, Security Awareness for Taxpayers
> Publication 5027, Identity Theft Information for Taxpayers
> Publication 4600, Safeguarding Taxpayer Information
> Publication 5367, Identity Protection PIN Opt-In Program for Taxpayers

Identity Theft

Data thefts at tax professionals' offices are on the rise. Every employee, both professional and administrative staff, should be educated about security threats and safeguards. Protecting taxpayer data is the law.

Note: Federal law now requires all tax preparers to create and implement a data security plan to protect their clients' data. Failure to do so may result in an investigation. Additionally, any failures that lead to an unauthorized disclosure may subject the preparer to penalties.

Identity theft occurs when someone uses another individual's personally identifiable information, such as their name, Social Security number, or credit card number, without permission to commit fraud or other crimes. Safeguarding taxpayer data has become a top priority for the IRS. Fraudulent refunds have become a major issue, and identity theft is considered one of the biggest challenges facing the IRS.

Innocent taxpayers are victimized by tax fraud because their refunds are subsequently delayed. The taxpayer may be unaware that this has happened until they attempt to e-file their own return and discover that a return had already been filed using their SSN. The IRS may send the taxpayer a letter saying it has identified a suspicious return using someone else's SSN.

Tax refund fraud involving stolen identities is referred to as SIRF, or Stolen Identity Refund Fraud.[87] SIRF is a growing type of crime that occurs when thieves file fraudulent refund claims using a legitimate taxpayer's identifying information, which they have stolen. This type of fraud can affect businesses as well as individuals.

Example: Alan is the sole shareholder of a C corporation in the State of California. In 2022, he receives a notice from the IRS about a large refund for an amended return that had been filed for his corporation. Alan never filed or signed an amended return. He later discovers that his former bookkeeper, who had worked for him in the prior year, had filed the return and directed the refund to her home address, intending to illegally cash the check using stolen documents that she took from the business. Alan immediately contacts the IRS to report the fraud.

---

[87] Stolen Identity Refund Fraud, or SIRF, has affected millions of taxpayers and results in more than $2 billion in losses annually to the U.S. Treasury.

Taxpayers who believe someone may have used their SSN fraudulently to file taxes should notify the IRS immediately. The IRS also recommends the following steps:

- Complete IRS Form 14039, *Identity Theft Affidavit*, if the taxpayer's e-file return is rejected because of a duplicate filing under the client's SSN.

- Request an IP PIN for the taxpayer and/or any other family member affected by ID theft.

- The taxpayer should continue to pay their taxes and file their tax return, even if they must do so by paper.

If the taxpayer had previously contacted the IRS and did not receive a resolution, they may contact the IRS for specialized assistance. The IRS offers an Identity Verification Service for taxpayers who receive an IRS notice regarding possible identity theft on their accounts.

Identity Protection PINs

As part of its crackdown on identity theft, the IRS is now allowing all taxpayers to request an identity protection personal identification number (IP PIN). An IP PIN is a six-digit number. The IP PIN helps prevent the misuse of a taxpayer's Social Security number or taxpayer identification number. If the taxpayer attempts to file an electronic return without his IP PIN, the return will be rejected.

> **Note:** The IRS now permits all taxpayers to apply for an identity protection personal identification number (IP PIN). Taxpayers who want an IP PIN can go to *www.irs.gov/ippin* to access the Get an IP PIN tool. Taxpayers who do not already have an account, must register with the IRS.

If the taxpayer loses their IP PIN and decides to submit a paper return, there will likely be a delay in processing, as the IRS will have to validate the taxpayer's identity. The IP PIN is only valid for a single year. A taxpayer will receive a new IP PIN every year for three years after reporting the identity theft incident to the IRS.

The IP PIN will be provided on a CP01N Notice. If a spouse also has an IP PIN, only the person whose SSN appears first on the tax return needs to input his or her IP PIN.

> **Example:** Bethany attempted to file her tax return electronically this year, but it was rejected. The IRS reject code stated that a tax return had already been filed for her. Bethany immediately contacted the IRS and reported the fraud. The IRS determined that she was a victim of refund fraud and placed an "identity theft indicator" on her account. Bethany is forced to file her return on paper this year, and the processing time for her return is increased. Next year, the IRS will automatically send her an IP PIN. Bethany will not be able to e-file her tax return without the IP PIN, which will help prevent refund fraud on her account in the future.

Employment-Related Identity Theft

Employment-related identity theft occurs when someone other than the valid owner of an SSN uses that SSN or other personal information for the purpose of obtaining employment. People may do this if they are not authorized to work in the United States or are trying to avoid child support payments, offsets, or other reasons.

251

This type of fraudulent activity can affect both individuals and business entities. Minor children, dependents and other non-filers can also be victims.

The true scope of employment-related identity fraud is unknown. A recent Government Accountability Office (GAO) report[88] on employment-related identity fraud identified more than 2.9 million Social Security numbers with "risk characteristics associated with identity theft."

> **Example:** Jose Chavez is 17 years old and still in high school. He just started his first after-school job in 2022. Jose is still claimed as a dependent by his parents. Jose earns $9,997 in wages, so he must file a tax return because his income is above the filing requirement. Jose's father, Alfonso, helps his son file his first tax return, properly marking Jose as a dependent. Six months after Jose files his first return, he receives a notice from the IRS, stating that he has unreported wages totaling $32,000. Jose examines the notice and realizes that the employer listed on his transcripts is in another state, where Jose has never lived. An identity thief has stolen Jose's SSN, and used it to work. Jose is a victim of identity theft. Jose and his parents must respond to the notice, and report the ID theft. Jose's parents (because Jose is a minor) should also file a Form 14039 for their son, and they should also consider requesting an IP PIN for Jose.

Warning Signs for Individual Clients

A taxpayer's SSN can be stolen through a data breach, a computer hack or even a lost wallet. A client's SSN has been compromised when:

- A return is rejected, and the IRS reject codes indicate the taxpayer's SSN has already been used, or that a dependent on the return has already been claimed by someone else.

- The client receives IRS notices regarding a tax return after all tax issues have been resolved, refund paid or account balances have been paid.

- The client receives a letter or other notice from the IRS inquiring about a business tax return for a business that does not exist, or that the client does not own.

- Clients who have not filed tax returns receive refunds.

- Clients receive tax transcripts that they did not request.

- An IRS notice indicates the client received wages from an employer unknown to them.

- The taxpayer's state or federal benefits were reduced or canceled because the agency received information reporting an income increase or change.

A tax practitioner must have a valid power of attorney (Form 2848) on file and authenticate the taxpayer's identity before any IRS employee can provide the practitioner with any taxpayer information regarding a ID theft or other fraud-related issue.

---

[88] Employment-Related Identity Fraud: *Improved Collaboration and Other Actions Would Help IRS and SSA Address Risks.* GAO-20-492. Published: May 06, 2020.

Example: Kendra hires Bruce, an enrolled agent, to file her tax return, which he files on time. A few months later, Kendra receives an IRS notice regarding her previous year's tax return. The notice includes a proposed adjustment based on a Form 1099-NEC for independent contractor compensation that was issued in her name. Kendra does not recognize the company on the IRS notice. She has never worked as an independent contractor. Kendra is a victim of identity theft. Kendra takes the notice to Bruce, who obtains a signed Form 2848 for Kendra, authorizing him to contact the IRS on her behalf. Once he has the signed power of attorney, Bruce contacts the Practitioner Priority Line, (PPS) a phone number just for tax practitioners at the IRS. He faxes the Form 2848 while he is on the phone with the operator, identifying himself as an enrolled practitioner. Bruce lets the operator know that Kendra, his client, is a victim of ID theft. The IRS operator immediately flags Kendra's account. Bruce will also respond to the notice and help Kendra to file an ID theft affidavit. The IRS will place an identity theft indicator on her account.

Warning Signs for Business Entities

Business identity theft (also known as corporate or commercial identity theft) happens when someone creates or uses the identifying information of a business to obtain tax benefits. Business identity thieves file fraudulent business returns to receive refundable business credits or to perpetuate individual identity theft. Business identity theft is more complex than individual identity theft. Many of the same indicators that signify simple filing or processing errors also hint at business identity theft. Examples of when a client's EIN has been compromised include when:

- The client's business return is accepted as an amended return, but the taxpayer has not filed an original return for that year.

- The business receives IRS notices about fictitious or non-existent employees.

- A business receives IRS notices regarding a defunct, closed, or dissolved business entity.

A large amount of business-related identity theft is initiated online by using fake or "spoofed" email accounts. The IRS does not initiate contact with taxpayers by email to request personal or financial information. This includes any type of electronic communication, such as text messages and social media channels.

Some of the individuals committing identity theft fraud are members of high-tech global rings engaged in organized criminal enterprises for stealing identities and profiting from that information. The Federal Trade Commission (FTC), the nation's consumer protection agency, provides guidance to businesses regarding information compromise and data theft schemes.

How to Avoid Being a Victim

Be suspicious of unsolicited phone calls, visits, or email messages from individuals asking about employees or other internal information. Do not provide personal information or information about an organization, unless you are certain of a person's authority to have the information. Do not reveal personal or financial information in an email and do not respond to email solicitations for this information, including following links received in an email.

Pay attention to the URL (web address) of a website. Malicious websites may look identical to a legitimate site, but the URL may use a variation in spelling or a different domain that looks or sounds similar to the genuine website.

If you are unsure whether an email request is legitimate, attempt to verify it by contacting the company directly by phone. Do not use the contact information provided on a website connected to the request; instead, check previous statements for contact information. Install and maintain anti-virus software, firewalls, and email filters to reduce some of this traffic. Consider reporting attacks to the police, and file a report with the Federal Trade Commission.

If a tax professional has a data breach where client information is compromised, the data breach must be reported to the IRS.

Phishing Attacks

Phishing attacks are a form of social engineering. Phishing attacks use email or malicious websites to solicit personal information by posing as a trustworthy person or organization. Phishing emails target a broad group of users in hopes of catching a few victims. For example, an attacker may send an email seemingly from a reputable credit card company, bank, or other financial institution that requests account information, often suggesting that there is a problem. When users respond with the requested information, attackers can use it to gain access to the accounts.

Phishing attacks may also appear to come from other types of organizations, such as charities. Attackers often take advantage of current events and certain times of the year, such as recent natural disasters or economic concerns (i.e., IRS scams), major political elections, and holidays in order to lure a response.

Most phishing emails have a "call to action" as part of their tactics, an effort to encourage the receiver into clicking a link or opening an attachment. Other phishing emails impersonate the IRS, or in some instances a private tax software provider. In those examples, preparers are warned that they must immediately update their account information or suffer some consequence. The link may go to a website that has been disguised to look like the login pages for IRS e-Services or a tax software provider.

IRS impersonation telephone calls, as well as other types of unwanted calls (e.g., telemarketing robocalls, fake grants, tech support, sweepstakes winnings, etc.) also remain popular scams.

Example: Paul receives an email alert from his brokerage firm, attempting to warn him of an "invalid login" to his account. The email urges him to click on a link in order to re-login to his account to update his personal data and verify his identity. Paul immediately clicks on the link within the email, not realizing that the link leads to a fake or "spoofed" website. Paul enters his username and password into the fake site, and the scammer records the numbers and is able to use them.

Protecting Clients from Phishing

There is no one action to protect your clients or your business from phishing. It requires a series of defensive steps. Tax professionals should consider these basic steps:

- Use strong, unique passwords. Use a phrase instead of a single word. Use different passwords for each account.

- Never take an email from a familiar source at face value; example: an email from "IRS e-Services." If it asks you to open a link or attachment, or includes a threat to close your account, think twice. Visit the e-Services website for confirmation.

- Consider a verbal confirmation by phone if you receive an email from a new client sending you tax information or a client requesting last-minute changes to their refund destination.

- Use security software to help defend against malware, viruses and known phishing sites and update the software automatically.

- Use the security options that come with your tax preparation software.

- Report all suspicious tax-related phishing emails to phishing@irs.gov.

Note: If you receive an email claiming to be from the IRS that contains a request for personal information, taxes associated with a large investment, or inheritance, do not reply. Do not click on any links or open any attachments. They can contain malicious code that may infect your computer or mobile phone.

Social Engineering Attacks

In a social engineering attack, an attacker uses social skills and human interaction to obtain information about an organization. An attacker may seem unassuming and respectable, possibly claiming to be a new employee, repair person, or researcher and even offering credentials to support that identity.

If an attacker is not able to gather enough information from one source, he or she may contact another source within the same organization and rely on the information from the first source to add to his or her credibility. Cybercriminals will sometimes pose as company executives in order to obtain sensitive personal information, such as names, birthdates, and payroll information.

Example: Cindy is the company bookkeeper for Cape Industrial Construction. The company has 150 employees. In late January, Cindy had just completed the Form W-2s for all the employees when she received an urgent email from the company's owner. The email stated: "I want you to send me the copies of all the employees' wage and tax statements for the year. You can send it as an attachment. Kindly prepare the lists and email them to me ASAP." Cindy immediately prepared the document and emailed it back to her boss. However, she did not realize that the email address had been "spoofed" or had a forged sender address. Cindy unknowingly sent sensitive employee information to a cybercriminal.

Identity Theft Prevention

Every day, the theft of personal and financial information puts people at risk of identity theft. Generally, thieves try to use the stolen data as quickly as possible to:

- Sell the information to other cybercriminals.
- Withdraw money from the victim's bank account.
- Make fraudulent credit card purchases.
- File a fraudulent tax return for a refund using victims' names.

To help stop identity thieves, the IRS says it now has dozens of identity theft screening filters in place to protect tax refunds. To educate taxpayers, the IRS has added a guide to identity theft on its website. Taxpayers are advised to be on the alert for possible identity theft if they receive an IRS notice or letter stating that any of the following has occurred:

- There was more than one tax return filed by the taxpayer.
- The taxpayer has a balance due, refund offset, or has had collection actions taken against him for a year in which he did not file a tax return.
- IRS records indicate the taxpayer received wages from an unknown employer.

The IRS will never seek financial or personal information by initiating contact with taxpayers by email. Many of these so-called "phishing" scams attempt to collect taxpayer Social Security numbers by contacting taxpayers using these methods. Phone scams with callers purporting to be from the IRS also have become widespread in recent years. Clients may also be victims of identity theft not related to tax administration if they:

- Receive bills for business lines of credit or credit cards they do not have.
- Notice that a credit report indicates credit or other open accounts they did not authorize.
- See unexplained bank account withdrawals.
- Suddenly stop receiving bills or other mail.
- Find unfamiliar accounts or charges on their credit report.

Even if the taxpayer has not been a victim of tax-related identity theft, but has been a victim of another type of fraud, it is still advisable for the taxpayer to fill out IRS Form 14039, Identity Theft Affidavit, as well as request an IP PIN, in order to help prevent future fraudulent activity.

Direct Deposit Account Limits

IRS procedure limits the number of refunds electronically deposited into a single financial account or prepaid debit card to a maximum of **three refunds**.[89] Any additional refunds attempted to be deposited to the same account will be converted to a paper refund check and

---

[89] Joint accounts most commonly have two account holders, but it is possible to have more. Often times an elderly person might rely on a joint account with multiple adult children in order to help manage financial affairs.

mailed to the taxpayer. The direct deposit limit is intended to prevent criminals from easily obtaining multiple tax refunds.

> **Example:** Barbara and Antoine are married and have a joint bank account. They get their paychecks direct deposited into the account. They choose to file separate tax returns, however. Barbara and Antoine can have their individual tax refunds deposited into their joint bank account, because up to a maximum of three refunds can be electronically deposited into the same bank account (but no more than three).

These limits are also designed to protect taxpayers from unscrupulous tax preparers who obtain payment for their services by depositing part or all of their clients' refunds into their own bank accounts, an action that is prohibited under the IRC and subject to discipline under Circular 230.

Safeguarding Taxpayer Data

Since tax return preparers are required to obtain and store client information, they have an important role to play in keeping this information secure. Tax practitioners can also become targets of cyber-criminals.

Thieves try to steal client data and tax preparers' identities that will allow them to file fraudulent tax returns for refunds. Since tax return preparers are also at risk of having their identities, and those of their clients, stolen, they should take special precautions to safeguard their clients' sensitive information.

Tax practitioners must report data losses or thefts immediately to the IRS so that appropriate precautions can be made to protect clients from fraudulent returns being filed in their names.

An "information security incident" is an adverse event that can result in an unauthorized disclosure, misuse, or destruction of sensitive taxpayer information. Information security incidents are events that give cybercriminals access to sensitive information without permission.

Types of incidents include: theft of taxpayer information, malicious attacks, and even natural disasters such as a flood, earthquake, or fire that destroys unrecoverable information and computer systems or networks. Preparers who experience a security incident or similar data breach are required to contact the IRS to report the incident within <u>one business day</u>.

> **Example:** Bernard is an enrolled agent. He proudly posts his EA certificate and Treasury Card on his website, which also contains his direct email address, and the email addresses of his staff. Bernard's secretary, Mary, received an email that she thought was from the IRS. She clicked on a spoofed link in the email from her workstation, unknowingly downloading financial malware to her computer and others on the network. Data thieves then 'hijacked' Bernard's identifying numbers, including his PTIN and his EFIN, which the cyberthieves then used to perform identity theft and file thousands of false tax returns.

Security controls are the management, operational, and technical safeguards you may use to protect the confidentiality, integrity, and availability of clients' information.

Examples of security controls are:

- Locking desk drawers and file cabinets.
- Locking doors to restrict access to paper and electronic files.
- Requiring passwords to restrict access to computer files.
- Using encrypted flash drives and using other encrypted procedures in electronically transferring a client's information to a third party—including e-mails.
- Keeping a backup of electronic data for recovery purposes.
- Redacting or truncating SSNs and other personal information.
- Shredding paper containing taxpayer information before throwing it in the trash.
- Using couriers and certified mail to ensure that the correct person receives the correspondence.
- Installing and requiring antivirus and other security software on all of the firm's computers.
- Requiring that all outside contractors maintain the same level of security protocols as the preparer.

> **Note:** Taxpayer data is defined as any information that is obtained or used in the preparation of a tax return (i.e., income statements, bookkeeping records, information statements, tax organizers, etc.).

Safeguarding taxpayer information is a top priority for the Internal Revenue Service. The *Gramm-Leach-Bliley Act* "safeguards rule" requires tax preparers and others who are significantly engaged in providing financial products or services that include preparation and filing of tax returns, to ensure the security and confidentiality of their customer's records and information.[90]

Enhanced Penalties Related to Identity Theft

IRC §7216 and §6713 provide criminal and civil penalties for tax preparers who improperly disclose taxpayer information. Enhanced penalties were added by the Taxpayer First Act for disclosures that relate to a crime of identity theft.

- **§6713 Penalty–** Disclosure or use of information by return preparers: for disclosure in connection with a crime related to identity theft, the penalty for each disclosure is $1,000 (normally $250) with an aggregate maximum per year of $50,000 (normally $10,000) under new §6713(b).
- **§7216 Penalty–** For disclosure or use of information by return preparers, the maximum fine is $100,000 (instead of $1,000) for violations to which §6713(b) apply.

---

[90] The Safeguards Rule, which is a law that took effect in 2003, requires tax professionals, data processors, and financial institutions to develop, implement and maintain a comprehensive information security program for handling customer information.

Example: Romina is a tax preparer that operated a notary and tax business with several other preparers. During the year, Romina electronically filed approximately 900 federal tax returns, all of them claiming fraudulent refunds, by using stolen identity documents. She directed that the IRS mail refund checks to various post office boxes which Romina had rented under her business' name. Romina's business was later raided by police, and evidence of the fraudulent refund scheme was discovered. Romina can be liable for criminal penalties, as well as enhanced penalties under §7216 and §6713 for her part in the identity theft scheme.

(Test yourself and then check the correct answers at the end of this chapter.)

1. Which type of plan is mandatory for every tax professional to implement?

A. Social engineering plan
B. Written security information plan
C. Risk management plan
D. Technical safeguards plan

2. Which of the following events would be considered an "information security incident"?

A. A client attempts to claim a false dependent.
B. An email containing sensitive client information is sent to incorrect recipients.
C. A taxpayer files their own tax return using online software.
D. A tax professional loses their internet access.

3. What is an IP PIN?

A. An alternative method of signing a tax return.
B. An alternative Social Security number.
C. A tax ID number for taxpayers who are ineligible for an ITIN or an SSN.
D. A six-digit number that helps prevent the misuse of a taxpayer's Social Security number.

4. Donald discovers that he is the victim of identity theft. Which IRS form should he use in order to alert the IRS to possible refund fraud on his individual tax account?

A. Form 14039.
B. Form 8821.
C. Form 2448.
D. Form 2106.

5. For how long is an IP PIN valid?

A. One year.
B. Two years.
C. Five years.
D. Indefinitely.

6. The maximum number of refunds that may be electronically deposited into a single financial account is:

A. One.
B. Two.
C. Three.
D. Five.

1. The answer is B. Federal law requires all tax preparers to create and implement a written security information plan (WISP), which is a type of data security plan to protect their clients' data.

2. The answer is B. The IRS requires tax professionals to report data breaches and other security incidents. An "information security incident" is an adverse event or the threat of an event that can result in an unauthorized disclosure, misuse, modification, or destruction of sensitive taxpayer information.

3. The answer is D. An IP PIN is a six-digit number assigned to eligible taxpayers that helps prevent the misuse of their Social Security number. All taxpayers are now eligible for an IP PIN, which can be requested on the IRS website.

4. The answer is A. Donald should fill out Form 14039, which is an identity theft affidavit. Even if the taxpayer has not been a victim of tax-related identity theft, but has been a victim of another type of fraud, it is still advisable for the taxpayer to fill out IRS Form 14039, Identity Theft Affidavit, in order to report the potential for future fraudulent activity.

5. The answer is A. An IP PIN is only valid for a single year. A taxpayer will receive a new IP PIN every year for three years after reporting the identity theft incident to the IRS.

6. The answer is C. To combat identity theft, IRS procedures limit the number of refunds that may be electronically deposited into a single financial account or prepaid debit card to **three**. Any additional refund(s) will be converted to a paper refund check and mailed to the taxpayer.

Index

international financial reporting laws, 21
interpretive regulations, 25
IP PIN. *See* identity protection PIN
IRB. *See* Internal Revenue Bulletin
IRC. *See* Internal Revenue Code
IRM. *See* Internal Revenue Manual
IRS Appeals Office, 218
IRS collections, 173
IRS divisions, 33
IRS information requests, 89
IRS notice, 27
IRS publications and forms, 28
IRS Restructuring and Reform Act of 1998, 31
IRS summons, 184

J

judicial branch, 22
jurat, 144

K

knowledge requirement, 119

L

Large Business & International Division, 33
legislation, 22
legislative branch, 22
legislative regulations, 24
levy, 182
lien, 182
limited practice, 45
LITC. *See* Low Income Taxpayer Clinic, *See* Low Income
    Taxpayer Clinic
long-term payment plan, 175
Low Income Taxpayer Clinic, 45, 50

M

mail advertising, 93
Maryland State Board of Individual Tax Preparers, 43
methods of payment, 173
monetary penalty, 164

N

negligence penalties, 141
no-change audit, 211
nonacquiescence, 30
notary public, performance as, 95
Notice of Deficiency, 220
Notice of Determination, 222
Notice of Federal Tax Lien, 182
notice of intent to levy, 182
not-practice before the IRS, 47

O

ODC. *See* credit for other dependents
offer in compromise, 192
office audit, 205
official complaint, 164
OIC. *See* offer in compromise
Oregon Board of Tax Practitioners, 43
original signatures, 96

P

Paid Preparer's Due Diligence Checklist, 117
paper returns, 242
penalties
    accuracy-related penalty, 138
    civil fraud penalties, 142
    disaster-related relief, 188
    due to an IRS error, 188
    failure to exercise due diligence, 123
    failure-to-file penalty, 136
    failure-to-pay penalty, 137
    for tax preparers, 145
    negligence penalties, 141
    practitioner sanctions, 164
    reliance on a tax advisor, 188
    trust fund recovery penalty, 144
penalty relief, 188
perfection period, 240
performance standard, 119
permissible disclosures, 73
personal identification number, 251
phishing attacks, 254
PLR. *See* private letter ruling
POA. *See* power of attorney
power of attorney, 66
    CAF number, 71
    Check Box authority, 72
    durable power of attorney, 68
    not required, 70
    revocations and withdrawals, 69
    signature authorizations, 70
practice before the IRS, 41
practitioner PIN method, 239
practitioner sanctions, 164
practitioner standards and misconduct, 159
pre-allegation notice, 165
preparer penalties, 147
preparer tax identification number, 47
preparer's identity theft penalties, 258
privacy regulations, 73, 75
private letter ruling, 27
procedural regulations, 25
prohibited actions during suspension or disbarment,
    166
proposed regulations, 25

This page intentionally left blank.

About the Authors

Joel Busch, CPA, JD

Joel Busch is a tax professor at San Jose State University, where he teaches courses at both the graduate and undergraduate levels. Previously, he was in charge of tax audits, research, and planning for one of the largest civil construction and mining companies in the United States. He received both a BS in Accounting and a MS in Taxation from SJSU and he has a JD from the Monterey College of Law. He is licensed in California as both a CPA and an attorney.

Christy Pinheiro, EA, ABA®

Christy Pinheiro is an Enrolled Agent and an Accredited Business Accountant. Christy was an accountant for two private CPA firms and for the State of California before going into private practice.

Thomas A. Gorczynski, EA, USTCP

Thomas A. Gorczynski is an Enrolled Agent, a Certified Tax Planner, and admitted to the bar of the United States Tax Court. Tom is also a nationally known tax educator and currently serves as editor-in-chief of EA Journal. He received the 2019 Excellence in Education Award from the National Association of Enrolled Agents. He earned a Master of Science in Taxation from Golden Gate University and a Certificate in Finance and Accounting from the Wharton School at the University of Pennsylvania.

See more information on our official website: *www.PassKeyOnline.com.*